IMAGES
of America

DESCHUTES NATIONAL FOREST

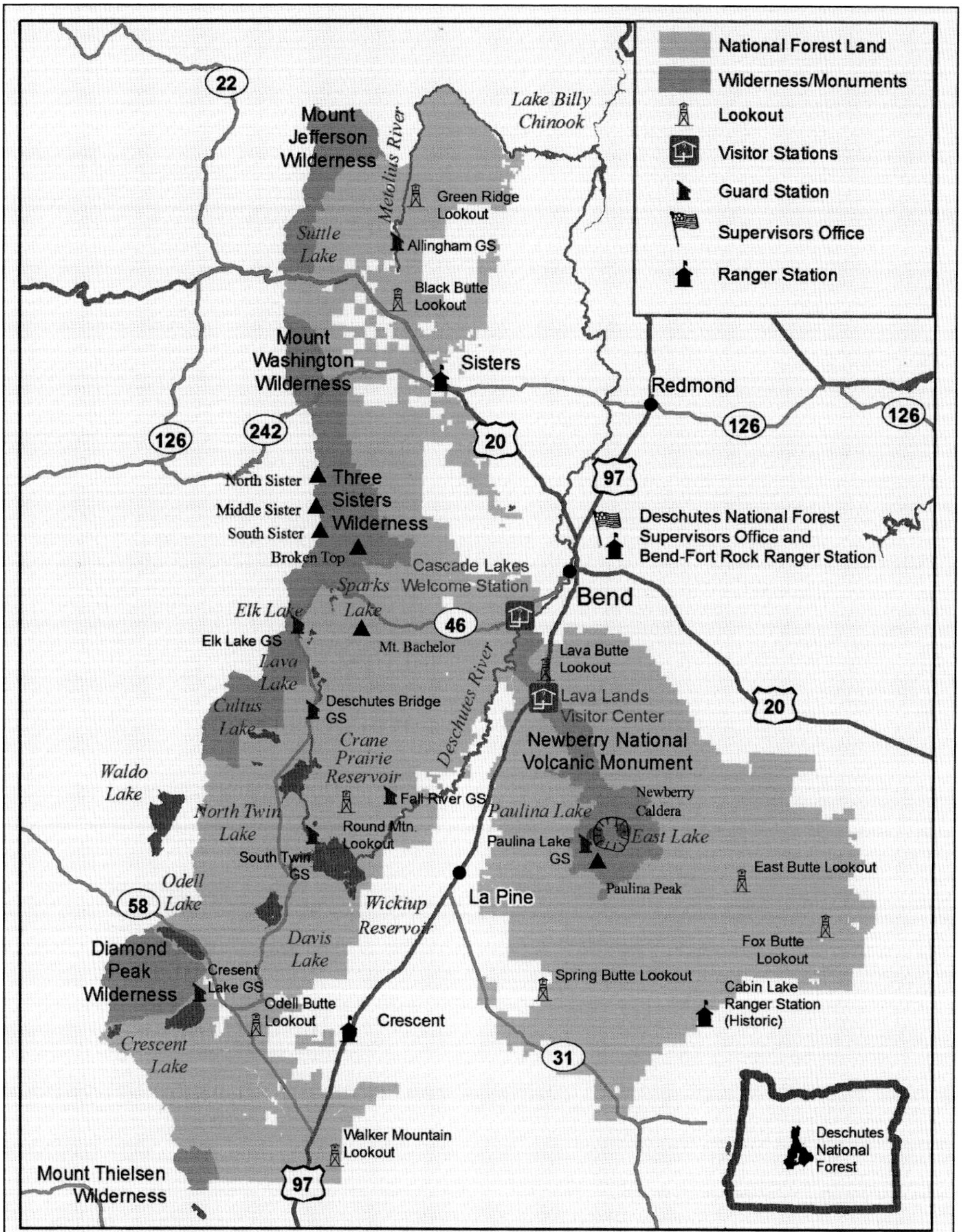

Within the boundaries of the Deschutes National Forest are almost 1.6 million acres of National Forest System land managed by the US Forest Service "for the greatest good of the greatest number in the long run." These lands include the 11,055-acre Pringle Falls Experimental Forest, the 56,300-acre Newberry National Volcanic Monument, and over 182,000 acres of National Wilderness Preservation System lands. (Deschutes National Forest.)

On the Cover: Janis and Paul Hosmer Sr. canoe on Mud Lake and admire the view of South Sister. In 1962, about six months after his death, Mud Lake was renamed Hosmer Lake in honor of Bend's well-known writer, photographer, and naturalist. (Deschutes County Historical Society.)

IMAGES
of America

DESCHUTES NATIONAL FOREST

Les Joslin

ARCADIA
PUBLISHING

ISBN 978-1-4671-2466-9

Published by Arcadia Publishing
Charleston, South Carolina

Printed in the United States of America

Library of Congress Control Number: 2016945218

For all general information, please contact Arcadia Publishing:
Telephone 843-853-2070
Fax 843-853-0044
E-mail sales@arcadiapublishing.com
For customer service and orders:
Toll-Free 1-888-313-2665

Visit us on the Internet at www.arcadiapublishing.com

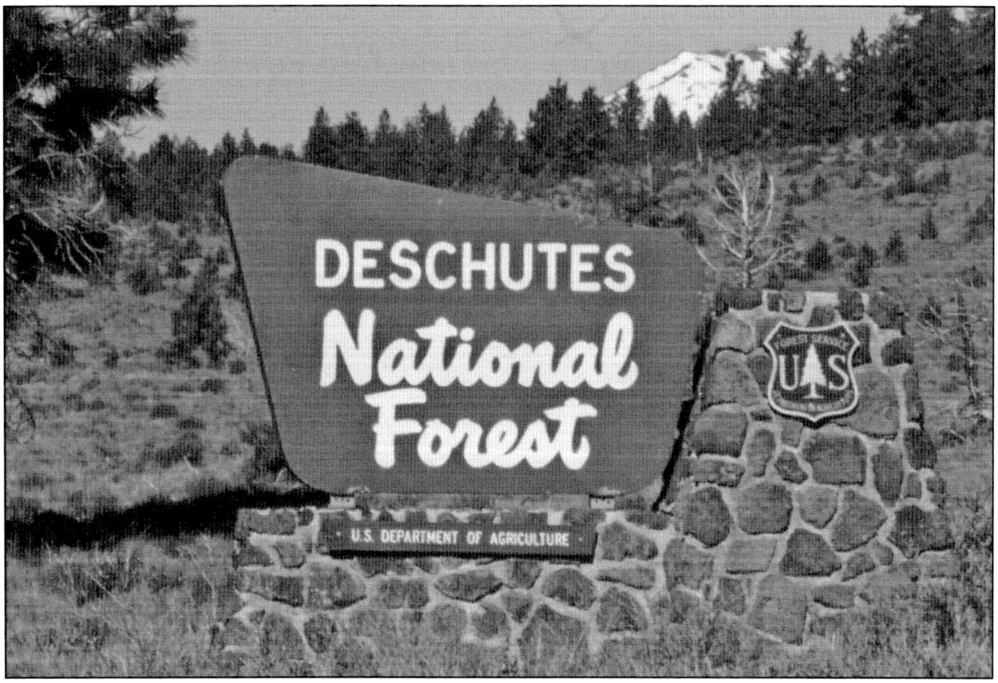

This look at the Deschutes National Forest and its natural and cultural resource stewardship heritage is dedicated to the citizen-owners of the National Forest System and those US Forest Service members who proudly and professionally pursue their "caring for the land and serving people" mandate. (Photograph by the author.)

Contents

ACKNOWLEDGMENTS

This effort to share at least some aspects of the complex story of the Deschutes National Forest through 10 thematic chapters comprising more than 200 captioned photographs has benefitted from the invaluable assistance and support of several.

First among these is fellow writer Tor Hanson of Bend, Oregon, without whose mastery of computer technology the compilation and integration of the images that illustrate this book would not have been possible. Thanks, Tor, for your invaluable contributions to this effort.

The majority of those images are from two sources: the Deschutes National Forest and the Deschutes County Historical Society. I greatly appreciate the generous support of this project afforded by forest supervisor John P. Allen and members of this staff. Forest archaeologist Penni Borghi and Bend–Fort Rock Ranger District archaeologists Dan Newsome and Jillian Gantt facilitated my access to the Deschutes National Forest historic photograph archive. Geographic information system specialist Dino Borghi prepared the excellent map on page 2.

I also appreciate the support of Deschutes County Historical Society executive director Kelly Cannon-Miller and the assistance of Des Chutes Historical Museum manager Vanessa Ivey and Des Chutes Historical Museum registrar Shey Hyatt, who provided access to the society's historic photograph collection and research resources.

Many others—including notable US Forest Service photographers of the past—are recognized in the individual photograph credit lines. Special thanks are due Apollo 7 astronaut Col. Walter Cunningham, US Marine Corps Reserve, retired, for permission to use the photographs on page 125.

And, of course, I acknowledge my wife, Pat, for her understanding of and patience with yet another writing project.

INTRODUCTION

The Deschutes National Forest in Central Oregon is one of 154 national forests (some managed as single forests, others as separate forests managed together, and still others as consolidated former separate forests), which, along with 21 national grasslands, comprise the 193 million-acre National Forest System managed for the American people—its citizen-owners—by the US Forest Service.

The story of the National Forest System began when Congress passed the Forest Reserve Act of 1891, which gave the president of the United States the power to set aside forest reserves from the public domain. Six years later, the Organic Act of 1897 specified the purposes for which forest reserves could be established; emphasized were protecting forests to secure water supplies and supply timber. The forest reserves were managed by the General Land Office of the US Department of the Interior. With the Transfer Act of 1905, administration of the forest reserves was transferred to the new Forest Service in the US Department of Agriculture.

Under founding forester Gifford Pinchot, the new agency was charged to administer the forest reserves—renamed "national forests" in 1907—for "the greatest good of the greatest number in the long run" and to do other federal forestry jobs. The Deschutes National Forest was established in 1908 with headquarters in Prineville, Oregon. As national forests in Oregon reorganized, those headquarters were moved to Bend, Oregon, in 1911.

The mission of the Forest Service is "to sustain the health, diversity, and productivity of the Nation's forests and grasslands to meet the needs of present and future generations." Accomplishing this mission involves three main jobs: managing the National Forest System, assisting state and private forestry interests and practices, and forestry research. All of these jobs are or have been evident on the Deschutes National Forest.

The largest and most visible Forest Service job in Central Oregon is management of the Deschutes National Forest. National forests, in the charge of federal officials called forest supervisors, are divided into several ranger districts managed by district rangers who, with their staffs, accomplish most of the on-the-ground work of a national forest. This includes management of timber, water, and forage resources and wildlife habitat as well as operation of campgrounds and picnic areas and maintenance of forest roads and trails. Unlike national parks, which are managed by the National Park Service of the US Department of the Interior as "public parks and pleasuring grounds" in a way that "preserves unimpaired the natural and cultural resources of the National Park System for the enjoyment, education, and inspiration of this and future generations," national forests are managed to produce a full range of commodity resources such as timber and grazing as well as amenity resources such as recreation and scenery.

After an early history of custodianship of national forest lands, which primarily involved protecting them from fire and trespass, many decades of multiple-use management—managing the national forests to optimize their timber, water, forage, wildlife, recreation, and other resources—have characterized National Forest System and Deschutes National Forest management. As a result of timber interest pressures during the late 1950s to increase timber cutting on the national forests, the Forest Service responded to "over use" and "single use" pressures by proposing that its long-standing multiple-use management policy be made law.

Congress passed the Multiple Use-Sustained Yield Management Act of 1960 that, as Wilkinson and Anderson put it in their 1987 book *Land and Resource Management in the National Forests*, "placed outdoor recreation, range, wildlife, and fish [resource management] on equal statutory footing with timber and watershed uses. However, [because of political pressure], the Act only required the agency to give equal 'consideration' to all resources, not administer them equally. Accordingly, the Forest Service . . . implemented . . . the Act by increasing its consideration of recreation, wildlife, and watershed through planning," while timber production continued to be emphasized in practice.

This emphasis on timber production was not always good for the health of the national forests. More recently, informed by an ethic that recognizes it cannot meet the needs of the American people without first securing the health, diversity, and productivity of their lands and waters, and aided by changing conditions and perceptions, the Forest Service has been changing the way it implements multiple use of national forest lands. In short, it is shifting its emphasis from commodity (timber) production to an ecosystem management approach that focuses on the health and what one past Forest Service chief termed "the long-term sustainability of watersheds, forests, and grasslands and the ecological, economic, and social benefits they can provide." Timber management remains an important forest health and ecosystem management tool.

Ecosystem management means using an ecological approach to achieve multiple-use management of national forests and grasslands by blending the needs of people and environmental values in such a way that national forests and grasslands represent diverse, healthy, productive, and sustainable ecosystems.

Ecosystem management is the basis of the Forest Service's natural resource management agenda for the 21st century and its focus on working with the American people to find ways to live within the limits of the land. This agenda emphasizes watershed restoration and maintenance, sustainable forest ecosystem management, forest road management, and outdoor recreation management. This agenda guides the Deschutes National Forest's management—as well as Forest Service management of the entire National Forest System—and the research and cooperation with state and private entities necessary to support this management.

Times are changing, and the relationships between the natural environment and human activity are changing. On the Deschutes National Forest and throughout the nation, a paradigm shift from an emphasis on commodity production to amenity uses of the National Forest System is evident. This book is intended to help you—as a citizen-owner of the National Forest System—visualize, understand, and appreciate the evolution of the Forest Service's stewardship of the amenity and commodity resources of the Deschutes National Forest.

That concept of the "citizen-owner" is the key to understanding that stewardship. It reflects the essential truth that the Deschutes National Forest and every other national forest and national grassland are your National Forest System land, not "Forest Service land."

With very few exceptions (such as non–National Forest System land acquired by the Forest Service for use as administrative sites or communication sites), and despite the frequent use of the term, there's no such thing as "Forest Service land."

It's "national forest land" that belongs to the people of the United States of America—the citizen-owners of the National Forest System—and is administered for them by the Forest Service as prescribed by law, not "Forest Service land."

A small point? A nitpick? Not at all!

It is an all-important distinction that informs—or should inform—the perceptions, and thus the operational realities, of the politicians, the public servants, and the public they serve of their respective roles, responsibilities, and prerogatives vis-à-vis the national forests and each other.

In addition to administering the Deschutes National Forest, the Forest Service in Central Oregon protects national forest and surrounding wildlands and communities from wildfire and pursues forestry research. Wildfire management is part of its state and private forestry job and is addressed in chapter 3. Forestry research is addressed in chapter 4.

One

Upper Deschutes Country

The Deschutes National Forest occupies about half of the upper Deschutes country—not a political entity but "the landscape to all horizons around" in the words of Ivan Doig. These horizons are defined in the west by the Three Sisters and other Cascade Range peaks northward toward Mount Jefferson and southward toward Diamond Peak; in the southeast by the Newberry Volcano, its surrounding Paulina Mountains, and the Walker Range; in the east by Pine Mountain, Horse Ridge, and Powell Butte; and in the north by the Crooked River Gorge.

This basin, the Upper Deschutes Basin, is drained toward the Columbia River by the spring-born Upper Deschutes River and its spring-fed tributaries including the Metolius River, the Little Deschutes River, and Paulina Creek.

In the rain shadow of the Cascades, the dry Upper Deschutes Basin is watered by snowmelt from the surrounding highlands. With elevation, its sagebrush and juniper lands transition to ponderosa pine, then lodgepole pine and mixed conifer forests, and lastly hardy alpine plant communities. Each environment is inhabited by adapted fish and wildlife species.

Human habitation is evidenced by an excavated 10,000-year-old Native American pit house at Paulina Lake and a more recent rock shelter on the Deschutes River. For several centuries before European American exploration and settlement, Northern Paiute groups from the arid sagebrush steppes to the east visited as part of their seasonal round of hunting and gathering.

European American exploration may have begun with the brief presence of displaced trappers in 1813. Peter Skene Ogden, a Hudson's Bay Company trapper, visited in 1825. Nathaniel Wyeth passed through in 1834, and Capt. John C. Frémont's expedition in 1843. In 1845, Stephen Meek led immigrants through en route to the Willamette Valley. Lt. Henry Larcom Abbot's Pacific Railway Survey party explored the area in 1855.

Settlement began in the 1870s, when Willamette Valley cattle ranchers sought new rangelands for their livestock. A settlement called Bend, based on irrigated agriculture and timber speculation, was incorporated in 1905. That same year, the US Forest Service, which soon administered the Deschutes National Forest to help sustain the upper Deschutes country economy, was founded.

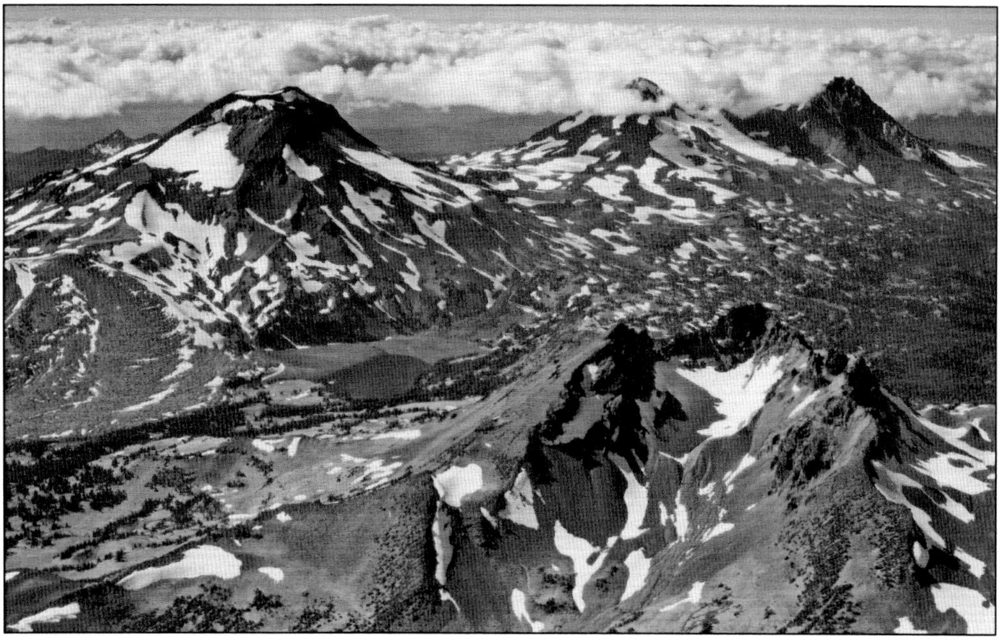

Moist air flowing westward from the Pacific Ocean cools as it rises over the Cascade Range—here, the Three Sisters—and releases its moisture as rain or snow. Between 80 and 125 inches of precipitation fall annually—mostly as snow—on western upper Deschutes country watersheds. This water percolates and flows into the Deschutes River system. (US Geological Survey.)

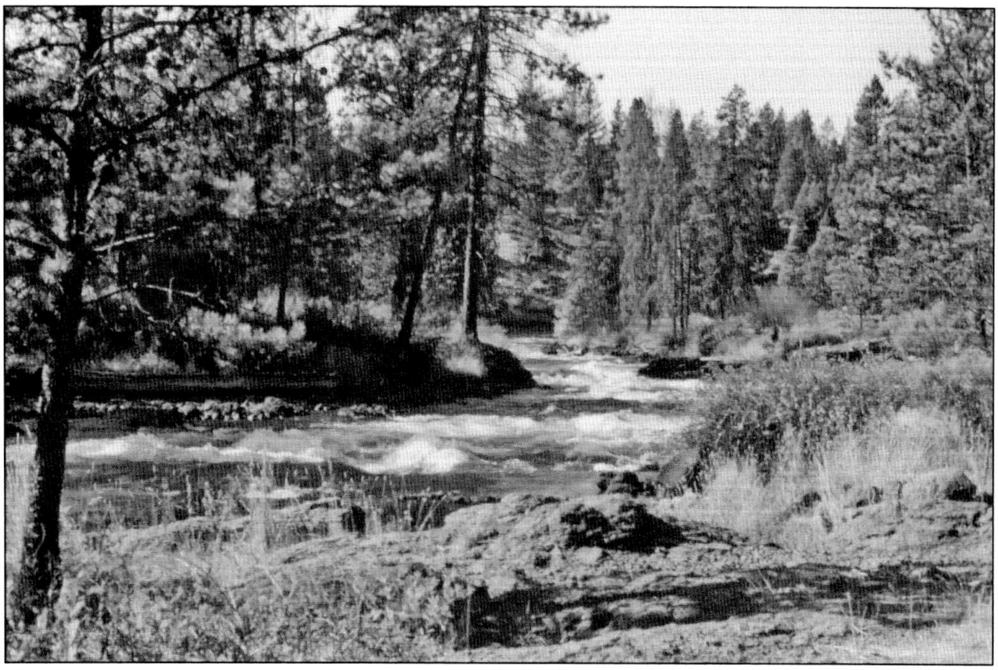

The Deschutes River and its tributaries drain the highlands of the upper Deschutes country as they flow through higher-elevation mixed conifer and lower-elevation ponderosa pine forests, then through more arid juniper woodland and sagebrush steppe landscapes toward the Columbia River. (Photograph by the author.)

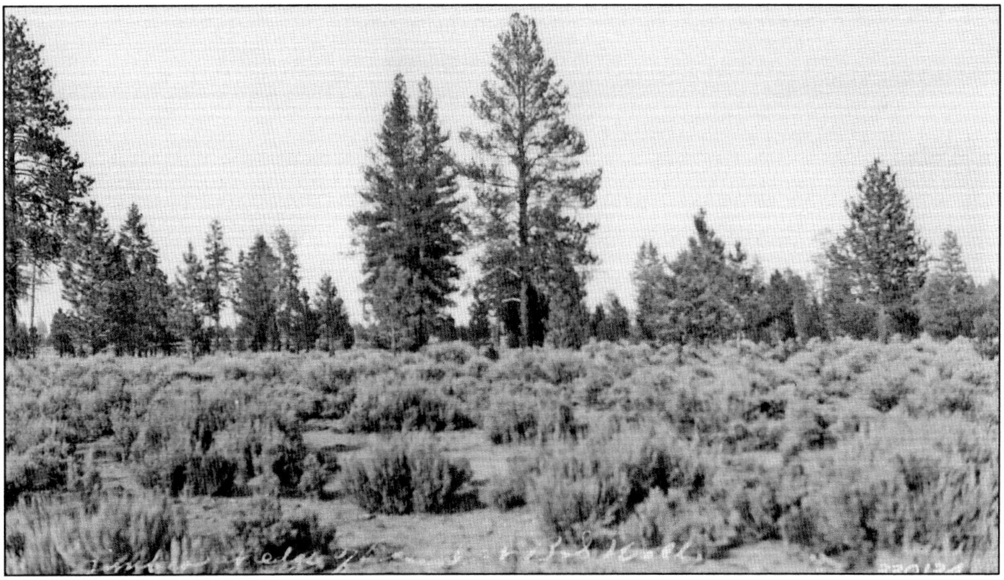

In the rain shadow of the Cascade Range, the eastern upper Deschutes country is an arid land in which ponderosa pine forests merge into high desert of juniper and sagebrush. Annual average precipitation is about 12 inches in Bend, on the edge of the ponderosa pine belt, and about 8 inches just a few miles to the east. (Deschutes National Forest, photograph by Carl B. Neal.)

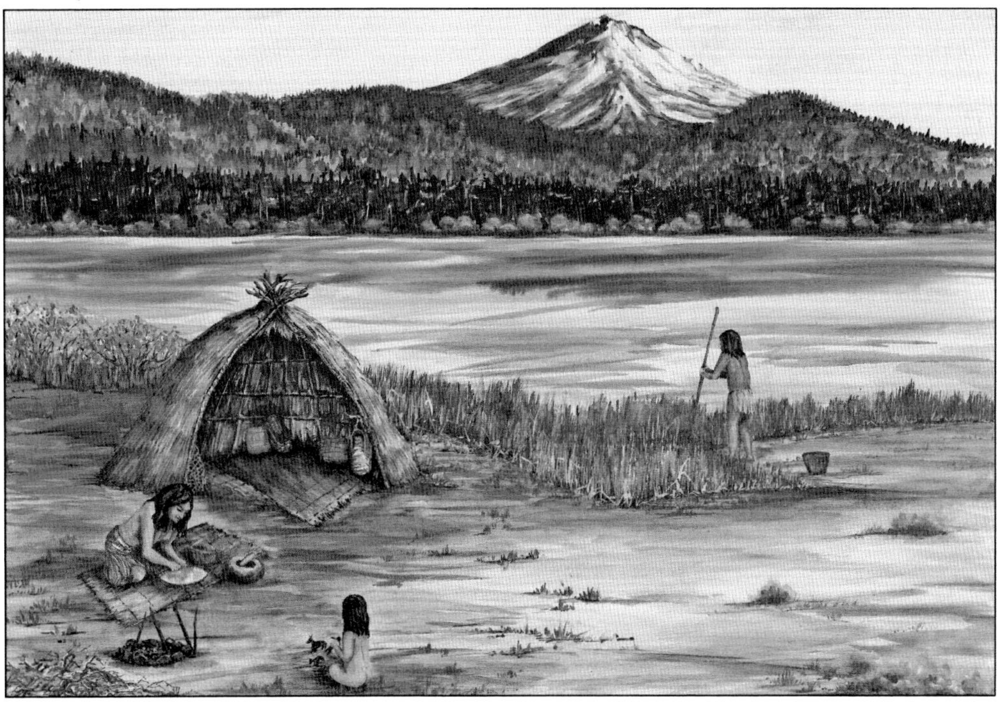

Centuries before European American exploration and settlement, Native Americans from the sagebrush steppes to the east visited the upper Deschutes country each year. Following seasonal hunting and gathering opportunities, they camped along the Deschutes River and on the banks of a long lake formed after Lava Butte's lava flow damned the river at Benham Falls. (Sunriver Nature Center.)

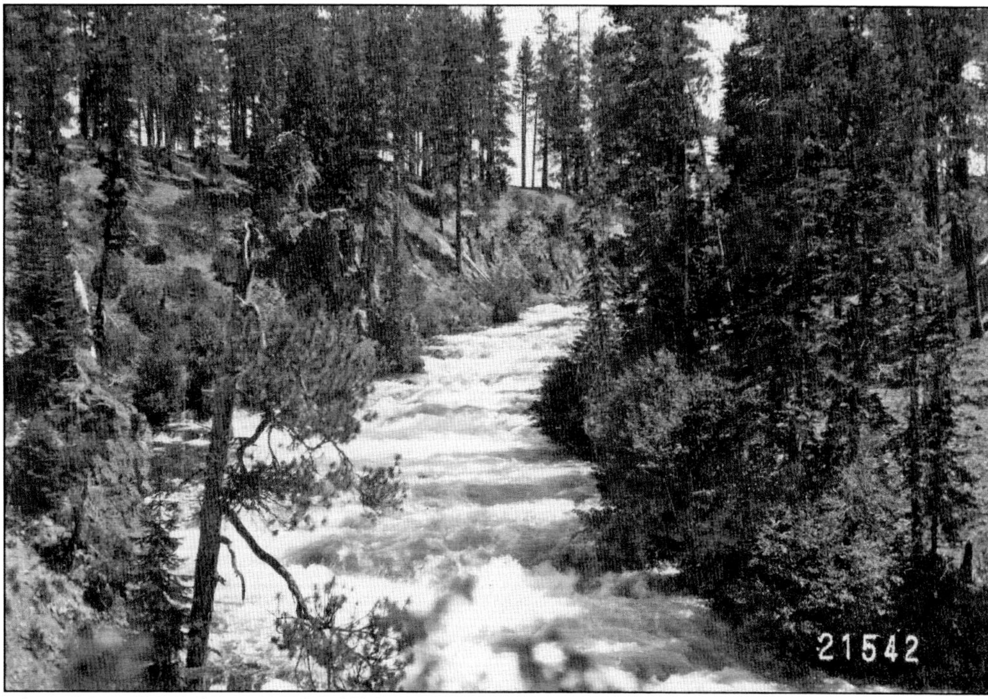

The timber, water, forage, and wildlife resources of the upper Deschutes country were appreciated by early conservationists as well as settlers and developers. Gifford Pinchot, then the 36-year-old chief of the Bureau of Forestry in the US Department of Agriculture, photographed Benham Falls, on the Deschutes River south of Bend, in August 1901. (Deschutes National Forest.)

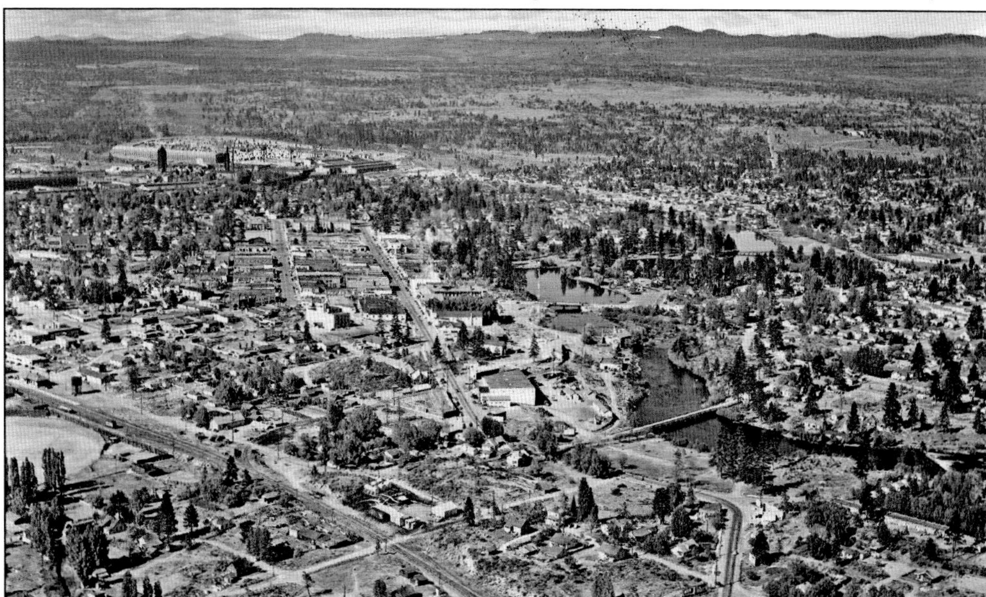

The natural resources of the upper Deschutes country—many within the Deschutes National Forest—have sustained the agricultural, industrial, and tourism-based economies of Central Oregon since settlement. Bend, which has grown from about 500 residents in 1905 to almost 90,000, is the region's largest urban area. (Deschutes County Historical Society.)

Two

Deschutes National Forest

After the Deschutes National Forest was established in 1908 and headquartered in Bend in 1911, a management system was developed for doing its job. In 1908, the year Gifford Pinchot decentralized national forest administration by establishing geographic districts ("regions" since 1930) run by district foresters ("regional foresters" since 1930) to whom forest supervisors reported, each national forest was subdivided into ranger districts overseen by district rangers. Since then, the supervisor of the Deschutes National Forest and as many as 25 other forest supervisors within what is now the Pacific Northwest Region have reported to the regional forester in Portland, Oregon.

Forest supervisors' offices were located in towns near the national forests and district ranger stations near or within those districts. The forest supervisor in Bend posted district rangers near Sisters, Pine Mountain, La Pine, Big River, and Crescent. These rangers, appointed under Civil Service Commission rules, were chosen from candidates who had passed a written examination and a practical field test that proved their ability to actually perform the duties of a forest ranger. Upon appointment, rangers were issued uniforms, the bronze Forest Service badge, and a 142-page pocket-size handbook called the *Use Book*, and posted to their districts.

The forest supervisor and his rangers early set about building the physical infrastructure—ranger stations, roads and trails, telephone lines, and more—essential to the early custodial management of the national forest. They also surveyed and marked the national forest boundaries and improved the maps of the national forest and its resources.

As the decades passed and national forest administration evolved from custodianship to active management of national forest resources, the Deschutes National Forest staff and infrastructure grew. College-educated foresters soon replaced the rough-and-ready, early-day rangers; in more recent decades, those foresters and their engineer partners have been joined by a diverse group of resource management specialists. The forest supervisor's headquarters occupied a succession of quarters in Bend, and for most of its history, four district rangers managed the Sisters, Bend, Fort Rock, and Crescent Ranger Districts. In 1995, the Bend and Fort Rock Ranger Districts were combined as one district.

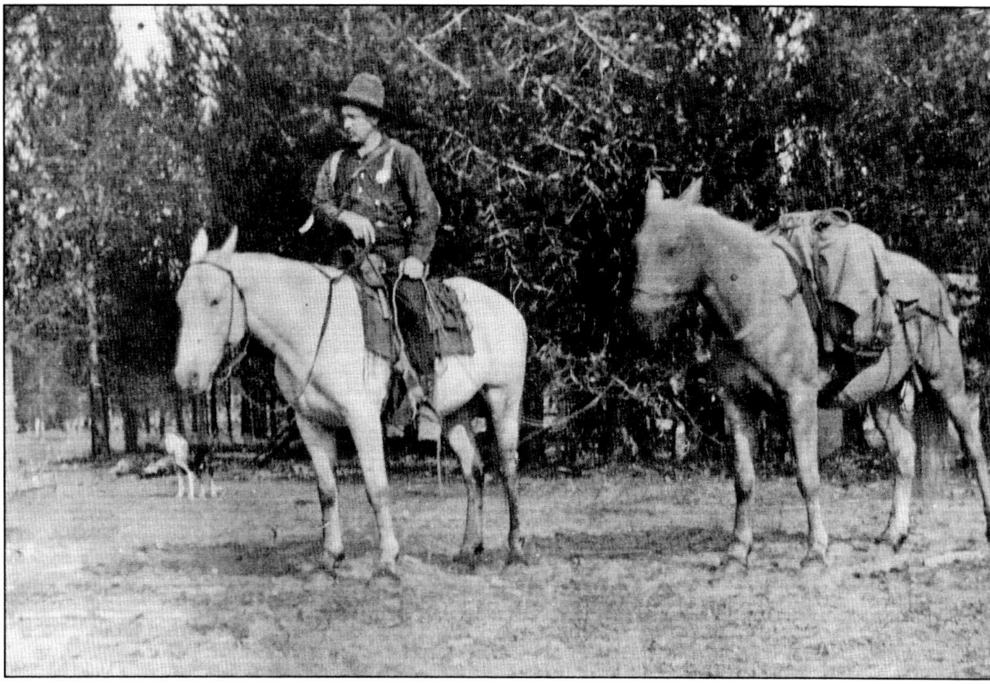

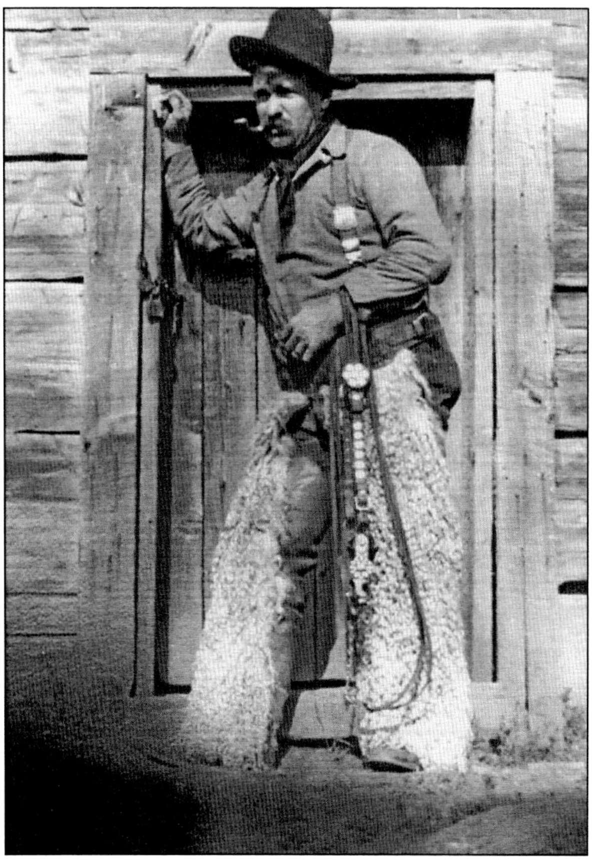

Appointed a US Department of the Interior forest ranger in 1903, Cy Bingham patrolled the Cascade Range Forest Reserve. He reputedly was the first to serve in that part of the reserve later included in the Deschutes National Forest. His pay was $75 per month, out of which he paid for his own saddle and packhorses, tools, and food. (Deschutes National Forest.)

After two years wearing the big round nickel-plated badge of a forest reserve ranger, Bingham pinned on the big bronze shield badge of the new US Forest Service in 1905 and continued his work. He became supervisor of the new Malheur National Forest in November 1907. He resigned from that post in 1920, served as Grant County, Oregon, sheriff until 1932, and died in California in 1937. (US Forest Service.)

Gifford Pinchot, the first American trained as a forester, worked with Pres. Theodore Roosevelt to establish the Forest Service in the US Department of Agriculture in 1905. Administration of the forest reserves was transferred from the Department of the Interior to the Forest Service in 1905, and in 1907, the forest reserves were renamed national forests. (US Forest Service.)

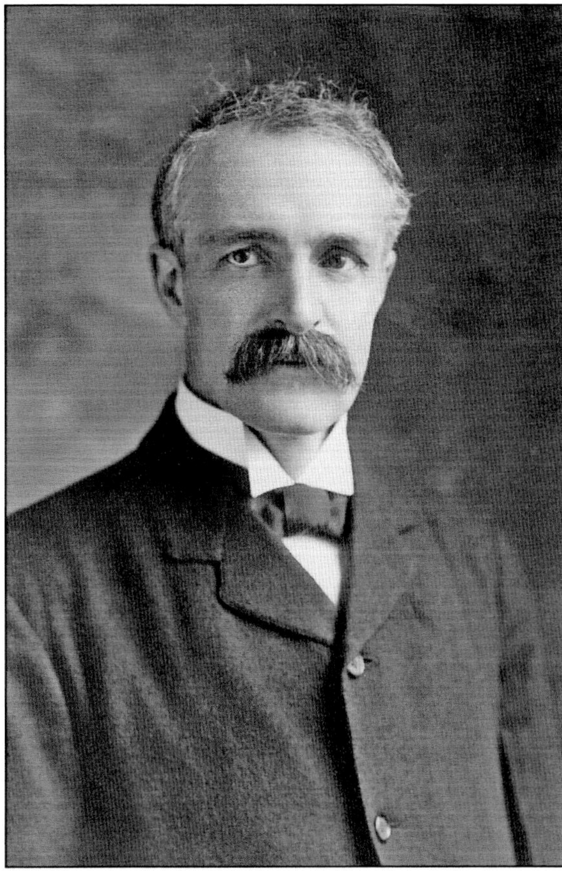

Pinchot accepted only the better Department of the Interior rangers—including Bingham—into his new Forest Service. Political appointment of rangers gave way to hiring under US Civil Service Commission rules. Ranger John Riis, who joined the Forest Service in 1907, served in Utah and California before he arrived on the Deschutes National Forest in 1911. (US Forest Service, photograph by Thornton Taft Munger.)

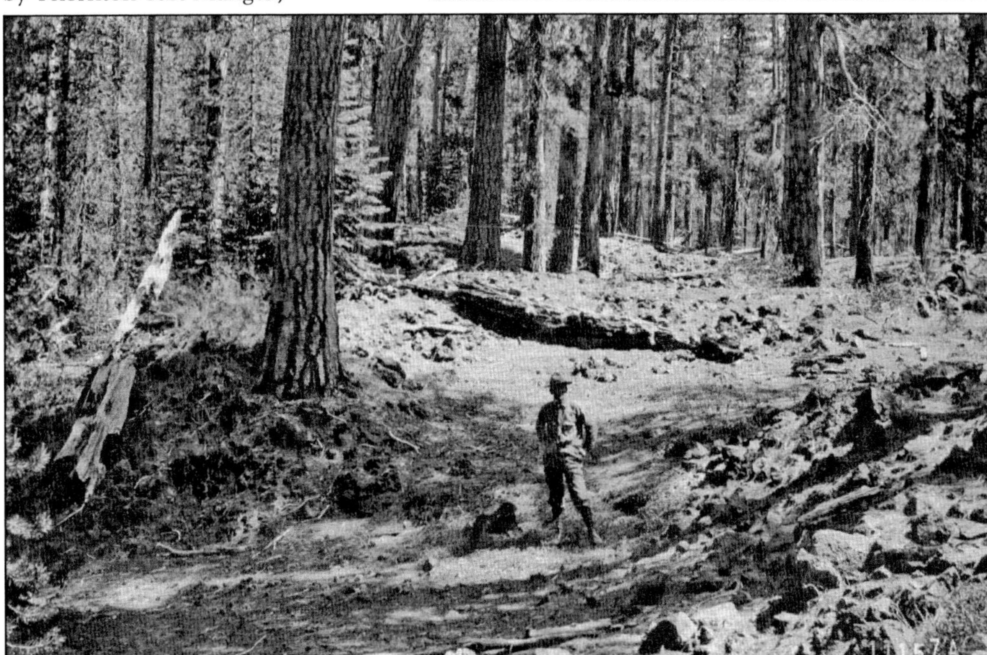

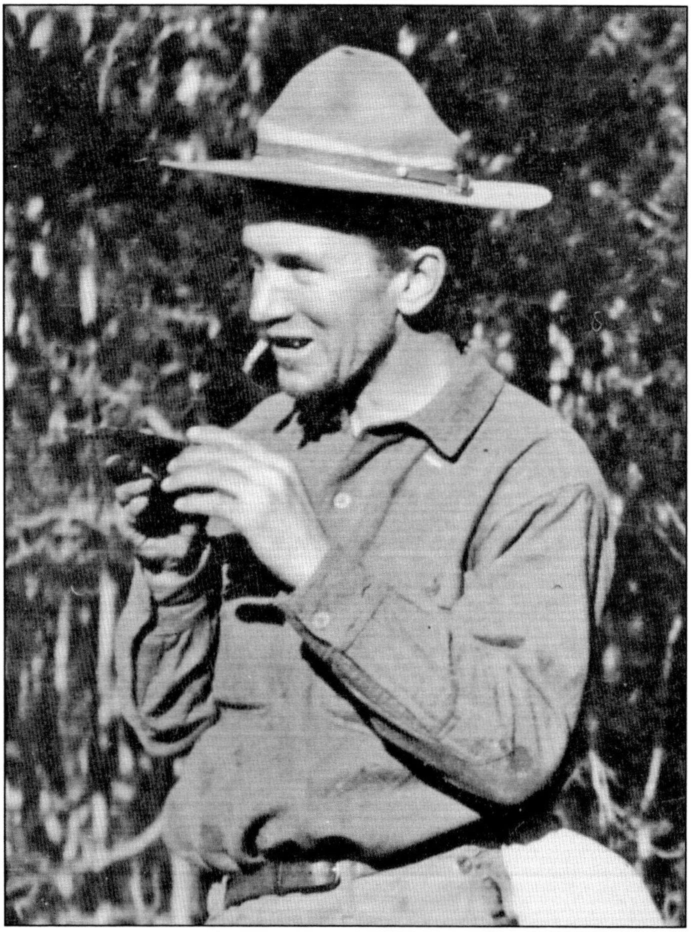

"A horse and a dog and a gun. What more could a man want?" rhapsodized former ranger John Riis (left) of the Big River Ranger District. "A comfortable cabin, pleasant work out under the sky where the lakes were blue gems set in the green hills; where trout leaped joyously in the sun and the waters were sweet and cool. I had it all." And, until he resigned in September 1913, he did at the Big River Ranger Station (below) on the Deschutes River, where his dog Pedro and his horse Bob patiently awaited the next adventure. A day's ride south of Bend, the ranger station was built in 1911 and used until 1917, when the district was combined with the La Pine Ranger District and its headquarters moved to La Pine. (Both, John Riis Group.)

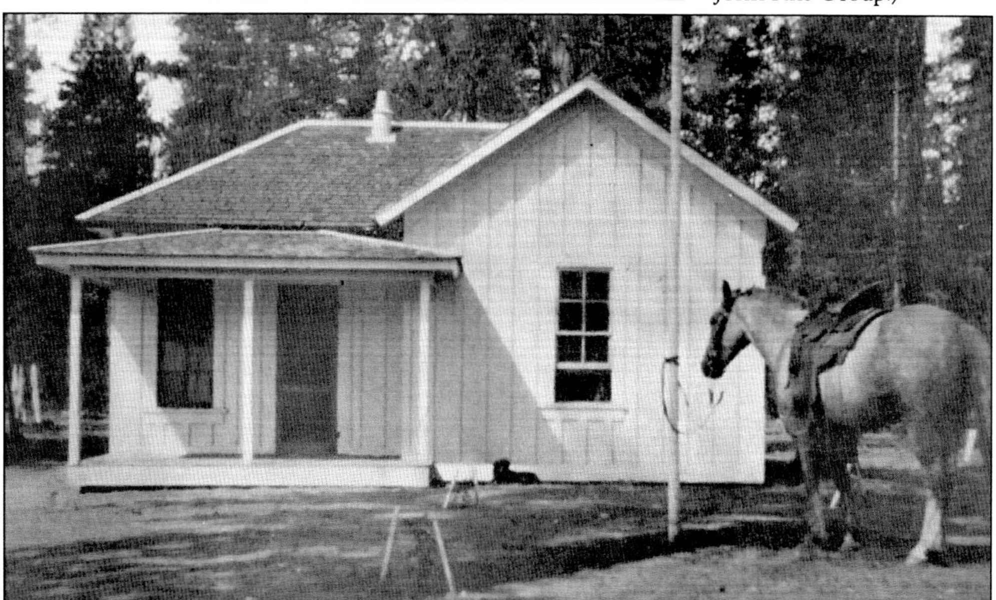

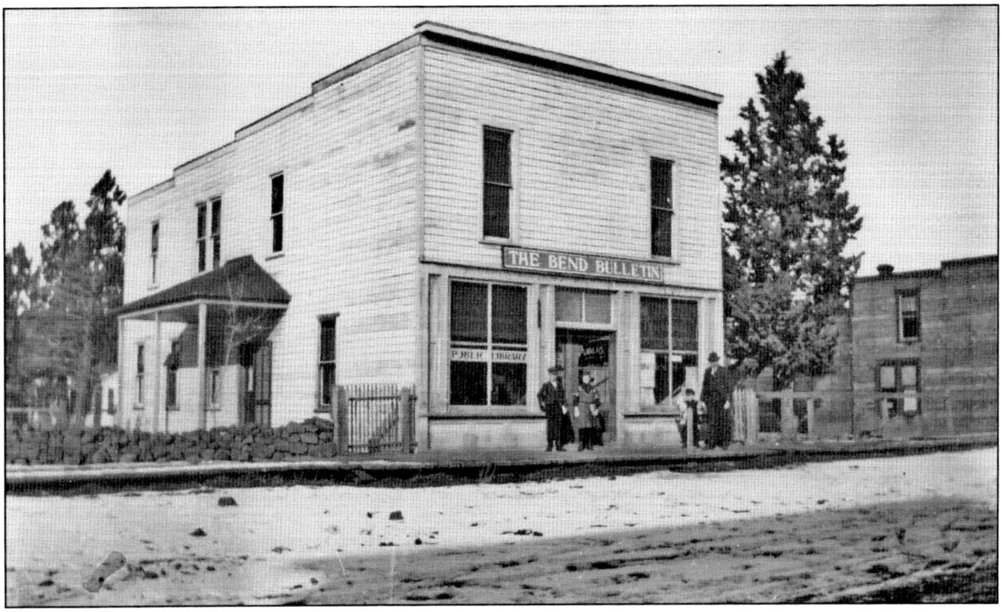

"The little town of Bend nestling at the food of the Cascades . . . was the Mecca of the Rangers on the Deschutes," former ranger John Riis writes in his 1937 book *Ranger Trails*. "We had to go to town every now and then to have our horses shod, replenish the larder, or for a few days of detail in the Supervisor's office" on the second floor of the Bend Bulletin Building. (Deschutes County Historical Society.)

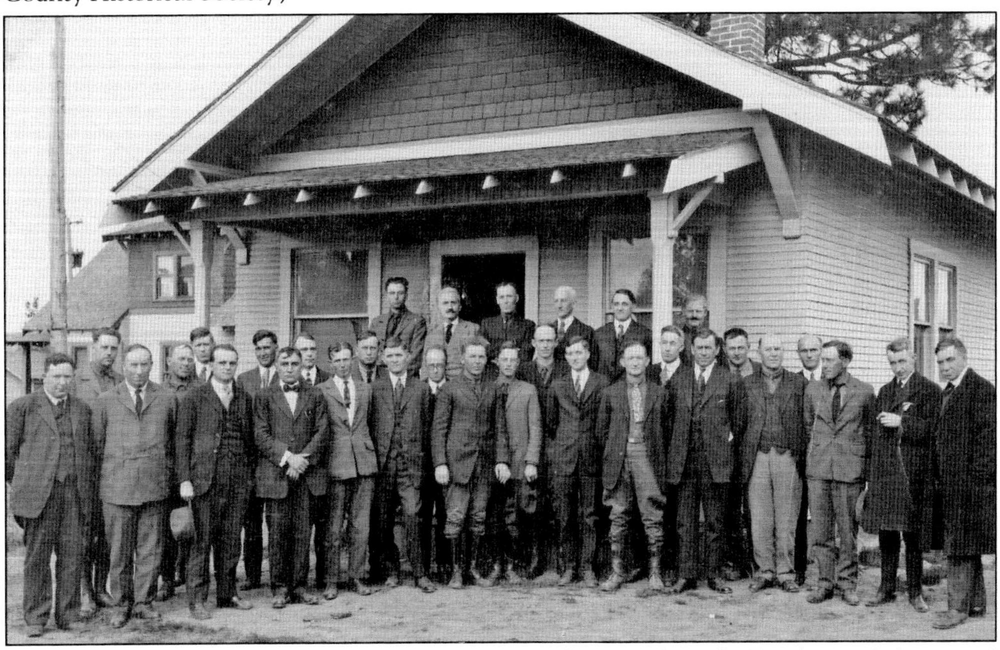

Early in their history, US Forest Service supervisors and rangers from the Deschutes, Ochoco, and Fremont National Forests and officials from the North Pacific District (now Pacific Northwest Region) office in Portland, Oregon, held annual three-day ranger meetings in Bend, such as this one in 1922. At those meetings, they planned for the coming year's field and fire seasons and associated ranger duties. (US Forest Service.)

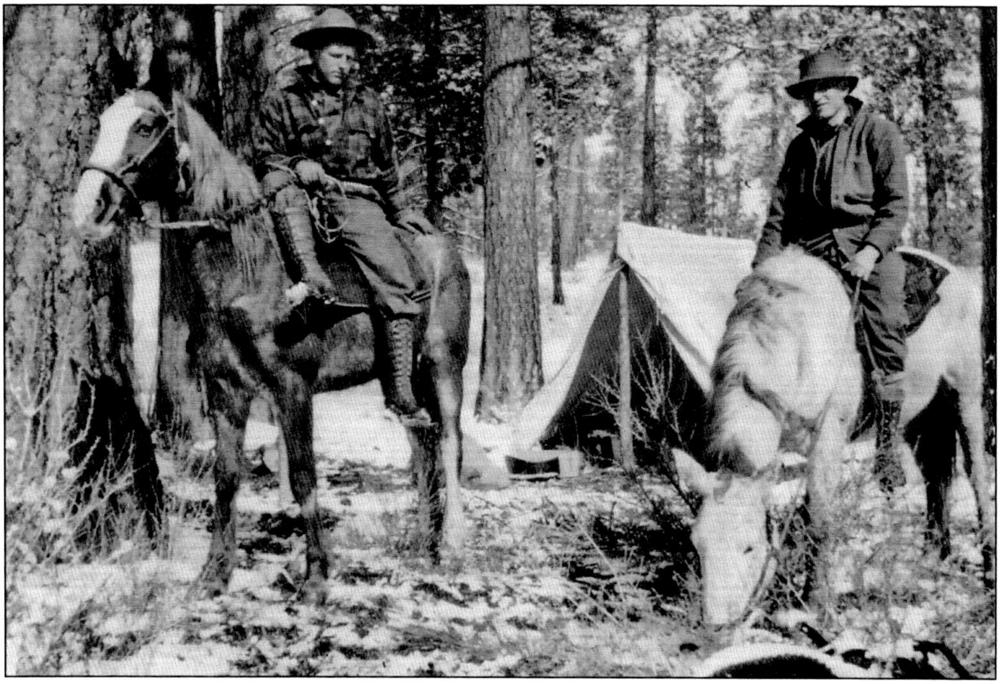

Ranger Harold E. Smith (left) of the Pine Mountain Ranger District from 1912 to 1918 was one of Riis's fellow Deschutes National Forest pioneer rangers. He and other early Forest Service personnel, such as forest assistant Will Sproat (right), often lived and worked under arduous conditions. (Stephen G. Petit.)

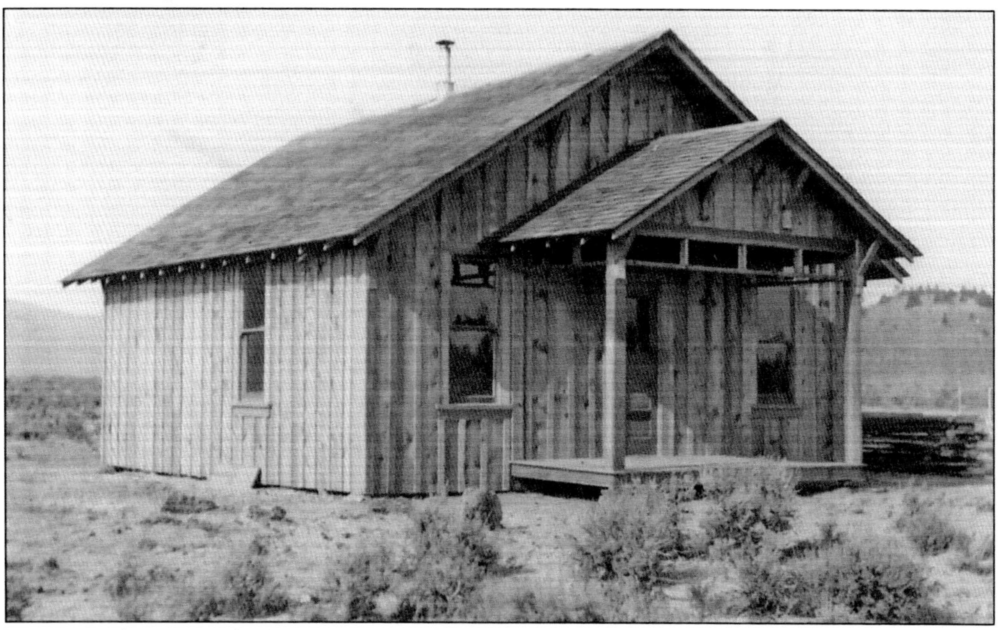

Living conditions on the Pine Mountain Ranger District improved in 1914. That year, with the help of ranger Harvey E. Vincent of the Sisters Ranger District, ranger Smith built this Pine Mountain Ranger Station building at Antelope Springs. He, his wife, and their daughter lived there until 1918. He served the rest of his Forest Service career in Alaska. (Stephen G. Petit.)

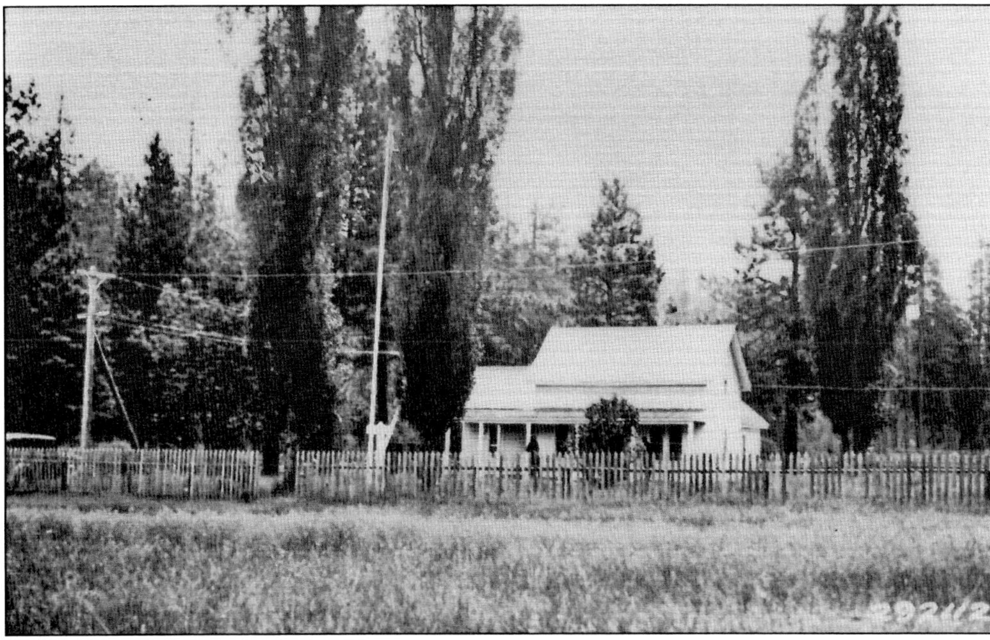

The old Allingham Ranch house, along the Metolius River about 13 miles north of Sisters, was the first Sisters Ranger Station. It was occupied by ranger Perry A. South in 1906 and later used as a guard station. Other Sisters Ranger District offices were on the north bank of Squaw Creek (renamed Wychus Creek) from 1909 to 1918, then over George Aitken's store in Sisters, which burned in 1923. (Deschutes County Historical Society.)

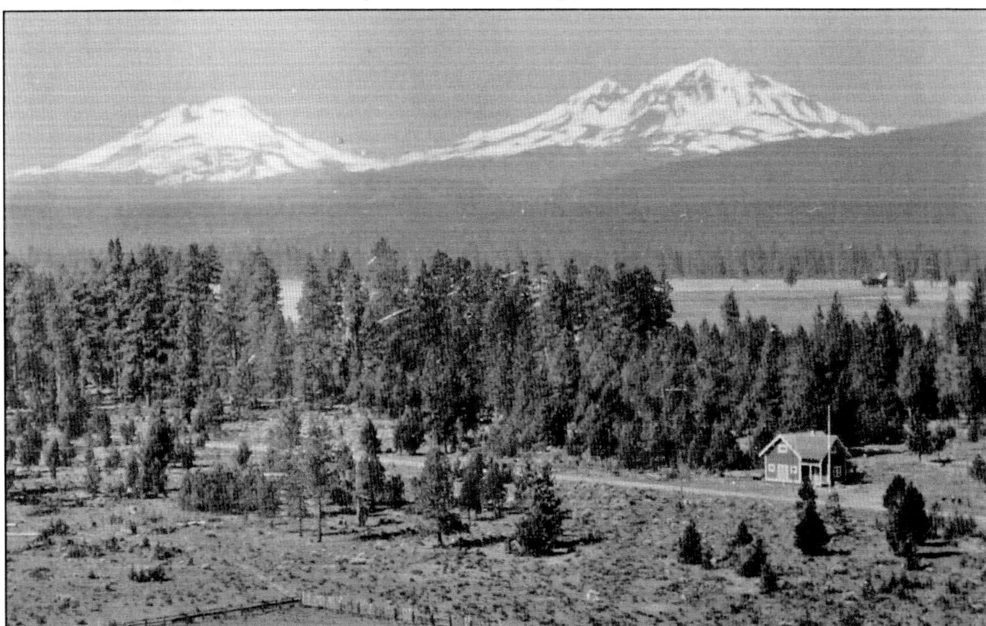

The fourth Sisters Ranger Station, shown with the Three Sisters behind it, was built on a site now well within Sisters in 1924. Adjacent land was purchased in 1936 on which a new Sisters Ranger Station compound was built in the late 1930s. The 1924 structure eventually was sold and moved to another location in town and remains as a private residence. (Nunzie Gould.)

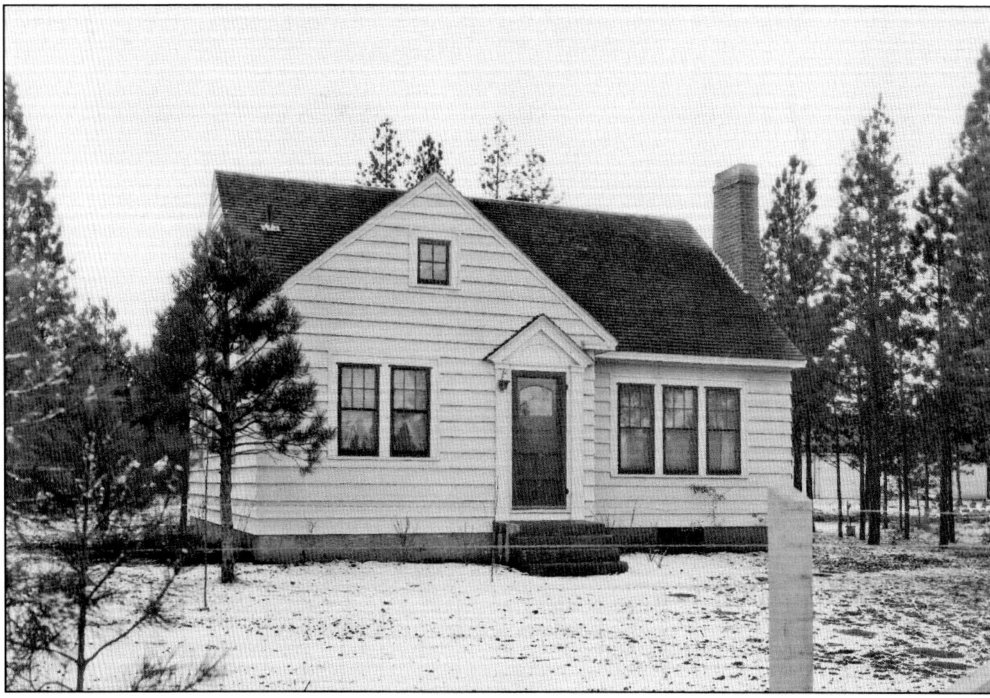

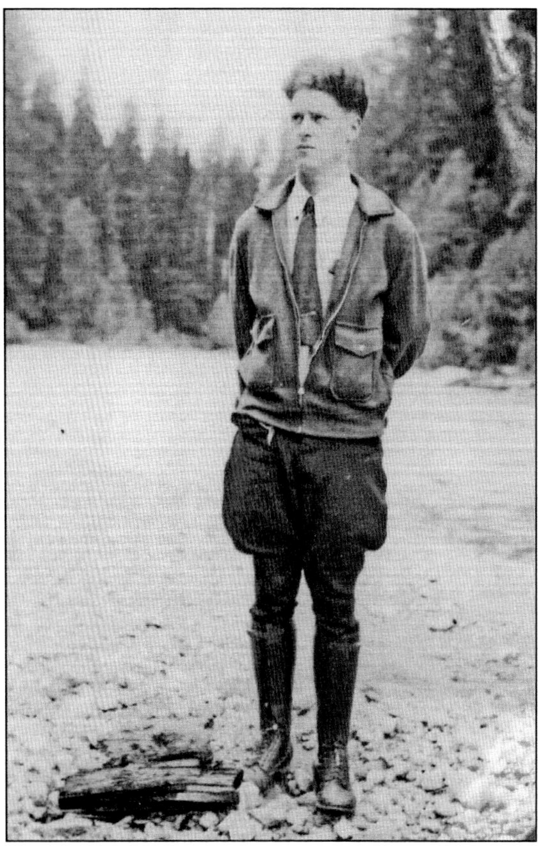

The fifth Sisters Ranger Station compound was built in the 1930s on the location of the current Sisters–Camp Sherman Fire Department station and the Sisters Village Green city park. In addition to this ranger's residence, it included an office building, a warehouse, three other cabins to house district personnel, and other buildings. (Deschutes National Forest.)

Lawrence Chapman, district ranger of the Sisters Ranger District from 1938 to 1940, and his wife lived in that new ranger's residence. Chapman transferred to the Malheur National Forest and eventually went to work in private industry. (Ann Chapman Brenda.)

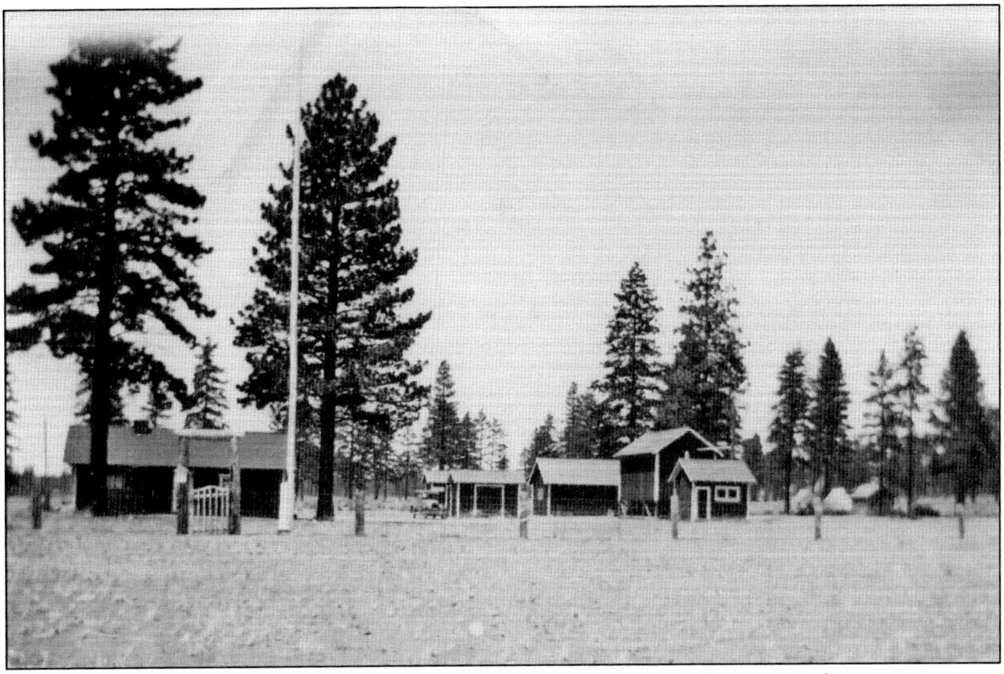

Forty miles as the crow flies south-southeast of Bend, where the ponderosa pine forest gives way to the sagebrush sea, remote Cabin Lake Ranger Station was headquarters for five Deschutes National Forest district rangers between 1917 and 1945. A well drilled in 1916 to improve grazing on the Fort Rock Ranger District made the site an attractive location for a ranger station. (Deschutes National Forest.)

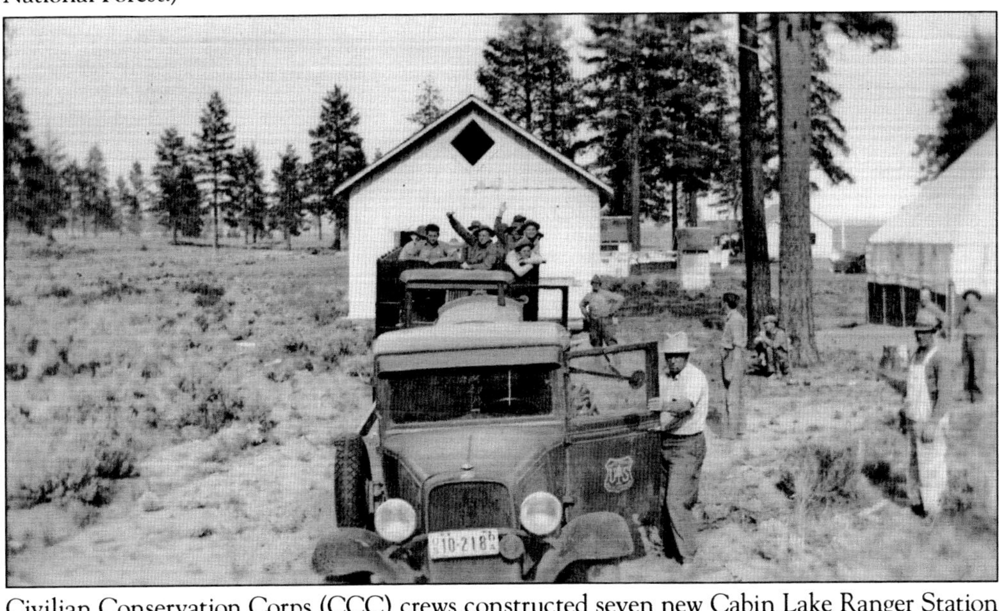

Civilian Conservation Corps (CCC) crews constructed seven new Cabin Lake Ranger Station buildings between 1934 and 1938. Six of these—a ranger's residence, two other residences, a warehouse, a shop, and a gas house—remain among the widely spaced ponderosa pines. Only the warehouse sports the pine tree logo found on many CCC-built ranger station buildings. The station's bunkhouse and pump house date from 1923. (Don Franks.)

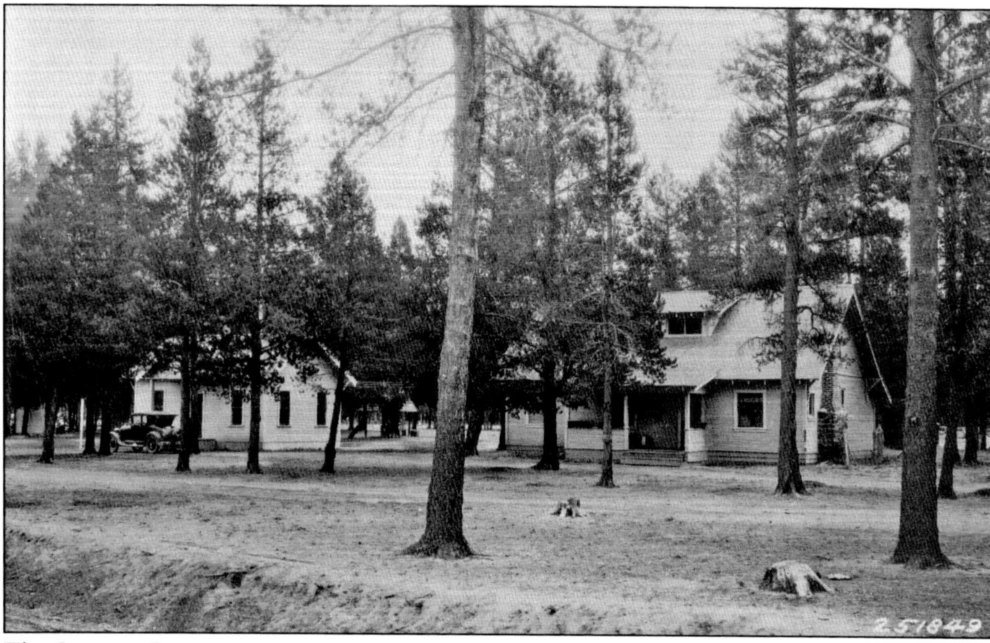

The Crescent Ranger Station office (left) and residence (right) were along US Highway 97 (then called The Dalles–California Highway) in 1930. The residence was moved from the abandoned Odell Guard Station site. While being reassembled along the highway, it wound up in the Great Northern Railway right-of-way. Twelve men moved it across the highway. (Deschutes National Forest.)

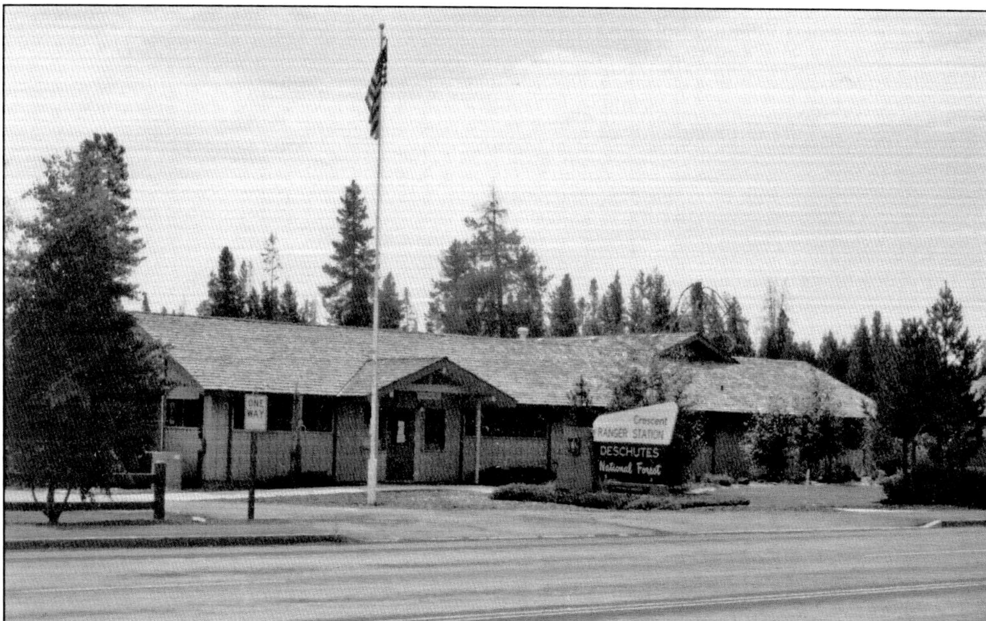

A new Crescent Ranger Station office building was built along US Highway 97 during the early-1960s era of new ranger station construction on the Deschutes National Forest. With additions, it served as the district ranger's office until a new office building was completed in 2015. (Deschutes National Forest.)

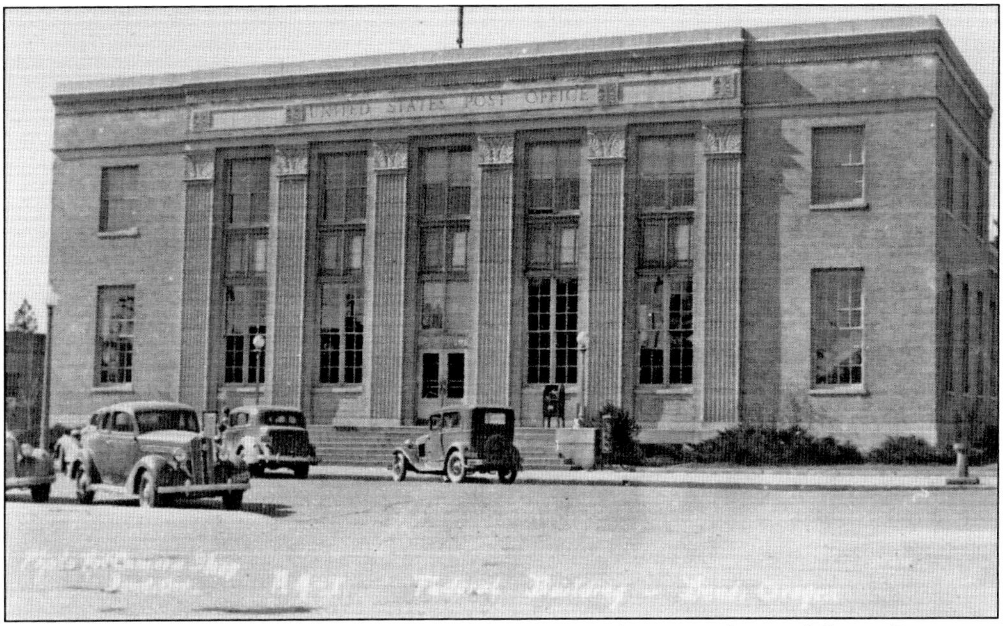

The Deschutes National Forest supervisor's office successively occupied second-floor office spaces in downtown Bend office buildings including the First National Bank Building, the O'Donnell Building, and the O'Kane Building. In 1933, the forest supervisor and his staff began an almost-three-decade residence on the second floor of the US Post Office Building on Wall Street. (Deschutes County Historical Society.)

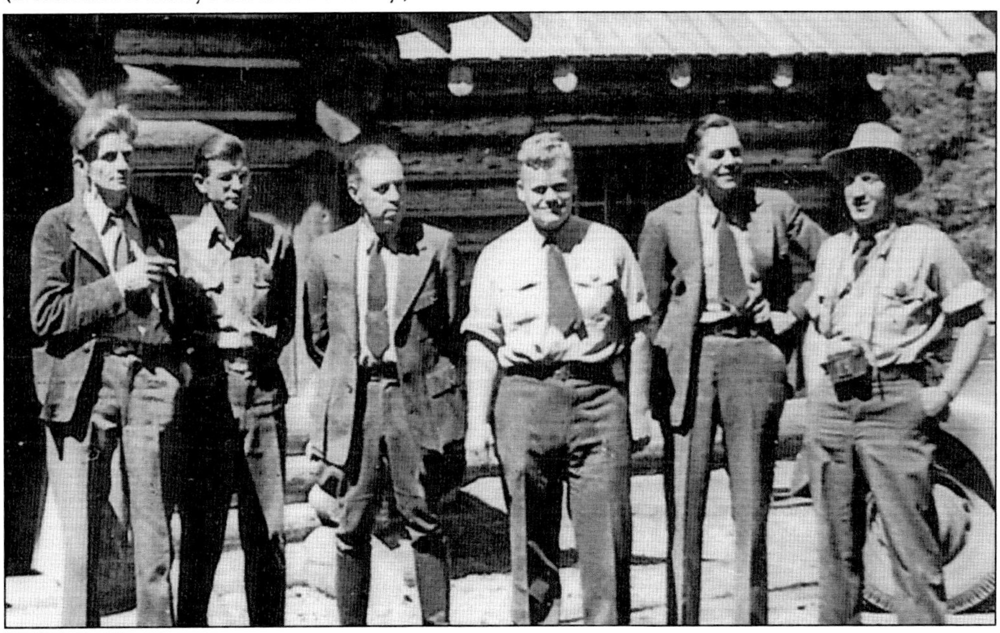

Deschutes National Forest supervisor Ralph W. Crawford (third from left) met with his district rangers and fire control officer at Skyliner Lodge in 1943. From left to right are Henry Tonseth, Fort Rock Ranger District; Harold Nyberg, Sisters Ranger District; Crawford; Homer Oft, Crescent Ranger District; Gail Baker, fire control officer; and Joe Lammi, Bend Ranger District. (Deschutes County Historical Society.)

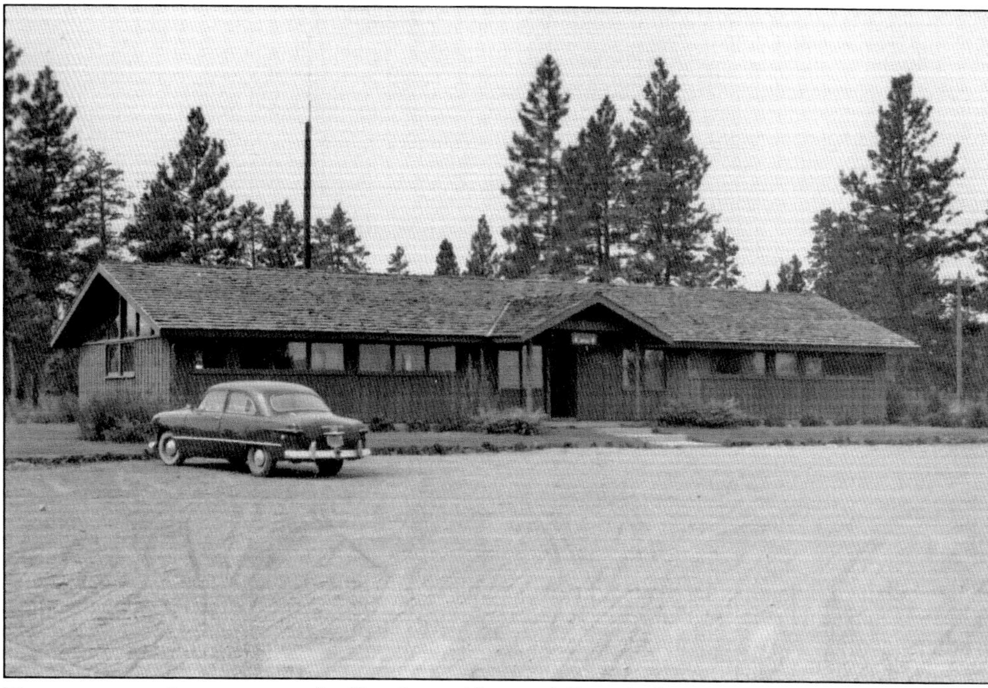

New ranger stations to meet the Deschutes National Forest's district rangers' increasing needs for office space were built during the early 1960s. A new Sisters Ranger Station for the Sisters Ranger District and the briefly revived Metolius Ranger District (above) was built on the west side of Sisters at the junction of US Highway 20 and Oregon Highway 242. With additions, this office and adjacent facilities continue to serve as the Sisters Ranger District headquarters. A new Bend Ranger Station (below) was built on Parrell Road on the southeastern side of Bend. (Both, Deschutes National Forest.)

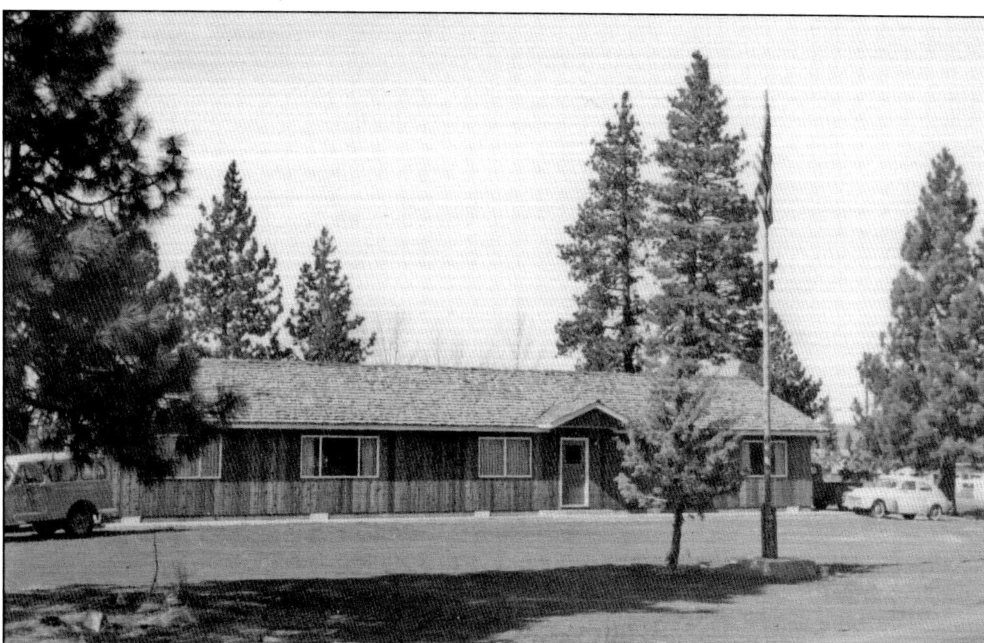

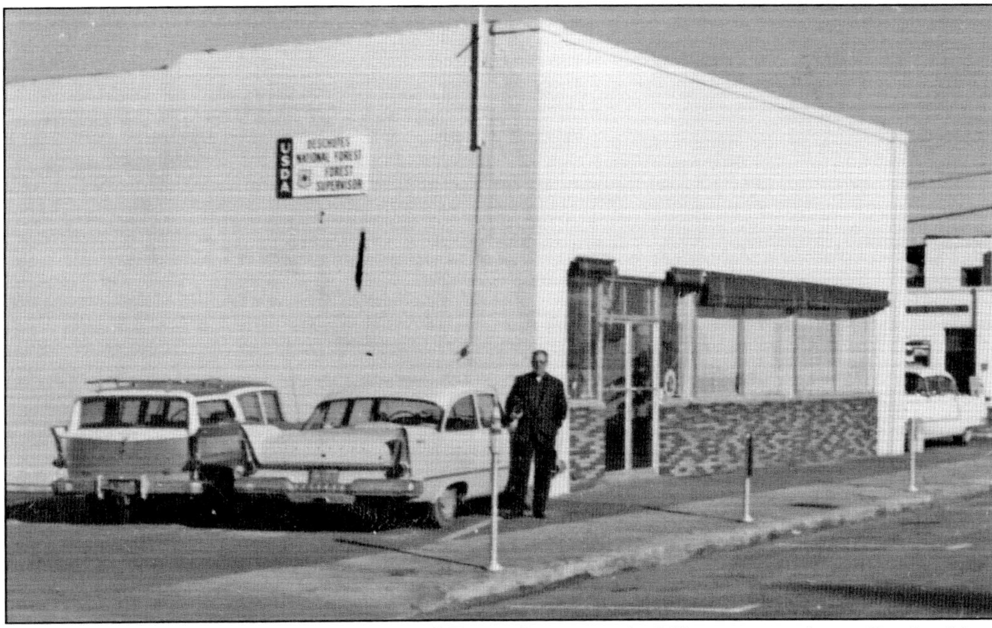

By the mid-1960s, the Deschutes National Forest Supervisor's Office occupied an office building on Bond Street in downtown Bend (above), and the Fort Rock Ranger District was housed in another office building at 760 East Greenwood Avenue on Bend's east side (below). District ranger Henry Tonseth, who led the Fort Rock Ranger District from 1934 to 1969—a 35-year term in office that remains a Pacific Northwest Region record for service as district ranger on one district—stands in front of his downtown office in this 1964 photograph. For the first decade of that 35-year tenure, his home and office had been at the remote Cabin Lake Ranger Station amidst the timber and grazing resources he managed and the loggers and ranchers he served. (Both, Deschutes National Forest.)

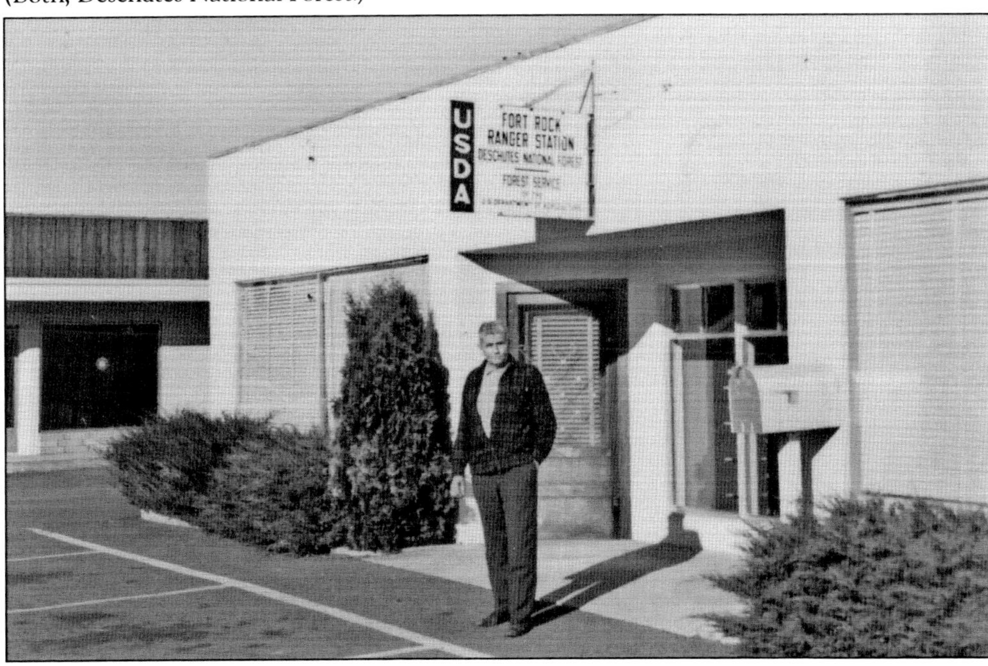

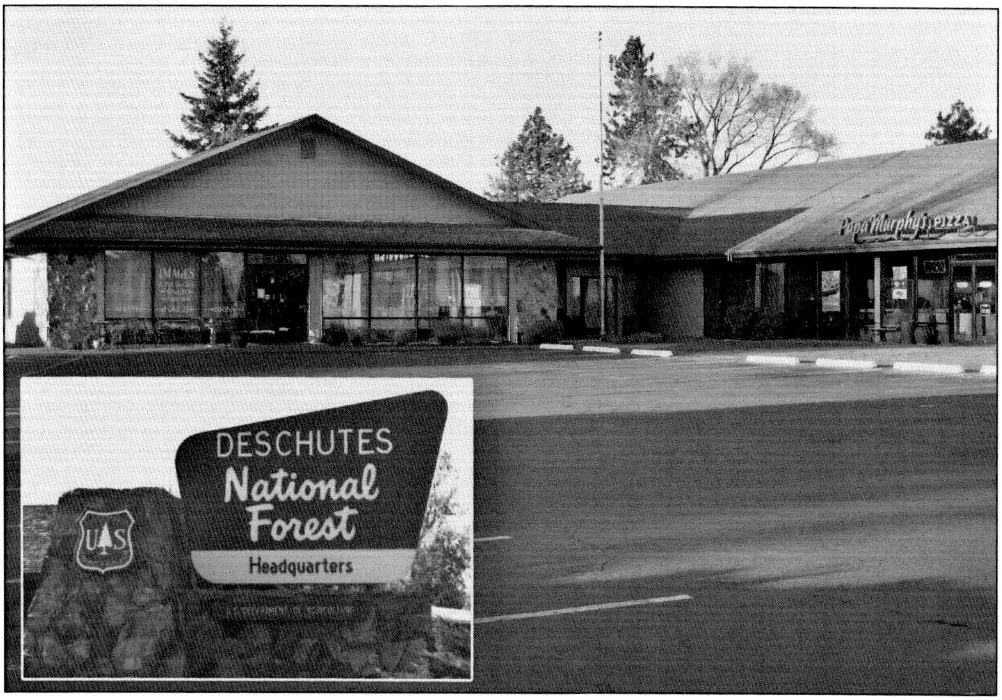

Before it housed strip-mall businesses, this Deschutes National Forest headquarters building at 211 Northeast Revere Avenue in Bend housed the forest supervisor, the Bend and Fort Rock district rangers, and their staffs from 1968 until 1983. "Now the public has only one building [at which to seek service] instead of three separate ones," forest supervisor Ashley Poust said of the new facility easily accessed from US Highway 97. (Inset, Deschutes National Forest, photograph by the author.)

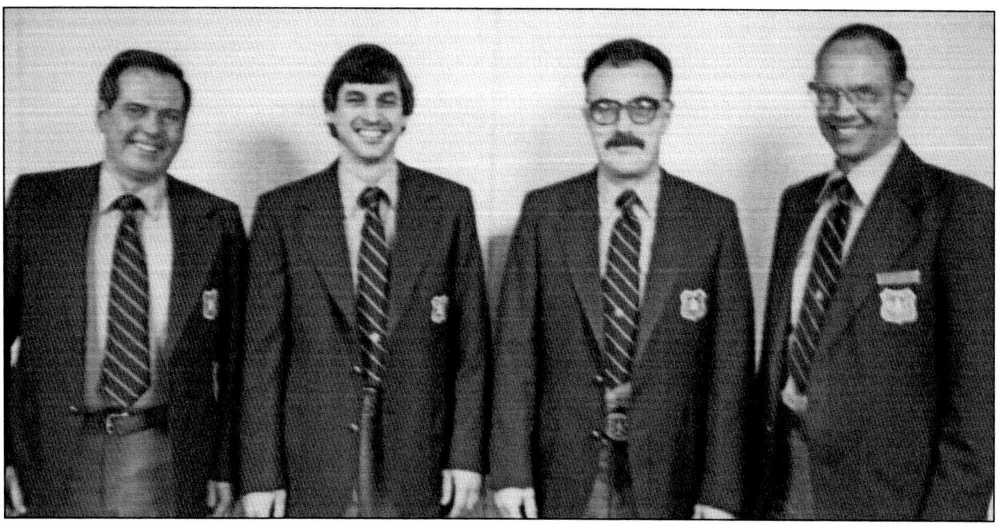

The four Deschutes National Forest district rangers in 1980 were, from left to right, George Chesley, Fort Rock Ranger District; Jeff Blackwood, Sisters Ranger District; Ted Lewis, Crescent Ranger District; and Walt Schloer, Bend Ranger District. Rangers Chesley and Schloer had offices in Bend, while ranger Blackwood was at Sisters Ranger Station and ranger Lewis was at Crescent Ranger Station. (George Chesley.)

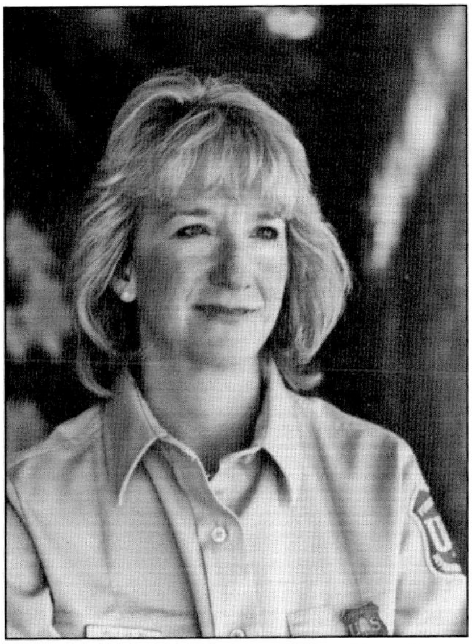

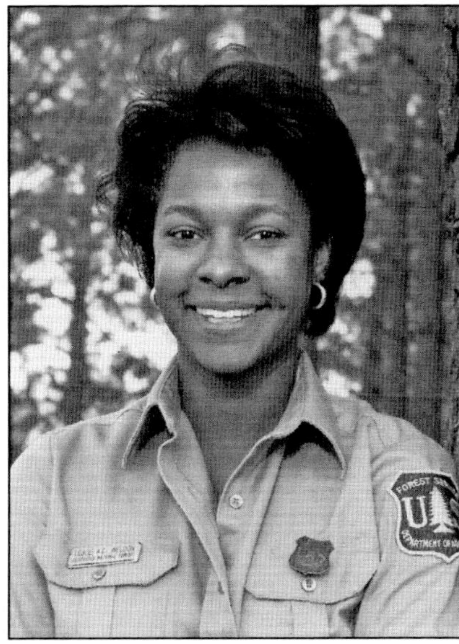

Two women have served as Deschutes National Forest supervisor. Sally Collins (left), forest supervisor from 1993 to 2000, went on to be associate chief of the US Forest Service. Leslie Weldon (right), forest supervisor from 2000 to 2008, then served as regional forester of the Northern Region and deputy chief for the National Forest System. (Left, Sally Collins; right, Oregon Forest Resources Institute.)

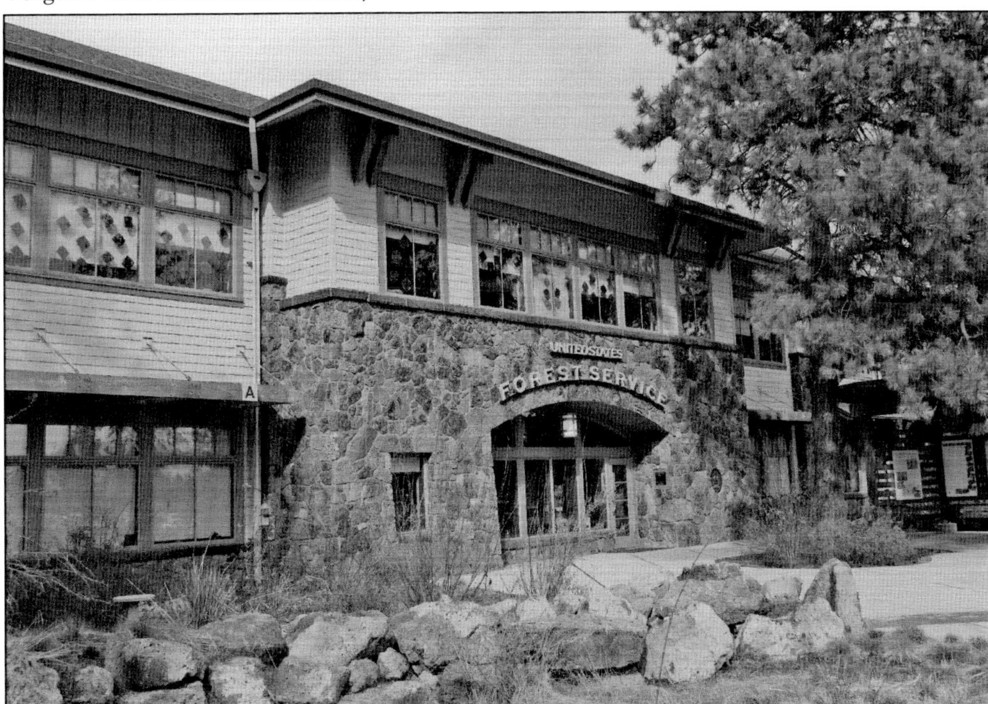

In 2011, during forest supervisor John Allen's administration, the Deschutes National Forest Headquarters staff and the Bend–Fort Rock Ranger District staff occupied this new facility in northeastern Bend on the site of the US Forest Service's former Bend Pine Nursery. Both had occupied rented office space. (Photograph by the author.)

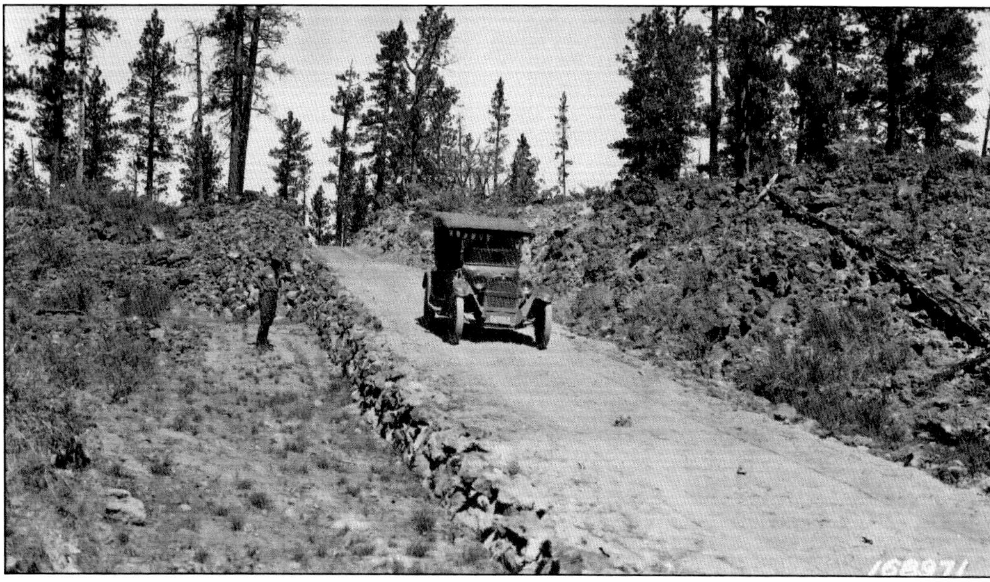

As the Deschutes National Forest developed and the age of the automobile advanced, better roads were needed to connect forest headquarters with ranger stations. Forest rangers needed them to access their satellite guard stations and fire lookouts, their resource management and protection jobs, and their growing clientele of loggers in the forest, ranchers on the range, and visitors at recreation sites including lodges, summer homes, and campgrounds clustered around scenic lakes. Roads also led to trailheads from which wilderness was and remains accessible only on trails traveled on foot or by horseback. The road above, photographed about a decade after the Deschutes National Forest was headquartered in Bend, wound some 60 miles to the remote headquarters of the Fort Rock Ranger District at Cabin Lake Ranger Station. By the middle of the 1920s, the road grader below was in use to construct Deschutes National Forest roads. (Both, Deschutes National Forest.)

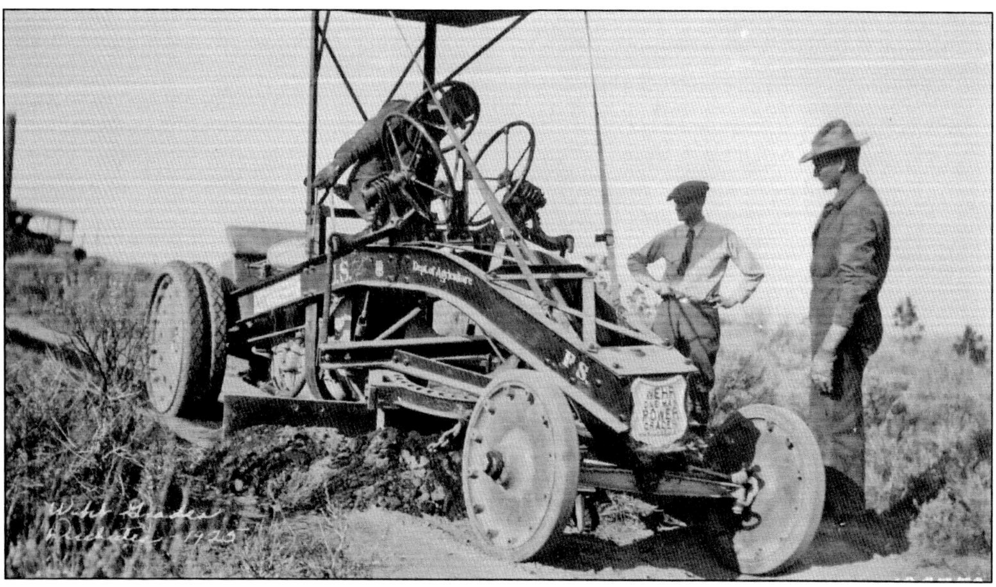

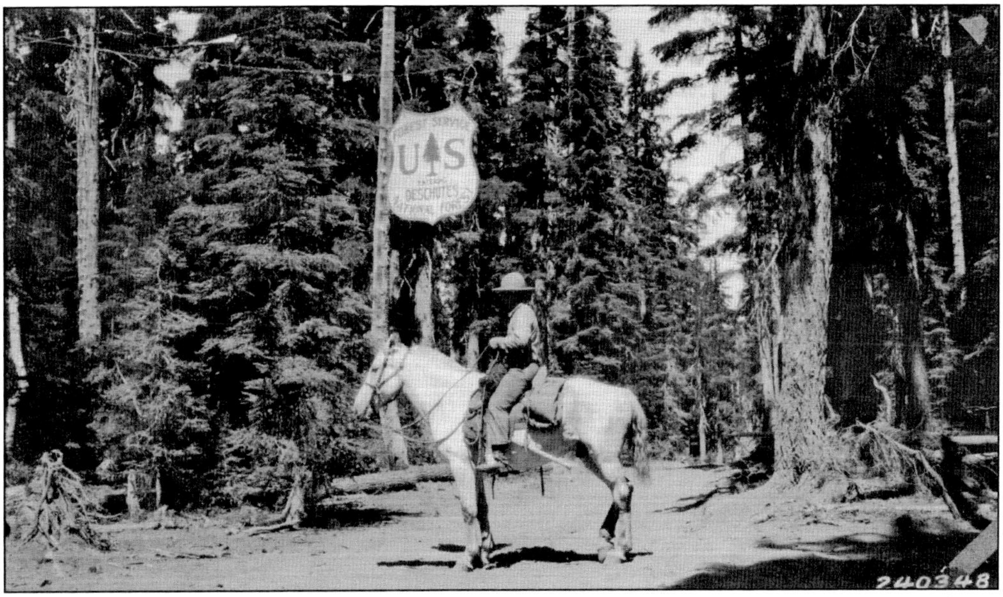

Road construction did not put horses completely out of business. On October 29, 1929, forest supervisor Carl B. Neal of the Deschutes National Forest photographed ranger Charles Thurston of the Umpqua National Forest on his horse Peter at the Windigo Pass boundary of the two national forests. (Deschutes County Historical Society.)

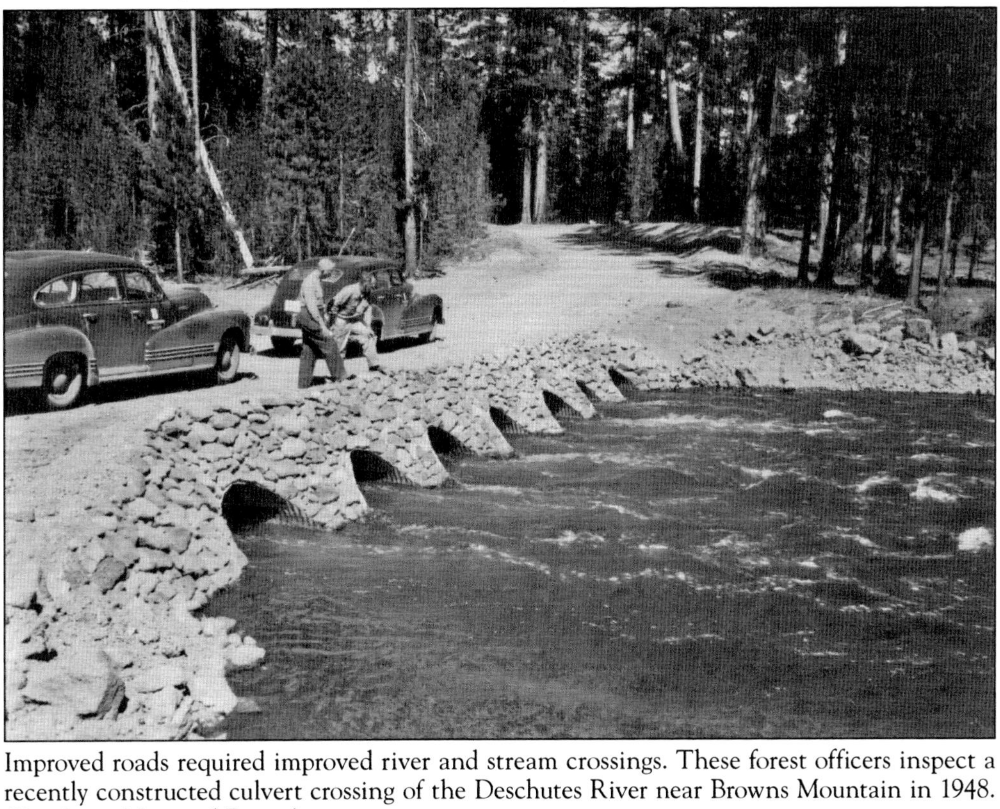

Improved roads required improved river and stream crossings. These forest officers inspect a recently constructed culvert crossing of the Deschutes River near Browns Mountain in 1948. (Deschutes National Forest.)

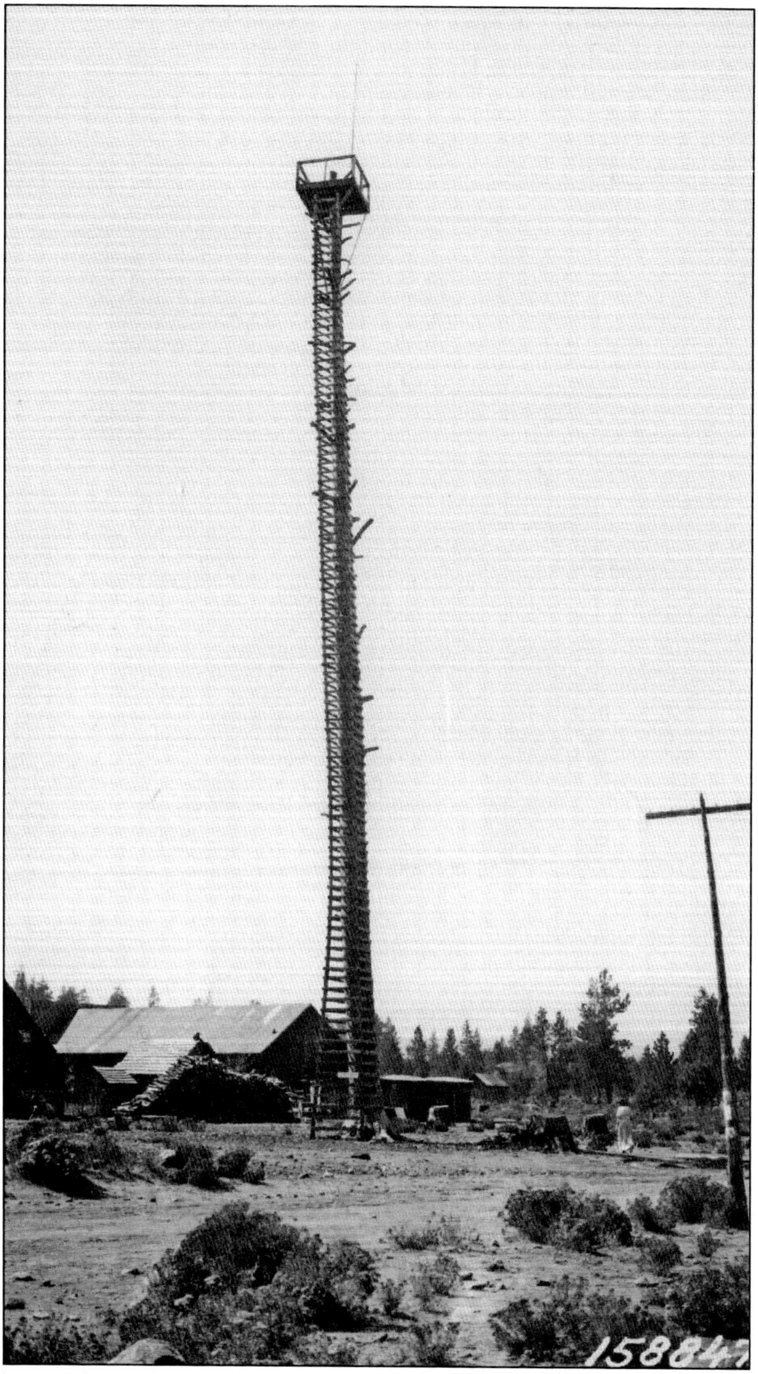

The fire lookout is the symbol of forest protection. The July 21, 1915, Deschutes Ranger column in the *Bend Bulletin* reports that "E.H. Howell, Deputy State Fire Warden, and Ranger H.E. Vincent [of the US Forest Service] are constructing a lookout tower in Sisters which will be about eighty feet high when completed." A June 27, 1921, news article refers to "a temporary lookout from a tree top at Sisters . . . in charge of Ben Smith." The tree lookout had to be cut down in 1926 because of decay. (Deschutes National Forest.)

Three

Forest Protection

Foresters protect the resources they manage from wildfire, insects, and disease as well as from theft and vandalism. Early-days rangers addressed those latter criminal threats to the forest as they went about their other duties. More recently, law and order in the national forests has been the province of Forest Service law enforcement officers.

Although there was recognition by some in the US Forest Service that fire plays a beneficial role in some forest ecosystems, disastrous experiences with wildfires early in the agency's history resulted in a strict policy of total wildfire suppression that was followed for more than half a century.

Deschutes National Forest foresters spent time and effort preventing, preparing to suppress, and suppressing wildfires to prevent loss of the timber and grazing resources in their charge and to protect the watershed, wildlife and their habitat, and recreation resources. Virtually all US Forest Service members played a role in the fire control mission. They cautioned forest visitors and users to prevent wildfires. They developed and maintained fire lookouts for detecting wildfires and guard stations at which fire guards and crews were assigned to quickly suppress wildfires. They adopted and developed new wildfire control technologies and techniques.

During the 1970s, fire control morphed into fire management that recognized beneficial effects of fire and employed prescribed burning under appropriate conditions to improve forest health and reduce the danger of catastrophic wildfires. Wildfires that threaten life and property—especially in the upper Deschutes country's growing wildland-urban interface in which many people have built homes in fire-prone forestlands—continue to be suppressed even as fire ecologists and fuels specialists employ fire as a management tool.

Less dramatic than fire management are Forest Service efforts to control insects and diseases that threaten forest health and forest resources. Late in the 20th century, a pandora moth epidemic defoliated many Deschutes National Forest ponderosa pines but killed relatively few. At the same time, a mountain pine beetle infestation that lasted well into the 21st century devastated many of the forest's lodgepole pine forests. Parasitic western dwarf mistletoe also threatens pine forests.

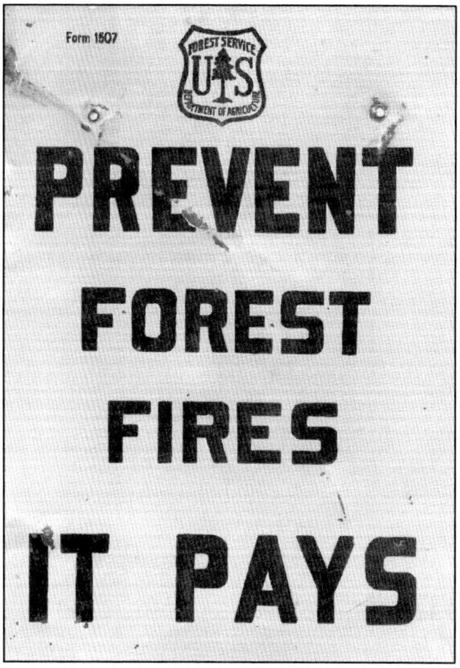

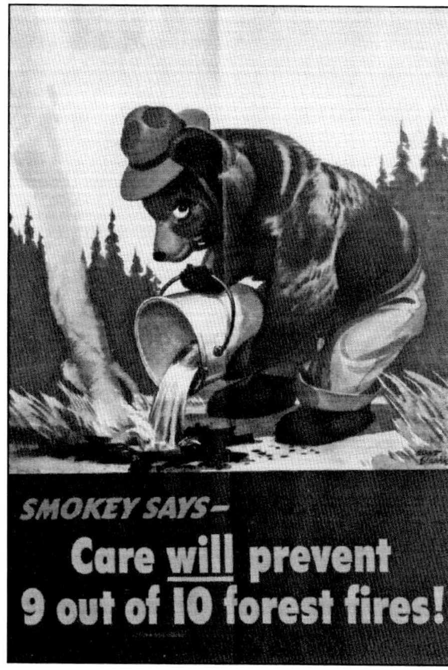

For more than a century, the US Forest Service has urged the public to prevent forest fires, more recently termed wildfires. Smokey, America's "forest fire preventin' bear" for over 70 years, first appeared in 1945 in this legendary poster painted by artist Albert Stahle. (US Forest Service.)

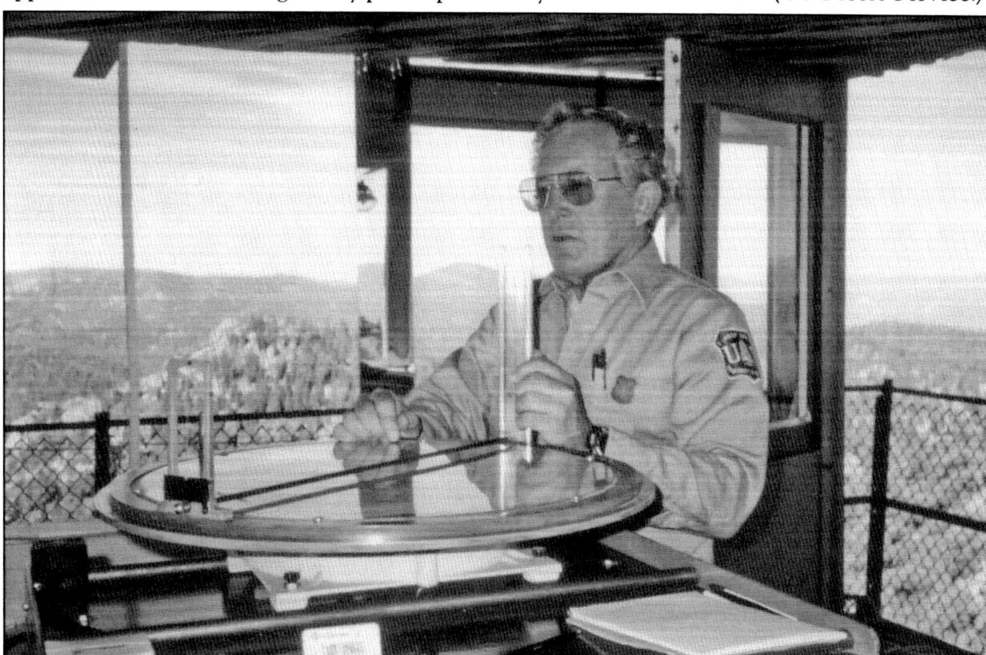

Whether ignited by human carelessness or lightning, wildfires are often detected by fire lookouts using the Osborne fire finder, invented by W.B. Osborne in 1915. Detection is also accomplished from fire patrol aircraft and by space-based remote sensing systems. Several fire lookouts remain in service on the Deschutes National Forest. (Photograph by the author.)

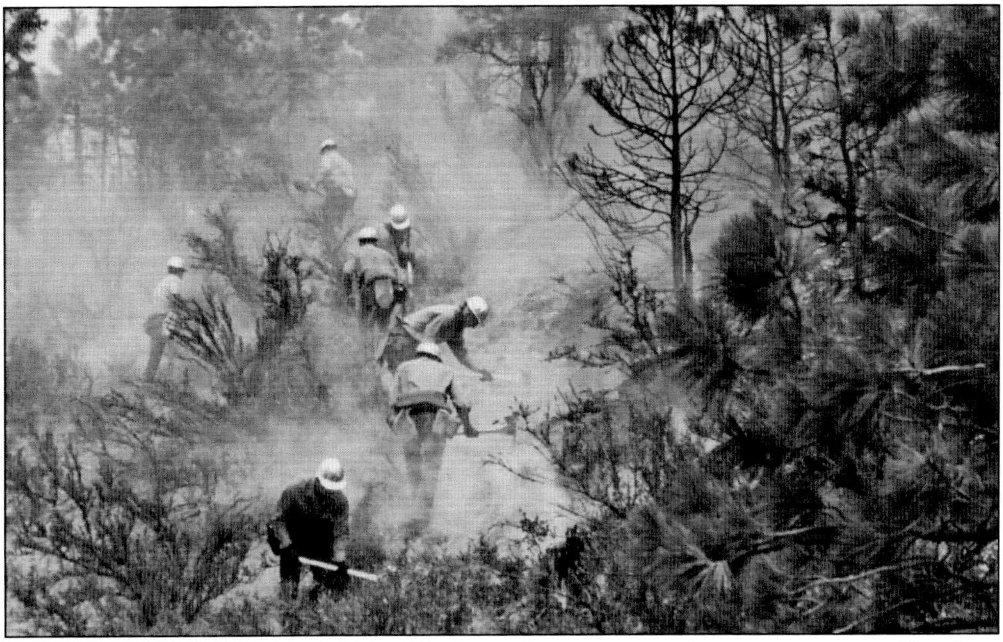

Regardless of how firefighters get to wildfires—walking, riding on fire apparatus, rappelling from helicopters, or parachuting from aircraft—firefighting always boils down to hot, hard, dirty, and dangerous work. These mid-20th-century Deschutes National Forest firefighters build a fire line to arrest a fire's spread by removing fuels. (Deschutes National Forest.)

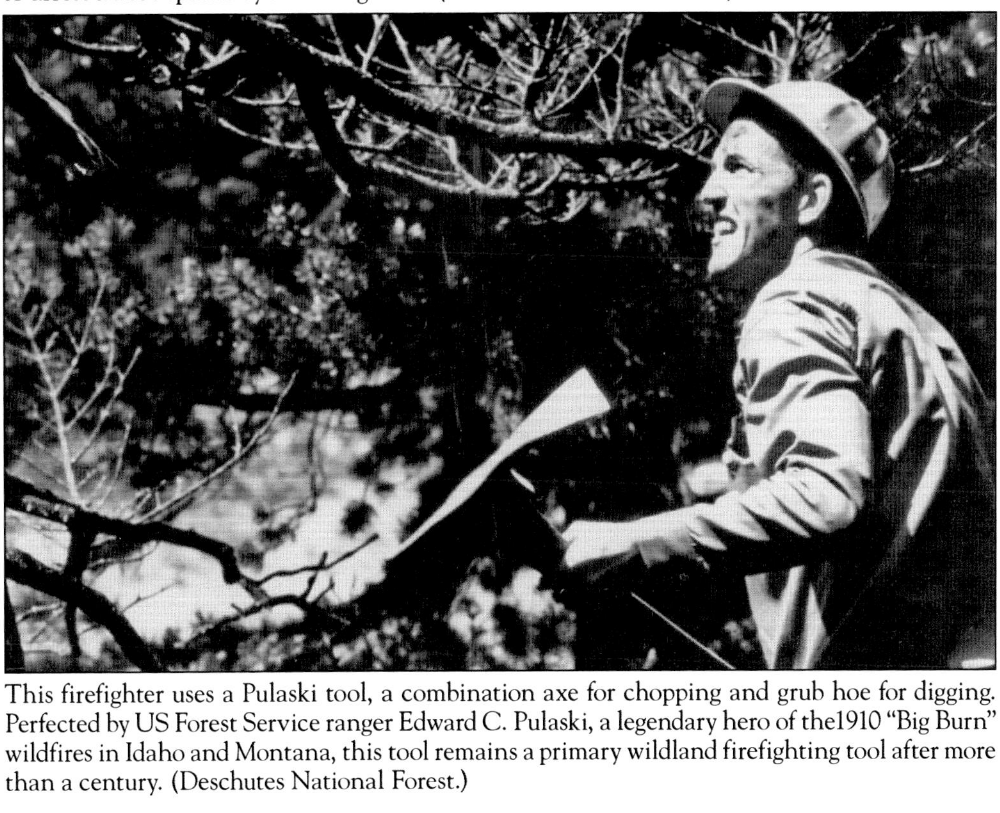

This firefighter uses a Pulaski tool, a combination axe for chopping and grub hoe for digging. Perfected by US Forest Service ranger Edward C. Pulaski, a legendary hero of the1910 "Big Burn" wildfires in Idaho and Montana, this tool remains a primary wildland firefighting tool after more than a century. (Deschutes National Forest.)

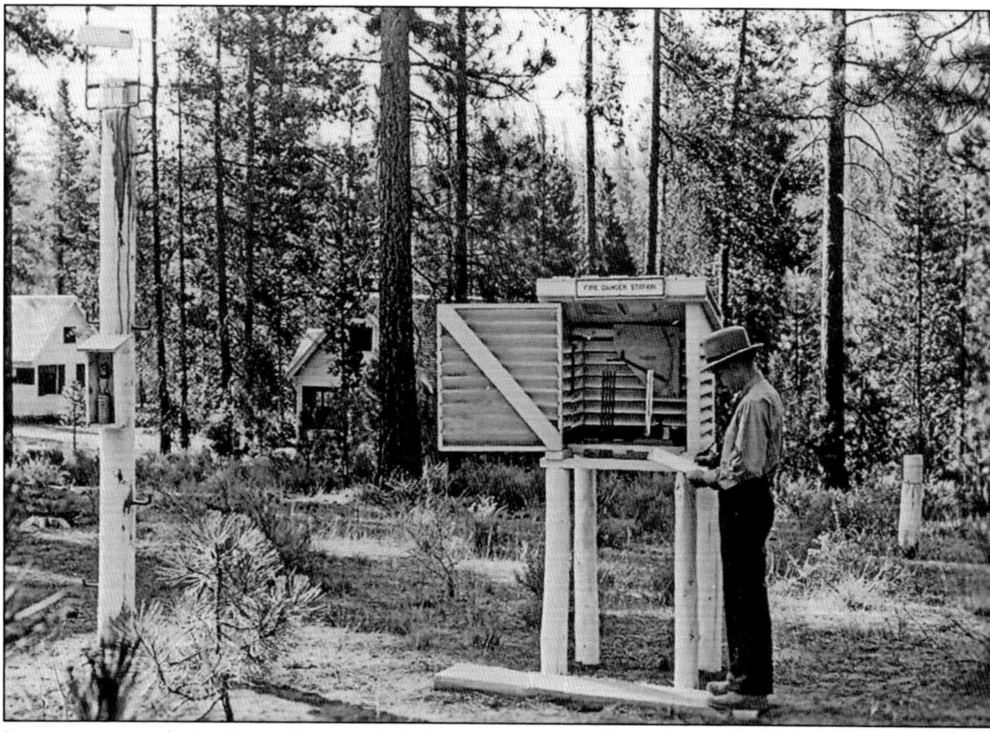

Temperature, relative humidity, rainfall, fuel moisture, and wind speed and direction contribute to how quickly wildfires spread once ignited. Forester Bill Morris, pictured at the Pringle Falls Experimental Forest fire danger station in 1945—and others throughout the Deschutes National Forest—recorded and reported daily readings of these factors to help determine wildfire danger and appropriate prevention and control measures. (Deschutes National Forest.)

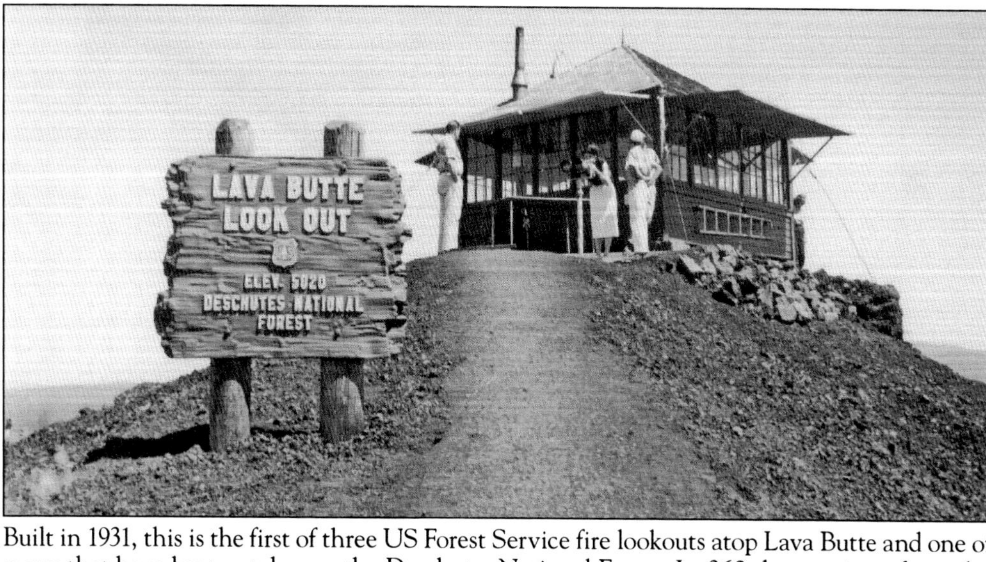

Built in 1931, this is the first of three US Forest Service fire lookouts atop Lava Butte and one of many that have kept watch over the Deschutes National Forest. Its 360-degree view of popular recreation lands, valuable timberlands, and now much of Central Oregon's wildland-urban interface communities makes today's modern Lava Butte Lookout invaluable. It normally detects more wildfires than any other lookout on the national forest. (Deschutes National Forest.)

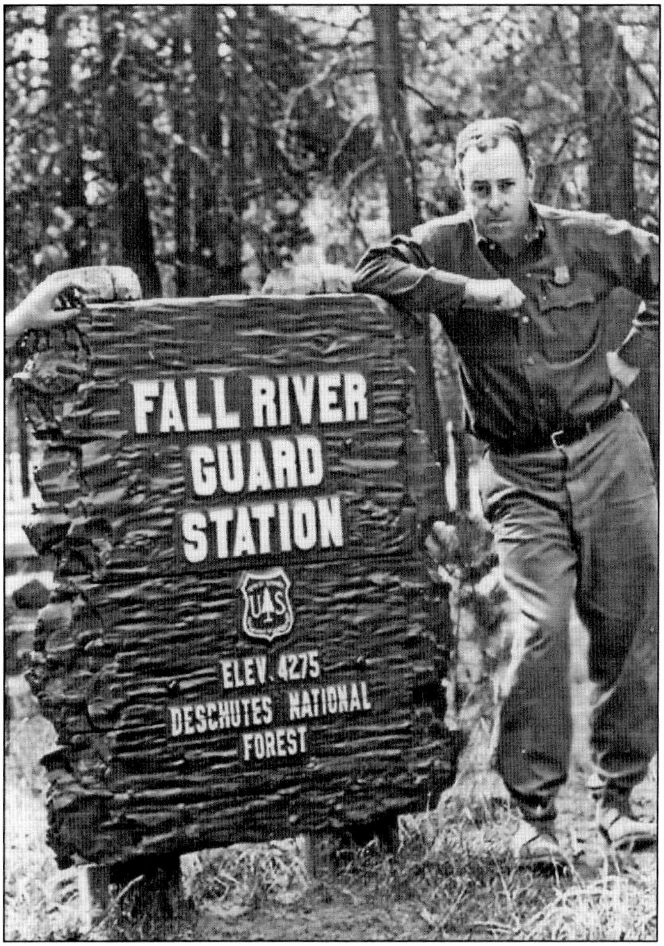

Forest supervisor Ralph Crawford (right) regularly stopped by the Fall River Guard Station (below), once a hub of Deschutes National Forest fire control. Fire lookouts reported fires to the dispatcher at this station, who sent firefighters to the fires. "Either in 1938 or 1939 was a horrendous fire season," recalled Bob Lindsay, the dispatcher's son. "Mother, running the switchboard, sat on a glass-bottomed stool. A lightning strike blew the switchboard up and knocked Mother off the stool and against the wall." A new switchboard with a safety switch was installed. After its dispatch years, the station was staffed every summer by fire guards and then by wildland fire engine crews until early in the 21st century. Restoration and use since as a recreation rental has preserved a heritage resource and developed a recreation resource. (Both, Deschutes National Forest.)

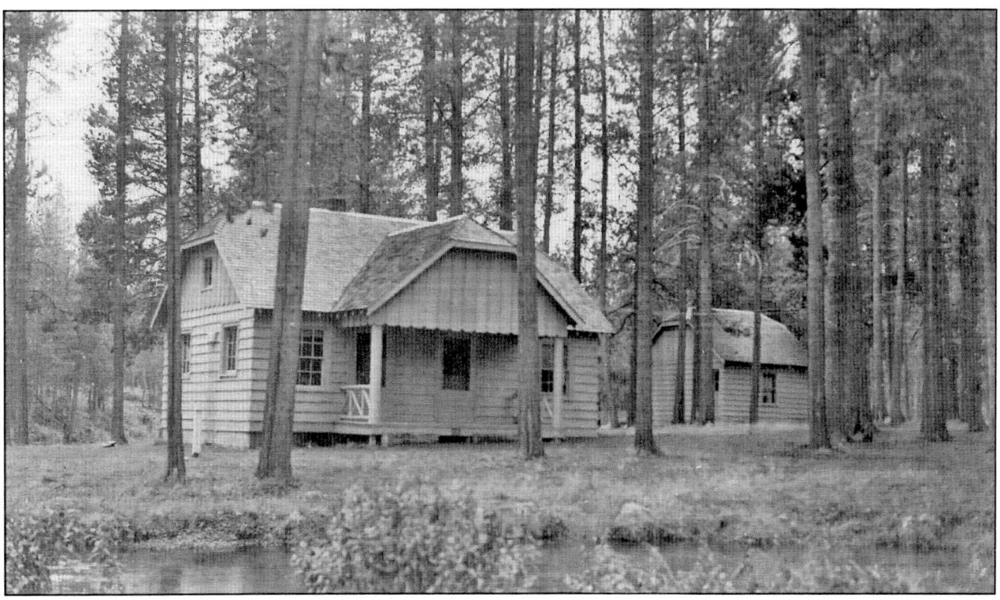

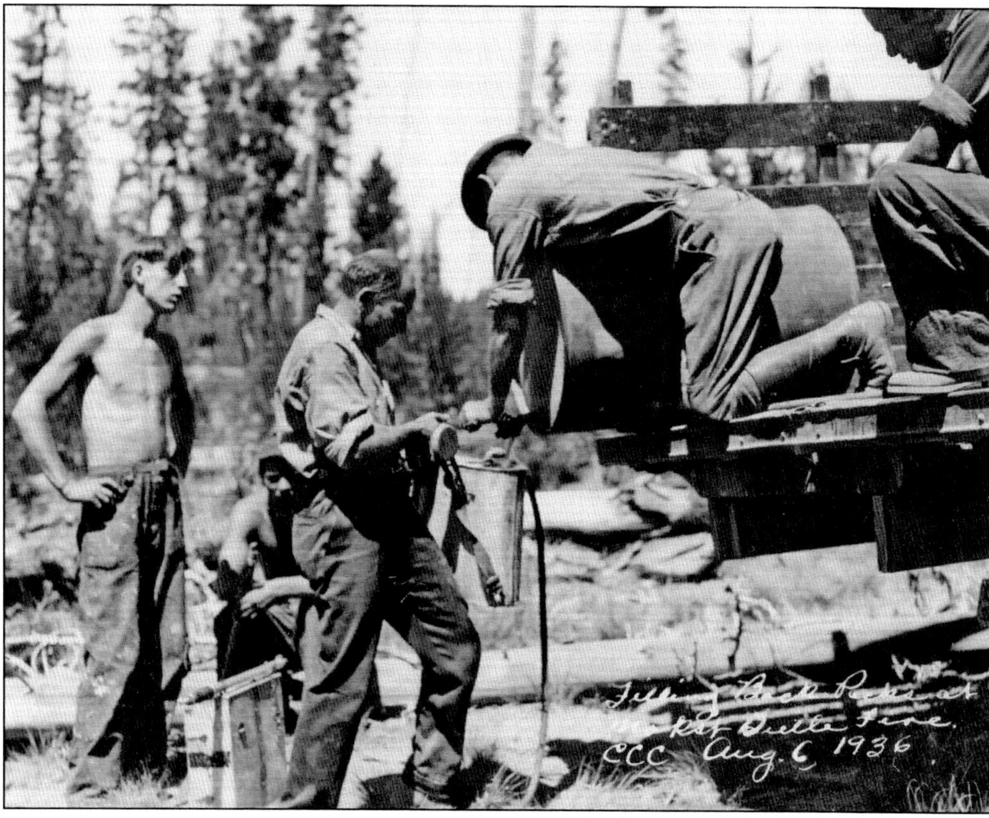

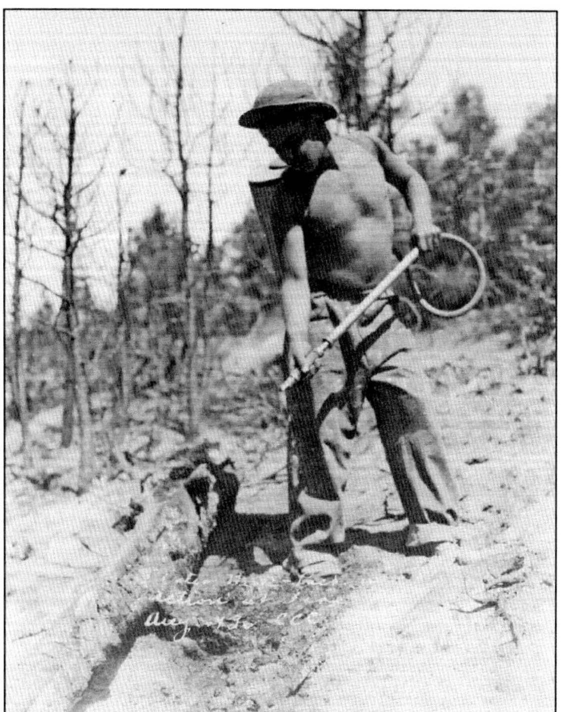

Before modern wildland fire engines arrived on the scene, water was a firefighting luxury. Squirting with water cools flames faster than throwing dirt. On August 6, 1936, this young CCC firefighter awaits his turn to fill his five-gallon backpack with water to help mop up the Mokst Butte Fire on the Deschutes National Forest. (Deschutes National Forest.)

Another CCC firefighter squirts water from a water backpack as he mops up the Mokst Butte Fire. Modern wildland firefighters are better dressed and equipped to fight wildfires. Never shirtless, they wear protective shirts and pants, have hard hats on their heads, and carry a pack filled with essential items that always include an emergency fire shelter. Pulaski tools and shovels remain the tools of their trade. (Deschutes National Forest.)

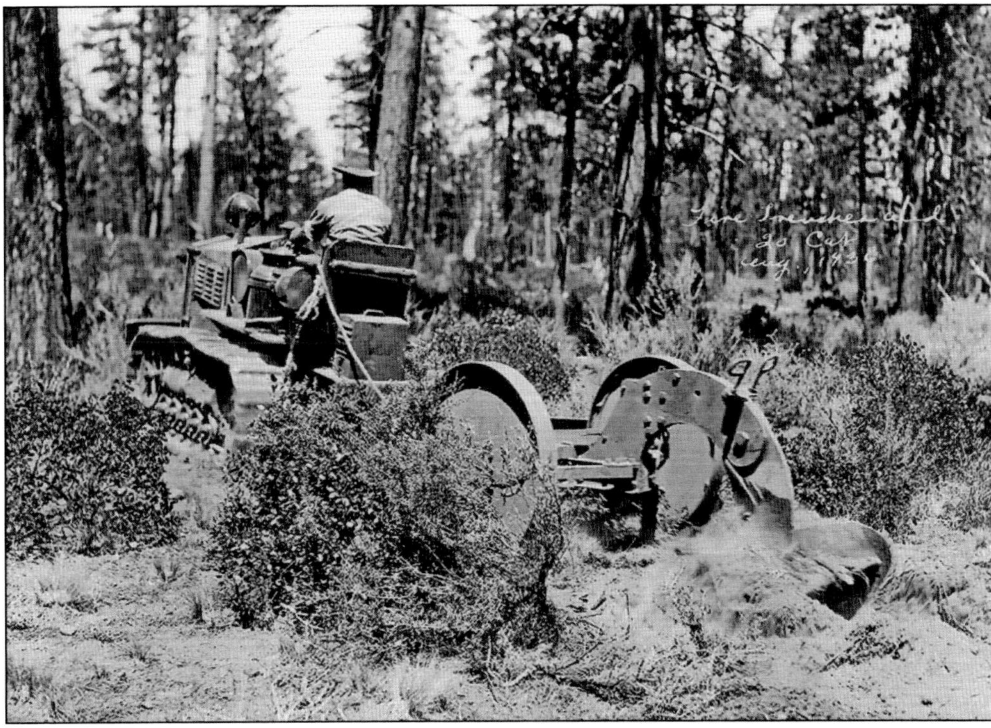

Where relatively flat terrain with soft pumice soils permitted, Deschutes National Forest firefighters were using fire trenchers such as this one pulled by a small Caterpillar tractor by 1936. Such equipment could expedite construction of fire control lines around wildfires and enable firefighters to begin mop-up operations sooner. (Deschutes National Forest.)

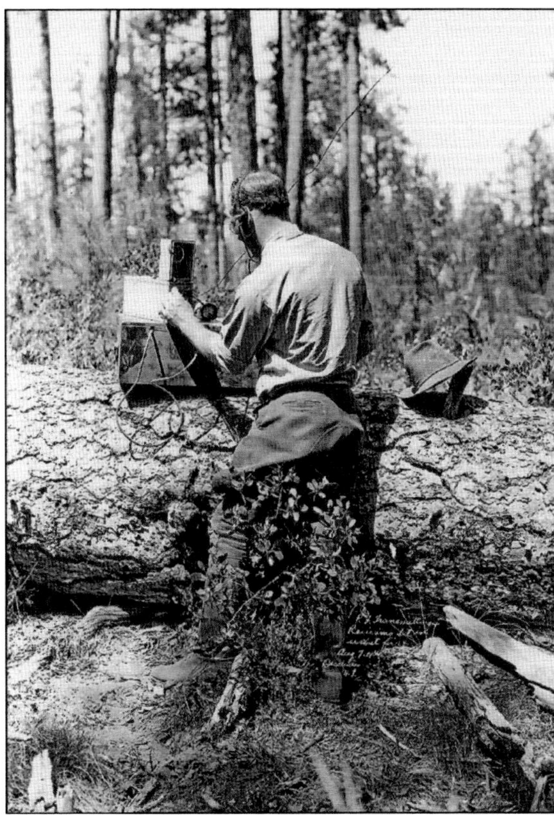

Advances in communications technology such as this transmitting and receiving radio set, used on a 1936 wildfire by Deschutes National Forest firefighter Bob Wakefield, also benefitted fire control operations. Fire bosses were better able to direct and receive reports from their line scouts, sector bosses, and crew bosses on the fire line. (Deschutes National Forest.)

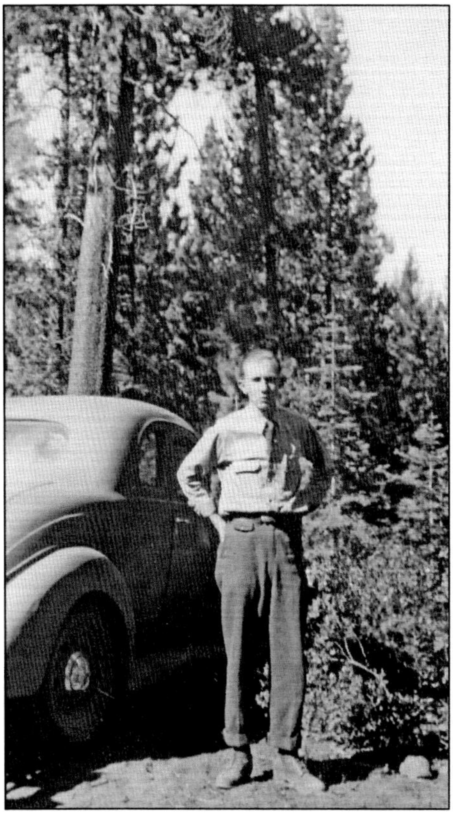

Service in the armed forces during World War II by many Deschutes National Forest personnel cost forest supervisor Ralph Crawford many of his experienced field men and fire crews. That slack was somewhat taken up by employing high school boys such as Wilmer Van Vleet Jr. of Bend to staff fire lookouts and fight wildfires. (Deschutes County Historical Society.)

Women, too, were pressed into service on the Deschutes National Forest to staff fire lookouts and were trained to fight wildfires. Here, members of the Women's Forest Service Reserve practice wildfire suppression on the Deschutes National Forest in 1945. Within just a few decades, women were completely integrated into US Forest Service work, including firefighting. (Deschutes National Forest.)

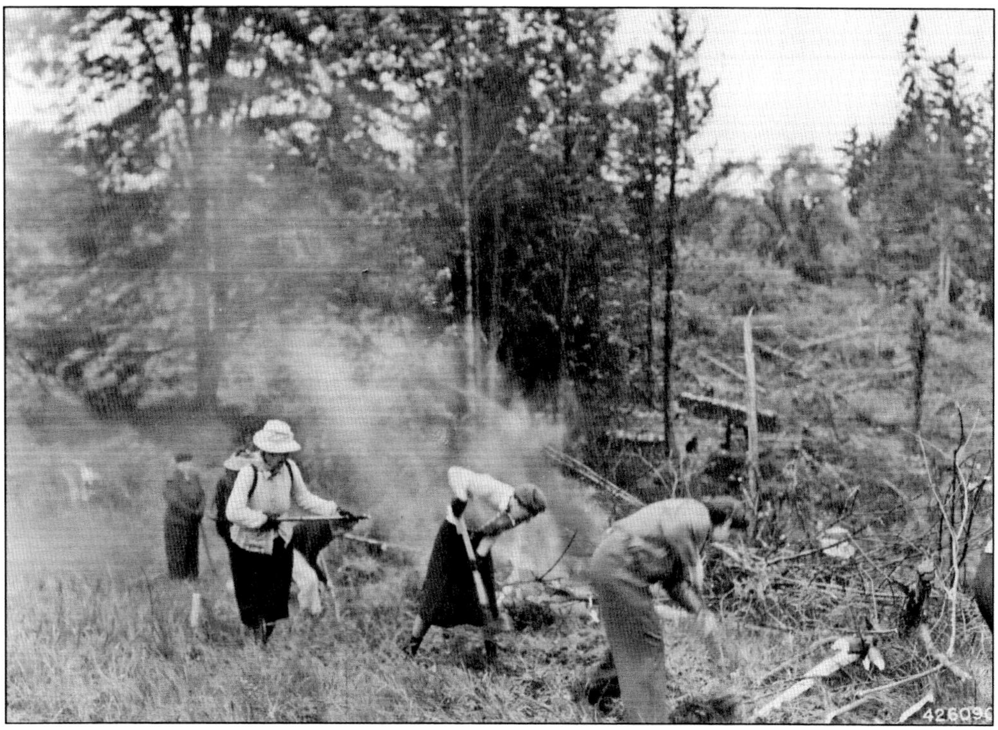

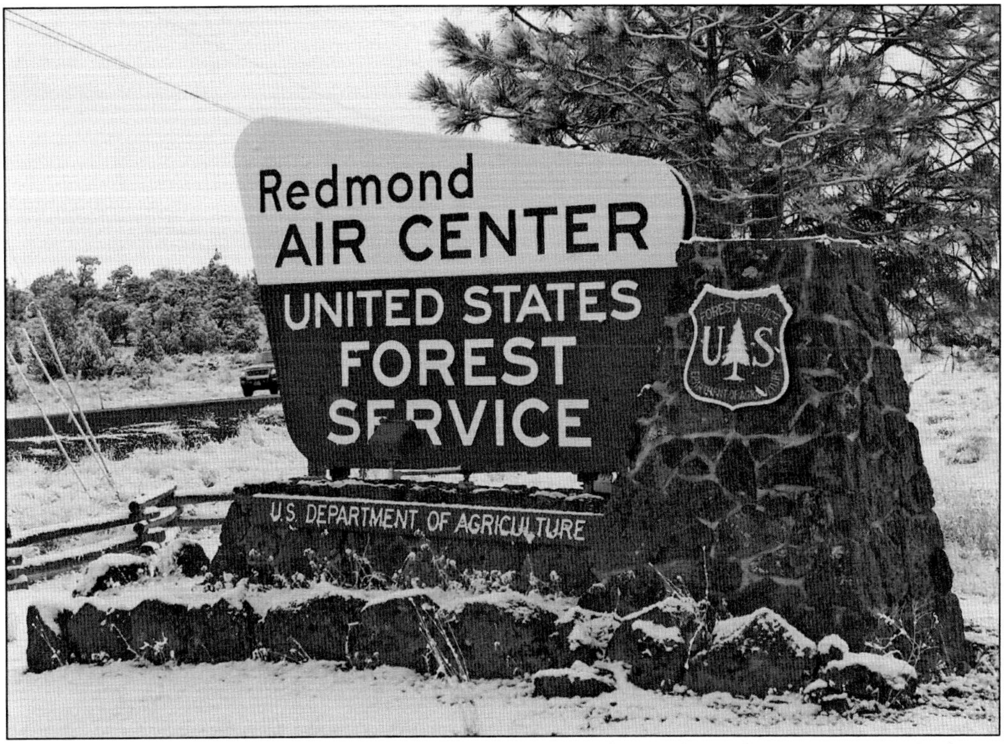

A hub of aerial firefighting in the Pacific Northwest, the Redmond Air Center at Roberts Field—less than two miles east of Redmond and about 15 miles north of Bend—is a home base for air tankers, smokejumpers, and hotshot firefighters. The nearness of these assets has been important to Deschutes National Forest wildfire management for more than half a century. (Photograph by the author.)

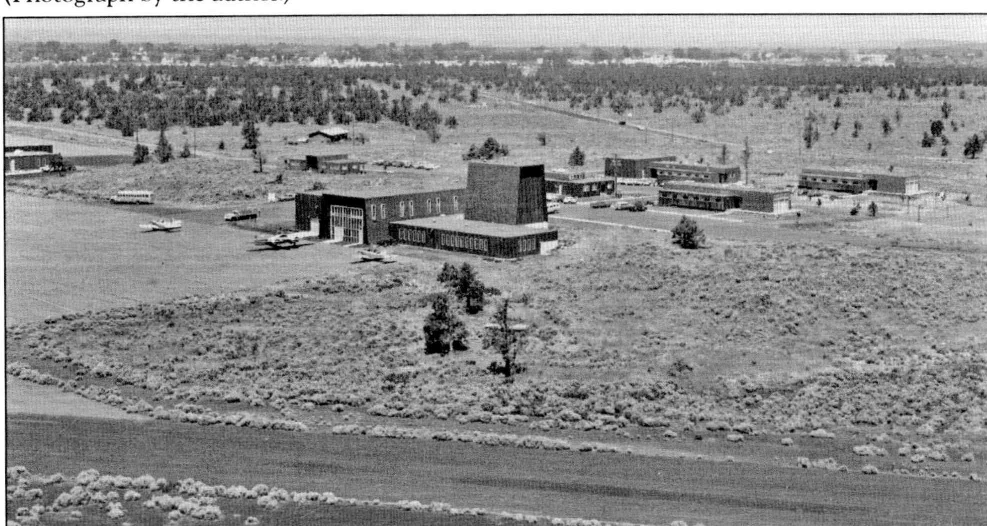

Redmond Air Center construction began in 1964 with an administration building and a residence, two 25-person barracks and a dining hall, and a parachute loft. Follow-on construction brought two aircraft hangars, a warehouse for a 500-person fire cache, and a smokejumper training center. (Deschutes National Forest.)

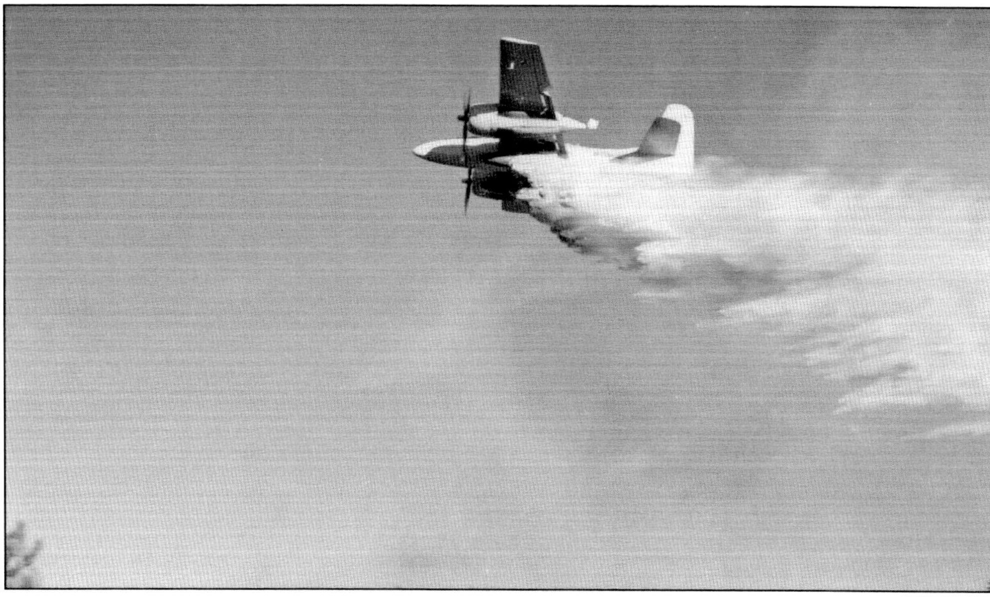

This converted US Navy F7F Tigercat air tanker based at Roberts Field drops 700 gallons of borate slurry that helped firefighters on the ground control a September 1959 timber fire on the Deschutes National Forest. Such operations demonstrated the usefulness of the future Redmond Air Center. (Deschutes National Forest.)

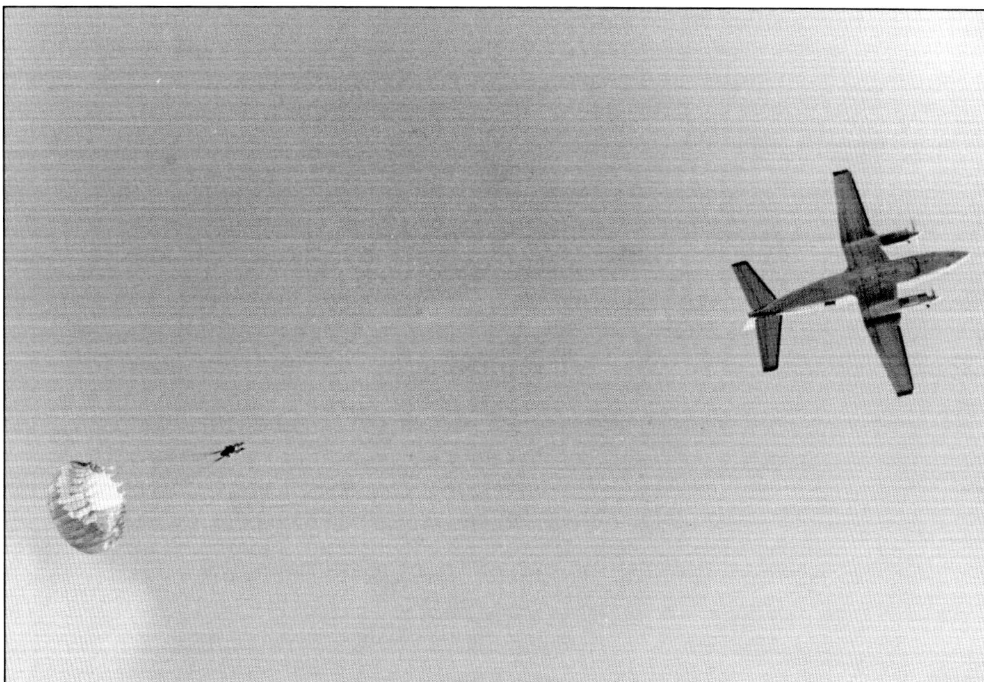

Smokejumpers trained and based at the Redmond Air Center since it opened have jumped on thousands of remote smokes all over the Pacific Northwest. Their rapid responses have kept most of these small fires from becoming large, destructive wildfires. (Deschutes County Historical Society.)

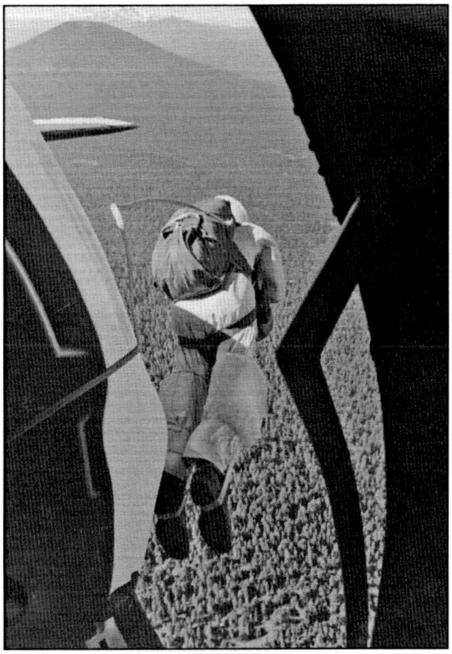

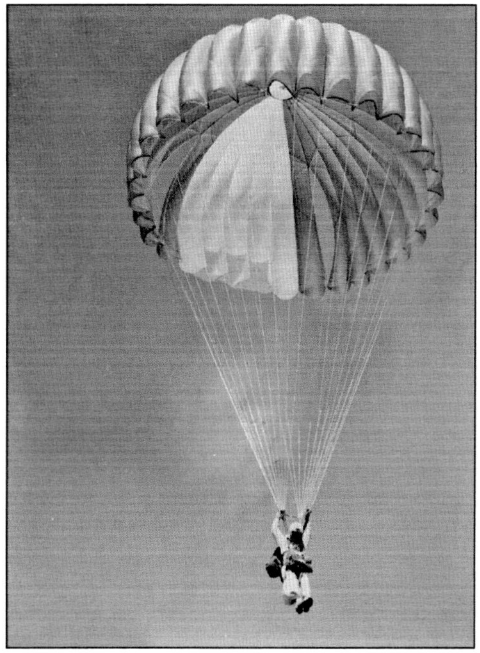

The instant after this smokejumper left the jump plane over the Deschutes National Forest—Black Butte and the Three Sisters are in the distance—the static line following him out the door opened his parachute (left). A moment later, the smokejumper prepares to land in the timber (right) and begin fighting a wildfire. (Deschutes County Historical Society.)

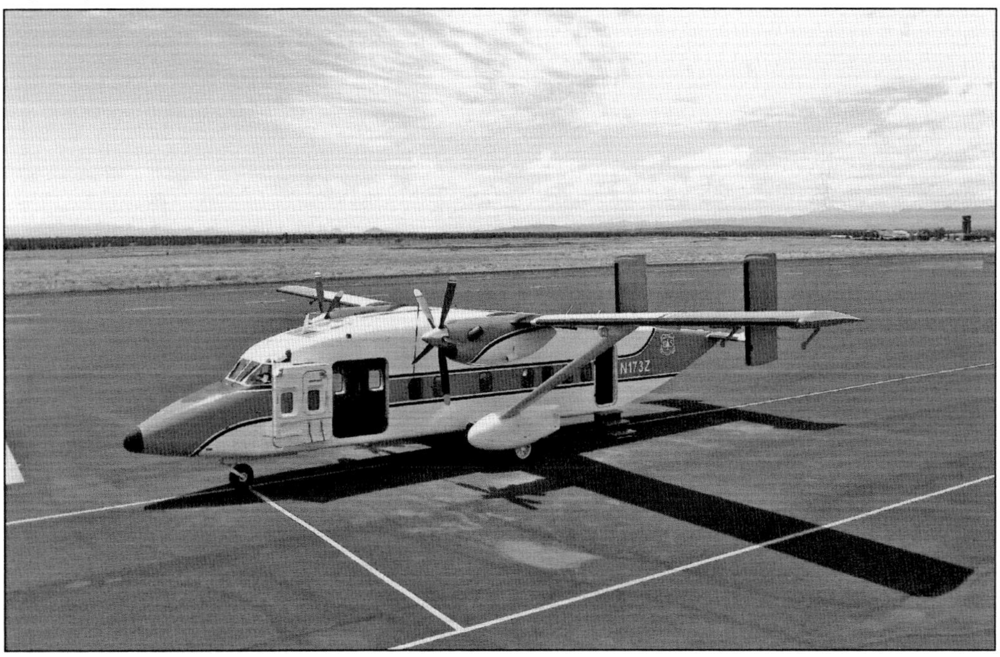

The US Forest Service has used a wide variety of aircraft over the 75-plus years of smokejumping. This Short 330 Sherpa, in service since the 1990s, follows such iconic aircraft as the Ford Tri-Motor, used from 1941 to 1969, and the Douglas DC-3 Dakota, used from the mid-1940s into the 2000s to deliver firefighters from the sky. (Photograph by Stan Collins.)

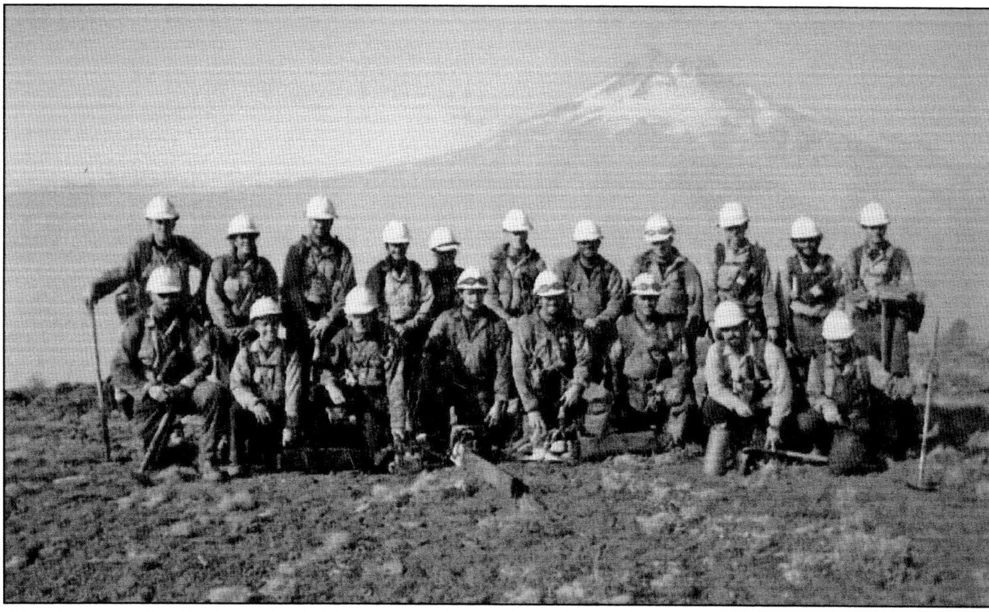

Also based at the Redmond Air Center are the Redmond Hotshots, one of about 100 twenty-person interagency crews of multiskilled professional wildland firefighters who may be sent anywhere in the United States to fight wildfires. The 2007 Redmond Hotshots were photographed near Mount Jefferson. (Redmond Hotshots.)

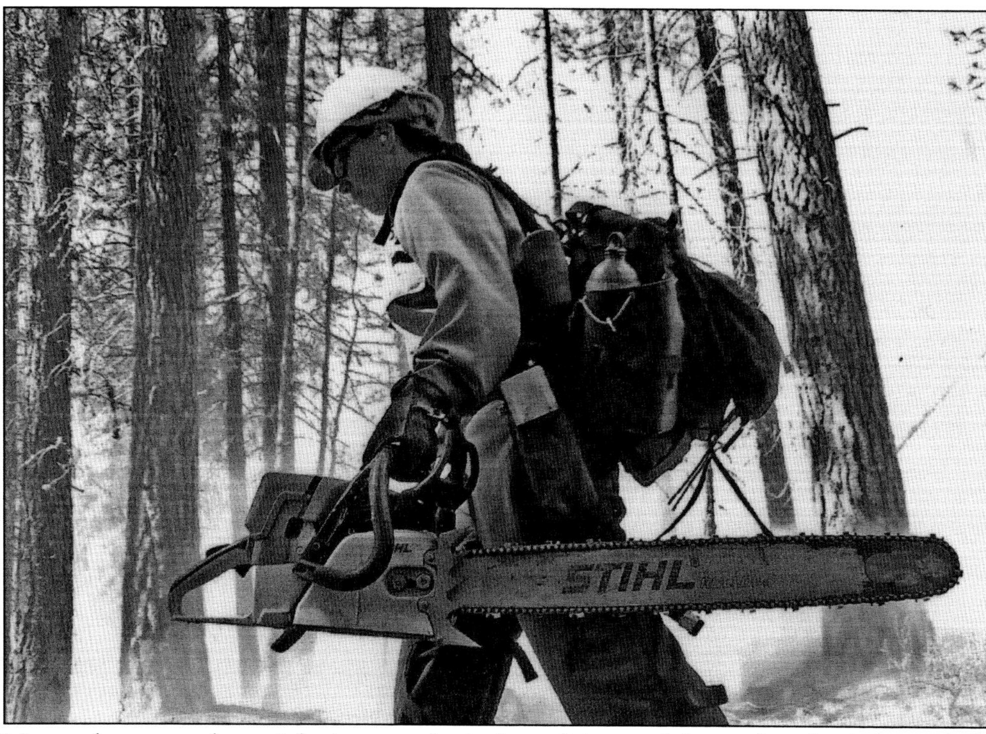

Men and women who satisfy rigorous physical condition and demanding firefighting skills requirements may serve on the interagency hotshot crews. Wendy Joslin, a professional forester and fire ecologist, served on the 2007 Redmond Hotshots. (Photograph by Shane Rountree.)

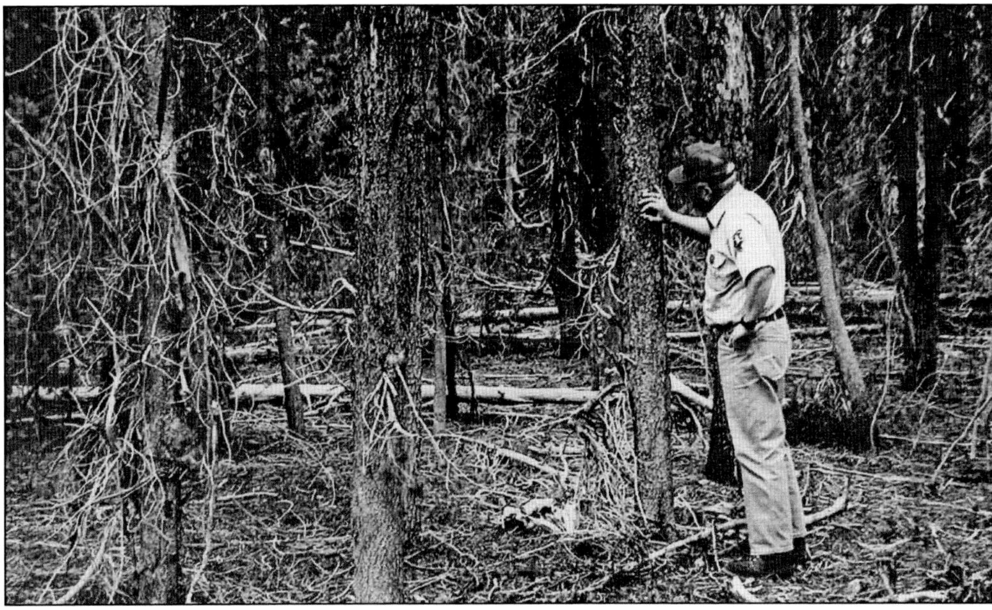

A US Forest Service officer who inspected a Deschutes National Forest lodgepole pine stand in May 2005 found that the mountain pine beetle had killed virtually all the lodgepole pines over six inches in diameter at breast height. Pitch tubes on the trunk evidence the tree is attempting to expel the beetles. (Photograph by Bill Peterson.)

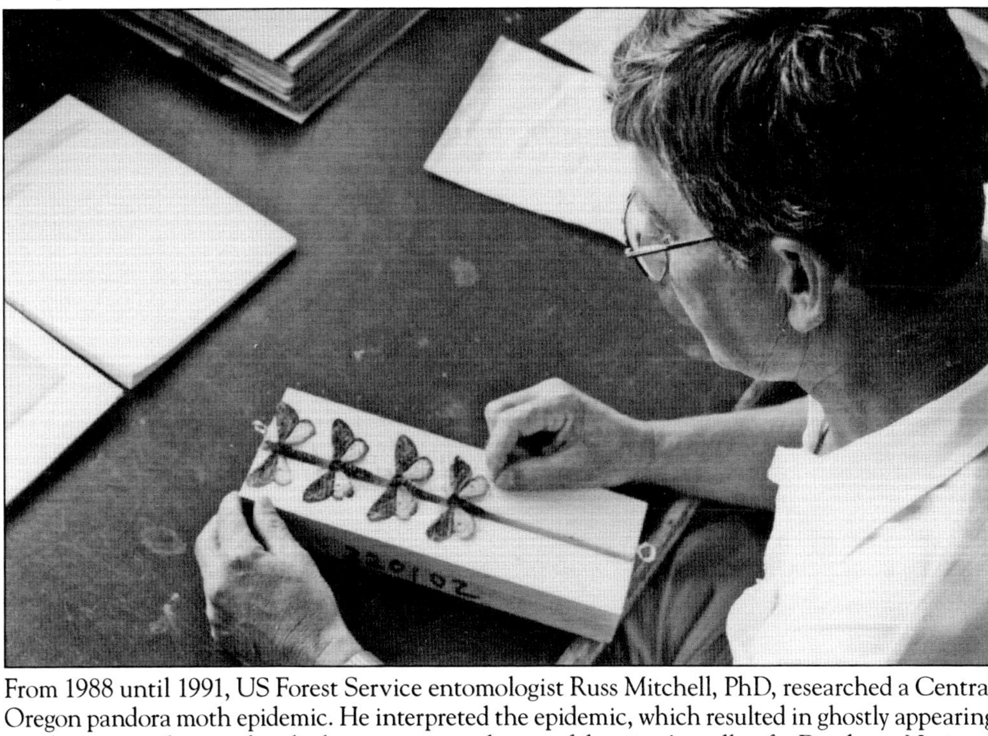

From 1988 until 1991, US Forest Service entomologist Russ Mitchell, PhD, researched a Central Oregon pandora moth epidemic. He interpreted the epidemic, which resulted in ghostly appearing ponderosa pine forests after the larvae consumed most of the pines' needles, for Deschutes National Forest managers and concerned citizens. (Pacific Northwest Research Station, photograph by Mark Reed.)

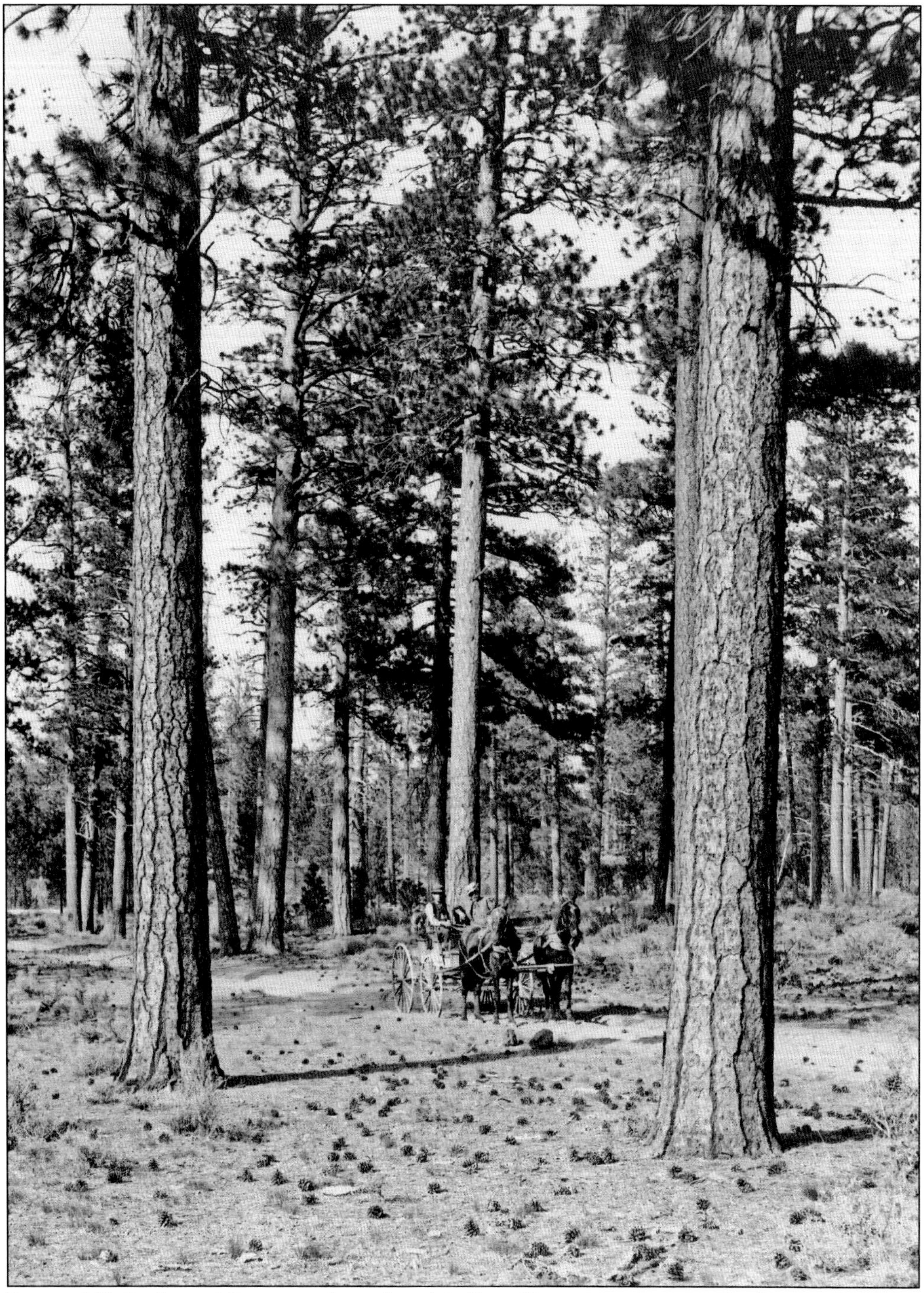

Pioneer US Geological Survey geologist Israel C. Russell was among many who foresaw the upper Deschutes country's timber future. "[The] yellow pine forests [in the] central part of Oregon are not only extensive but contain magnificent, well-grown trees, which will be of great commercial value when railroads . . . bring them within reach of markets," he writes in his 1905 *Preliminary Report on the Geology and Water Resources of Central Oregon*. (Deschutes County Historical Society.)

Four

Timber Resources

As the upper Deschutes country was settled, a few pioneer woodsmen supplied logs to a few small sawmills that provided lumber to a local market. In anticipation of a railroad that would transport the area's timber to markets all over the West and beyond, land speculators began a timber rush. By the early 1900s, large chunks of formerly public domain timberland had passed into private hands—sometimes legally, sometimes not. This went on until July 1903, when Pres. Theodore Roosevelt included the remaining public timberlands in a federal forest reserve that in 1908 became the Deschutes National Forest.

Within five years of the Oregon Trunk Railroad's arrival in Bend in 1911, a great increase in logging supplied the giant Brooks-Scanlon and Shevlin-Hixon sawmills, which began production in 1916. Within a decade, these and other companies' private timberlands were mostly cut over. They turned to the Deschutes National Forest for trees to sustain their production and the area's economy.

The General Exchange Act of 1922 allowed the lumber companies to exchange their cutover timberlands—incorporated into the national forest—for rights to cut national forest timber under US Forest Service supervision. By the middle of the 20th century, the Deschutes National Forest had grown by over 350,000 acres—almost a quarter of its current acreage—through land exchanges. Scientific management coupled with reforestation established and maintained healthy second-growth ponderosa pine forests on national forest lands, including those previously private cutover lands.

To advance the science of growing timber crops on the Deschutes National Forest and other forests east of the Cascade Range in Oregon and Washington, the Forest Service founded the Pringle Falls Experimental Forest on the Deschutes National Forest in 1931 and the Deschutes Research Center in Bend. In 1964, the research center evolved into the Bend Silviculture Laboratory, which also focused on timber production.

Bend is no longer a timber town. Its last sawmill sawed its last log in 1993. Timber now grown on the Deschutes National Forest is shipped to a mill in Gilchrist, Oregon, and other more distant processing plants and managed for future production of a wide range of forest products and benefits.

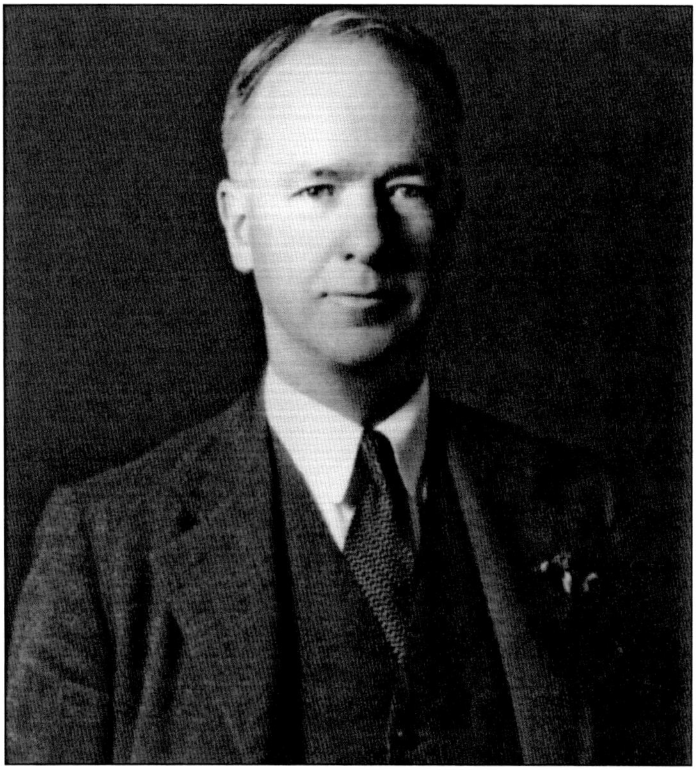

Thornton Taft Munger, a young Yale forester new to the US Forest Service, was sent to Central Oregon in 1908 to study national forest timber resources that soon supported the region's timber economy. Munger's peregrinations stimulated the early asking, if not the conclusive answering, of the kinds of questions he and those who worked for him researched at the Pringle Falls Experimental Forest and at the Bend Silviculture Laboratory for decades. (Pacific Northwest Research Station.)

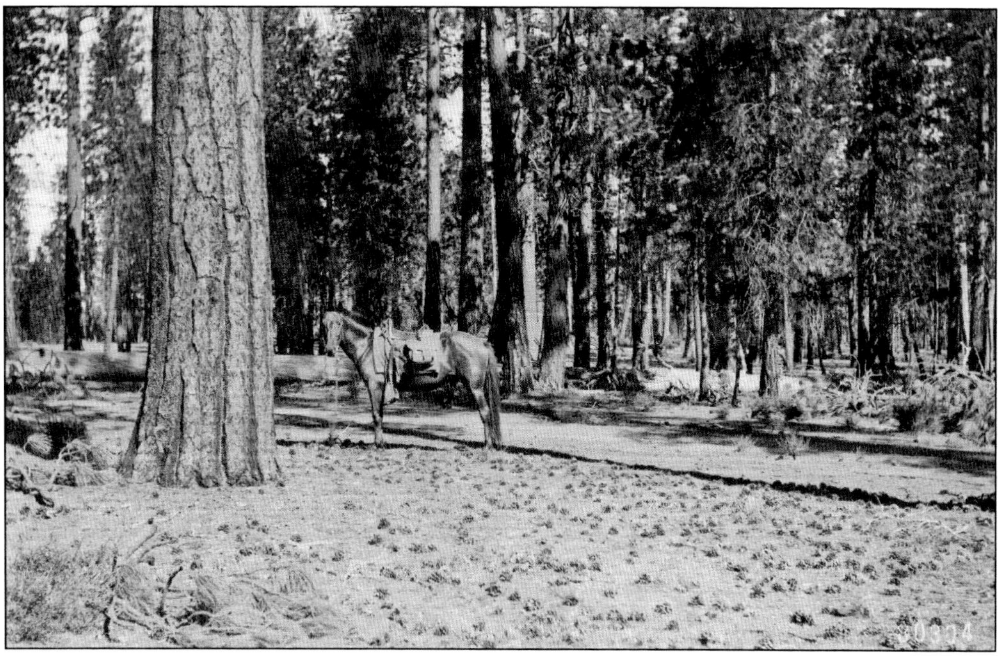

Munger used his horse for scale when he photographed this ponderosa pine stand near Crescent. "It has since struck me how audacious or naïve it was . . . to assign a forest assistant with no experience . . . to such a study that now would be assigned only to subject specialists with Ph.D.s," Munger mused in 1962 of his 1908 sojourn. (Pacific Northwest Research Station.)

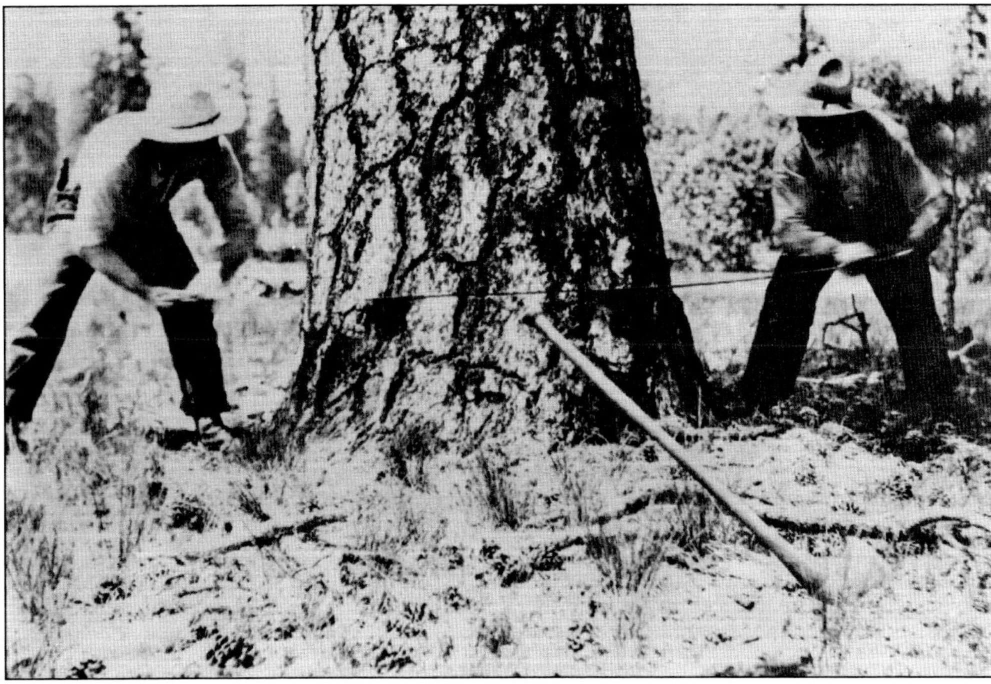

As scientists such as Russell and Munger studied and wrote, early loggers with two-man crosscut saws called "misery whips" felled large western yellow pines (called ponderosa pines since the 1930s) in the forests around Bend (above). The logs they cut supplied several small sawmills that provided lumber for local use and, beginning in 1911, to regional markets by rail. One of these, the Bend Company Sawmill (below), prospered until it burned in 1915. (Both, Deschutes County Historical Society.)

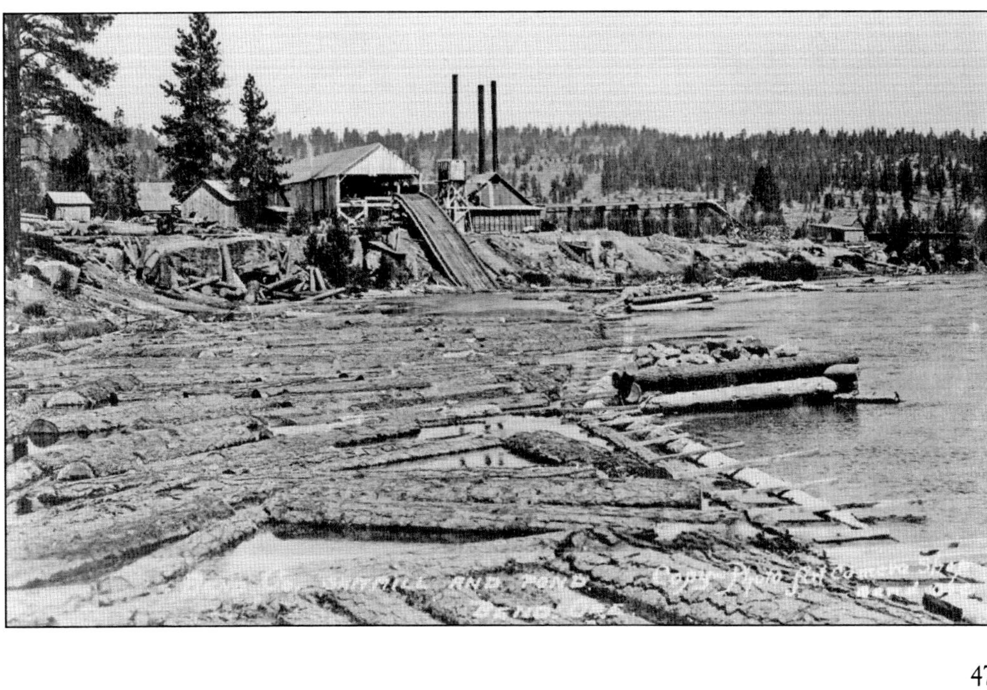

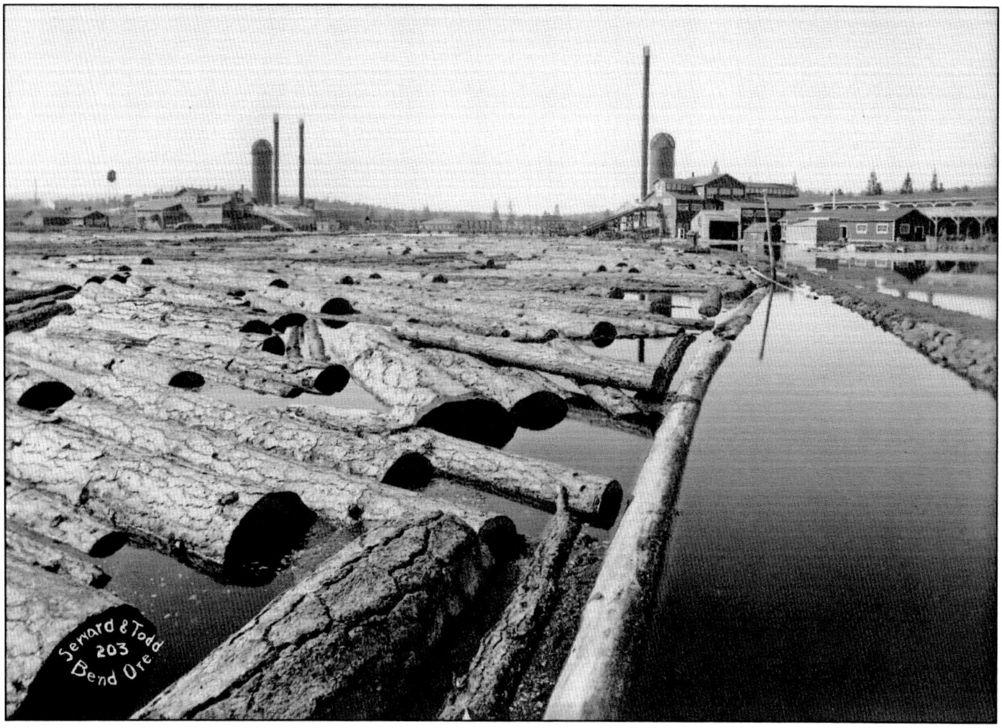

Within five years of the arrival of the Oregon Trunk Railroad in Bend in October 1911, the large Shevlin-Hixon Company sawmill (left) and Brooks-Scanlon Company sawmill (right) faced each other across the Deschutes River. Bend's two new sawmills, which began production in 1916, were designed to cut a million board feet of lumber each day between them. (Deschutes County Historical Society.)

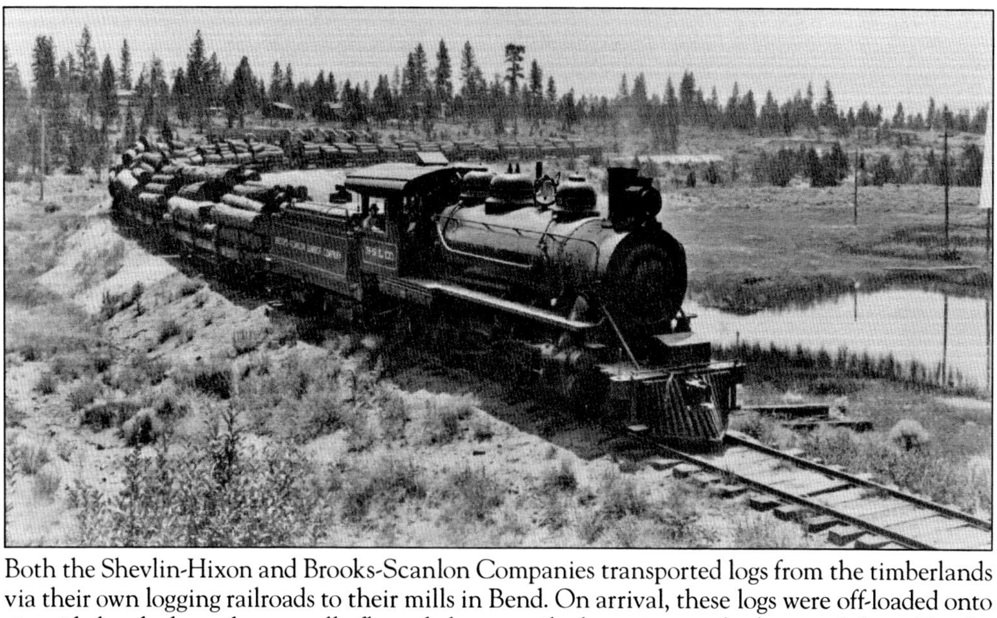

Both the Shevlin-Hixon and Brooks-Scanlon Companies transported logs from the timberlands via their own logging railroads to their mills in Bend. On arrival, these logs were off-loaded onto riverside log docks and eventually floated about a mile downriver to the log pond shared by the two mills. (Deschutes County Historical Society.)

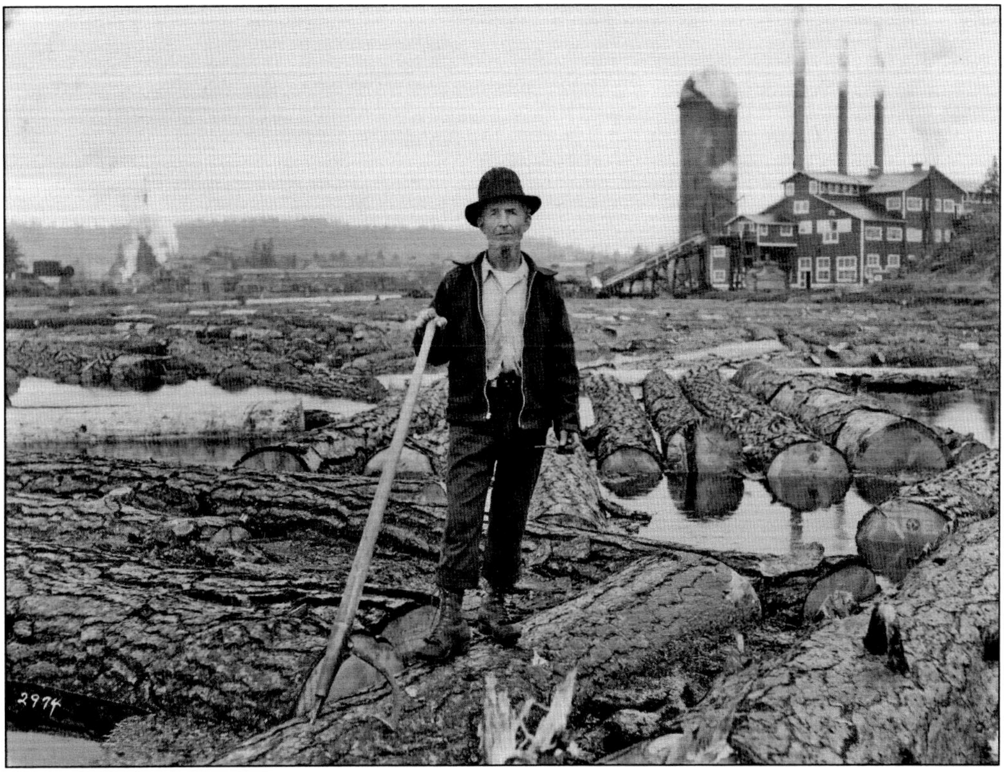

It was Brooks-Scanlon Company "pond monkey" Dan McLennon's job to herd those logs to the log pond to await their date with the saw. Agile in corked boots, he hopped from log to log with a peavey in hand. The tool was used to push a log with the point or roll a log with the attached cant hook. (Deschutes County Historical Society.)

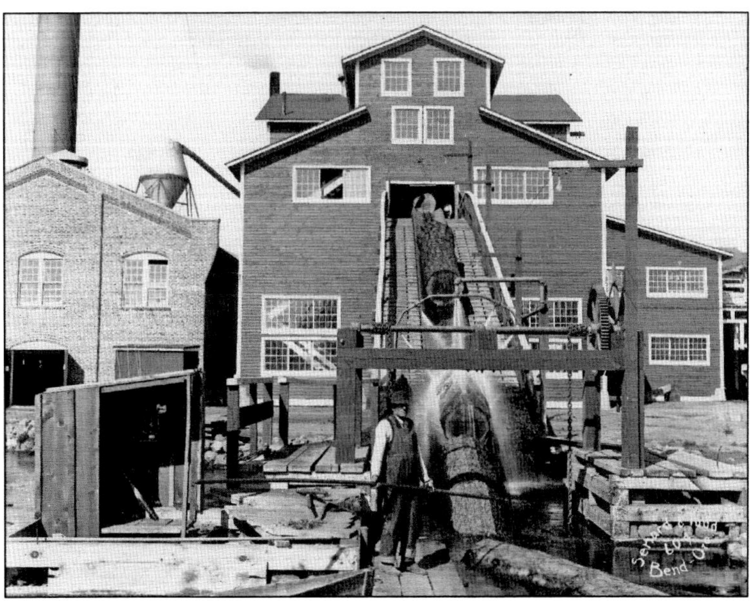

Logs were chained out of the millpond into the mill, where a headsaw cut them into cants for further sawing and edging into boards. After air-drying and planing into finished dimension lumber of various sizes and grades, the lumber was ready to ship to market. (Deschutes County Historical Society.)

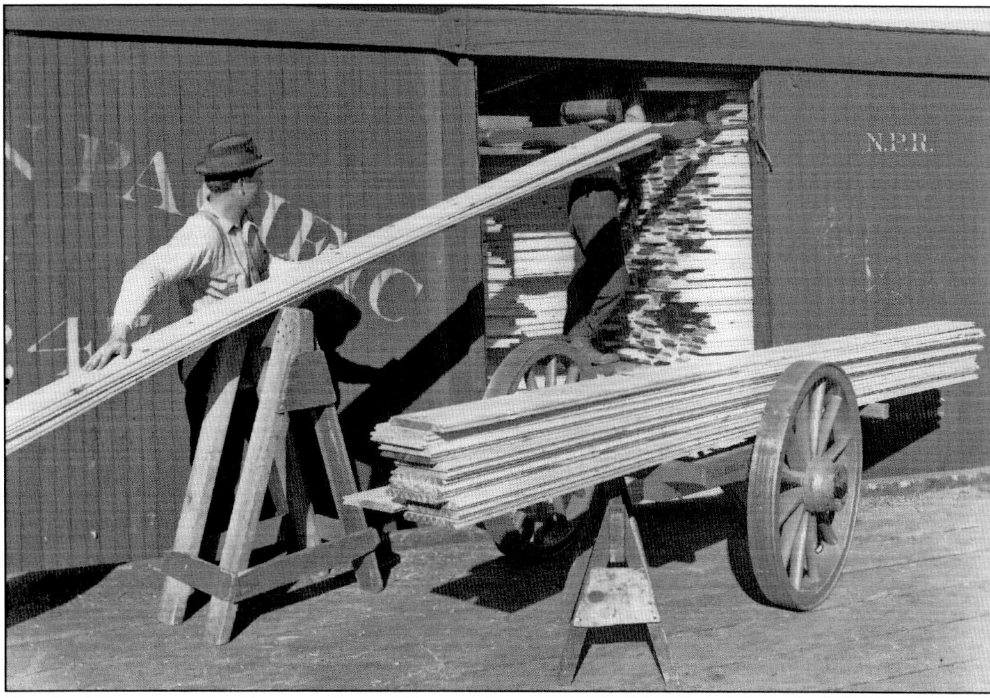

Finished dimension lumber was shipped by rail from both the Shevlin-Hixon and Brooks-Scanlon mills to a national market. In addition to lumber, the mills processed wood into products ranging from specialty building materials to boxes to ironing boards. (Deschutes County Historical Society.)

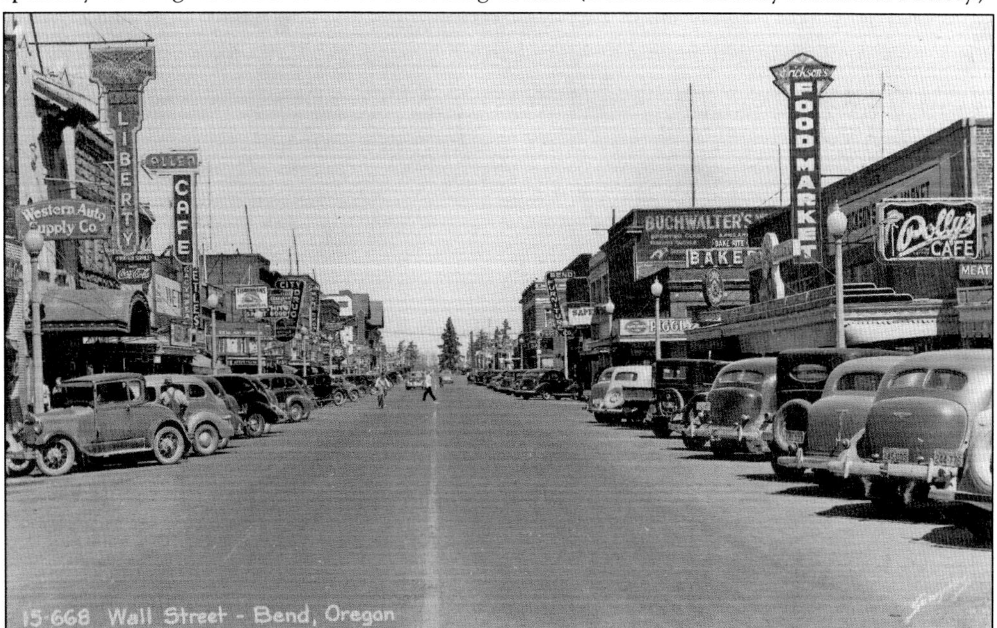

As new mills were built and operated, Bend—a town of about 500 souls when it incorporated in 1905—grew to 5,000 by 1918 and kept on growing. With the timber soon supplied by the Deschutes National Forest, the two sawmills were the economic mainstays of Bend for several decades. (Deschutes County Historical Society.)

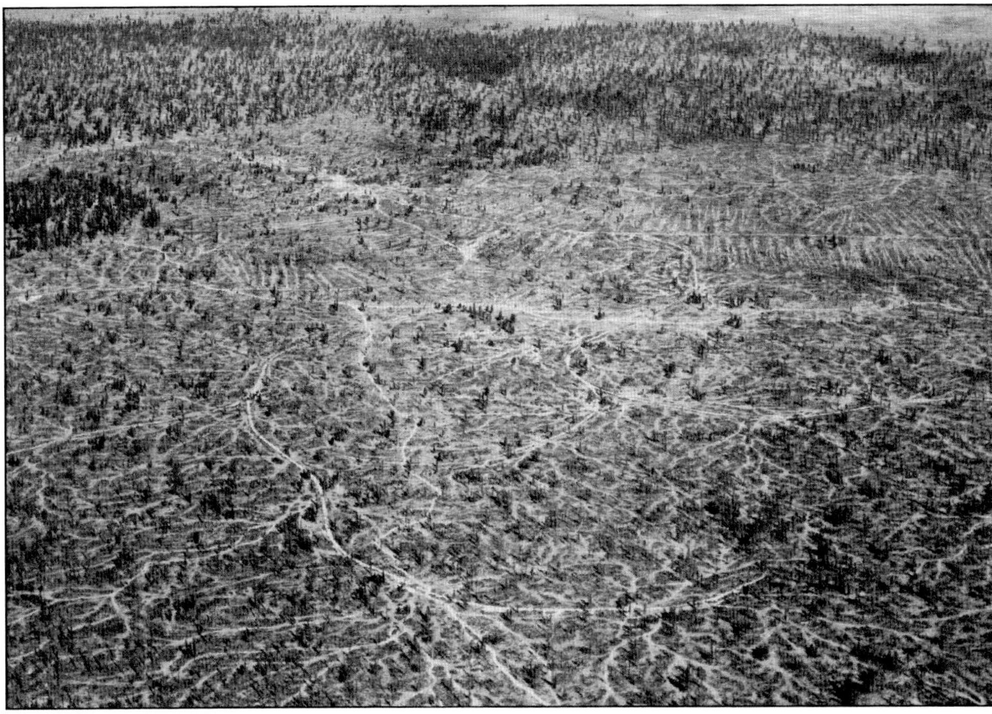

Private timberlands in the upper Deschutes country were soon cut, and the region's lumber companies large and small turned to the Deschutes National Forest to sustain their production and the economy. Congress passed the General Exchange Act of 1922, which allowed companies to exchange their cutover timberlands such as these south of Bend for rights to cut national forest timber under US Forest Service supervision. (Deschutes National Forest.)

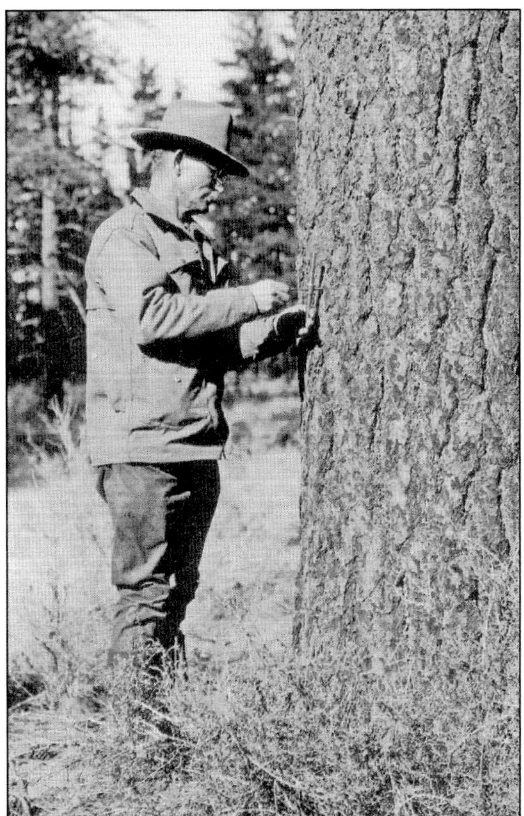

In 1925, the US Forest Service transferred Walt Perry, an experienced forester with a forward-looking timber ethic, from the Carson National Forest in New Mexico to the Deschutes National Forest. As chief lumberman, Perry managed the companies' logging operations on the national forest. (US Forest Service, photograph by Carl B. Neal.)

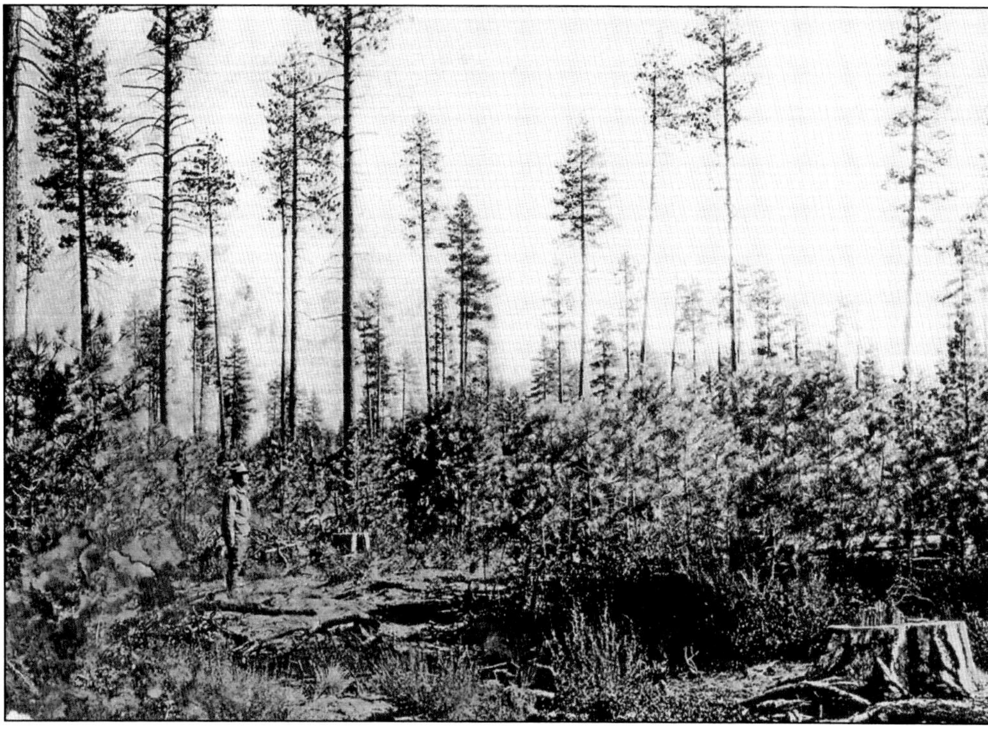

Chief lumberman Perry inspects a Deschutes National Forest timber sale to the Shevlin-Hixon Company in July 1930. Harvesting national forest timber on a sustained-yield basis promised a more secure future for Central Oregon's timber economy. (US Forest Service.)

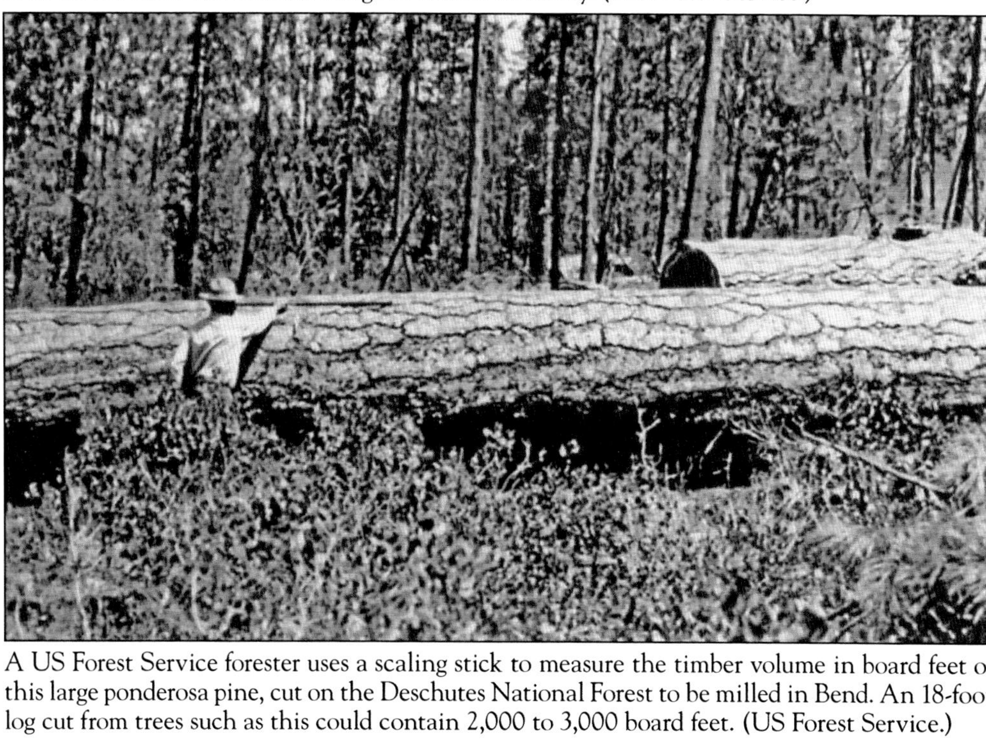

A US Forest Service forester uses a scaling stick to measure the timber volume in board feet of this large ponderosa pine, cut on the Deschutes National Forest to be milled in Bend. An 18-foot log cut from trees such as this could contain 2,000 to 3,000 board feet. (US Forest Service.)

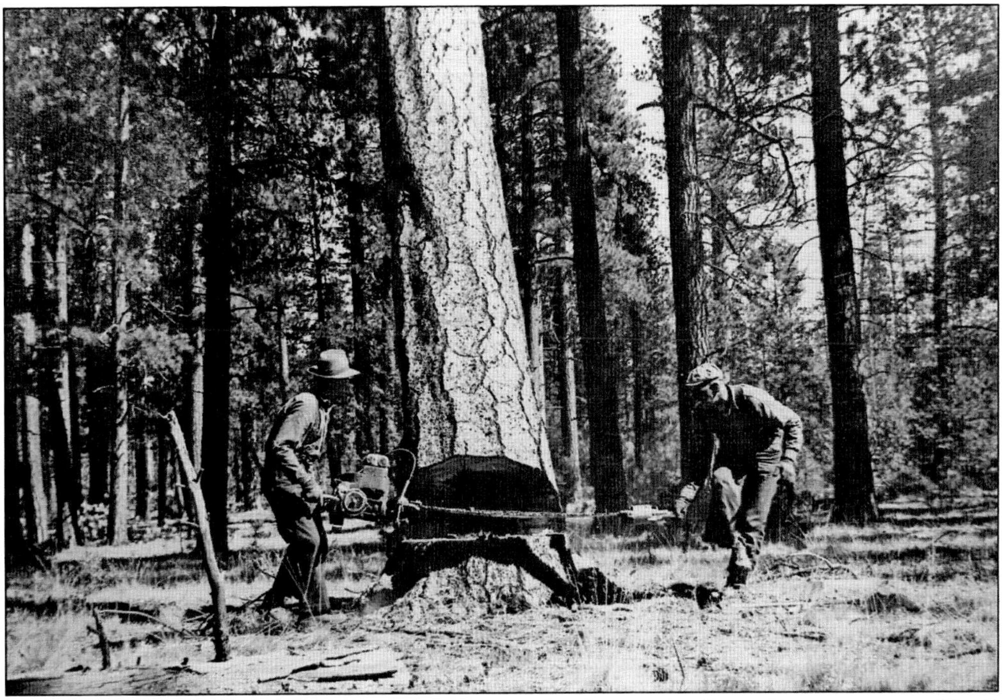

Central Oregon's lumber industry continued to evolve during the Great Depression and World War II years. Replacement of "misery whips" by power saws, for example, was a major change. In 1943, the Brooks-Scanlon Company began using power saws, first for bucking tree trunks into logs and later for felling trees. Here, timber fallers use a two-man power saw to cut a ponderosa pine. (US Forest Service.)

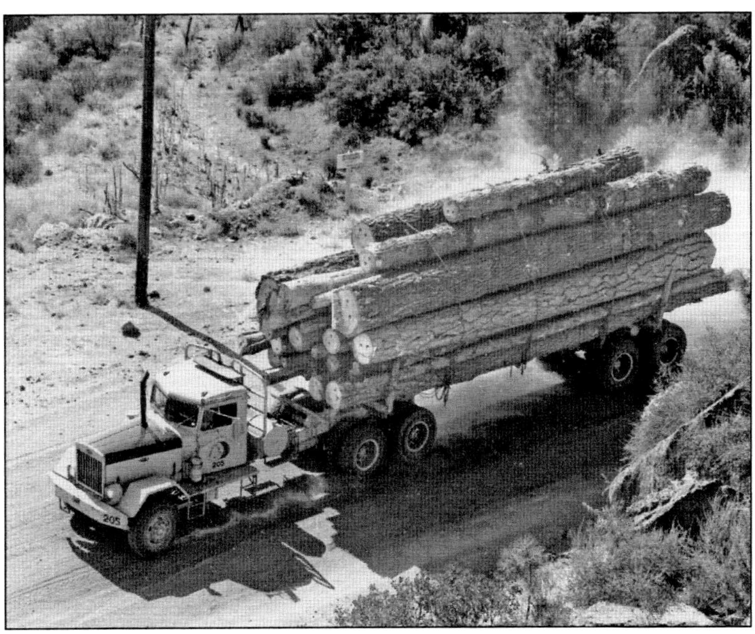

During the 1950s, truck logging replaced railroad logging in Central Oregon. Here, Brooks-Scanlon Company log truck No. 205 approaches the log decks on the Deschutes River about a mile upriver of the company's mill. (Deschutes County Historical Society, photograph by Paul Hosmer.)

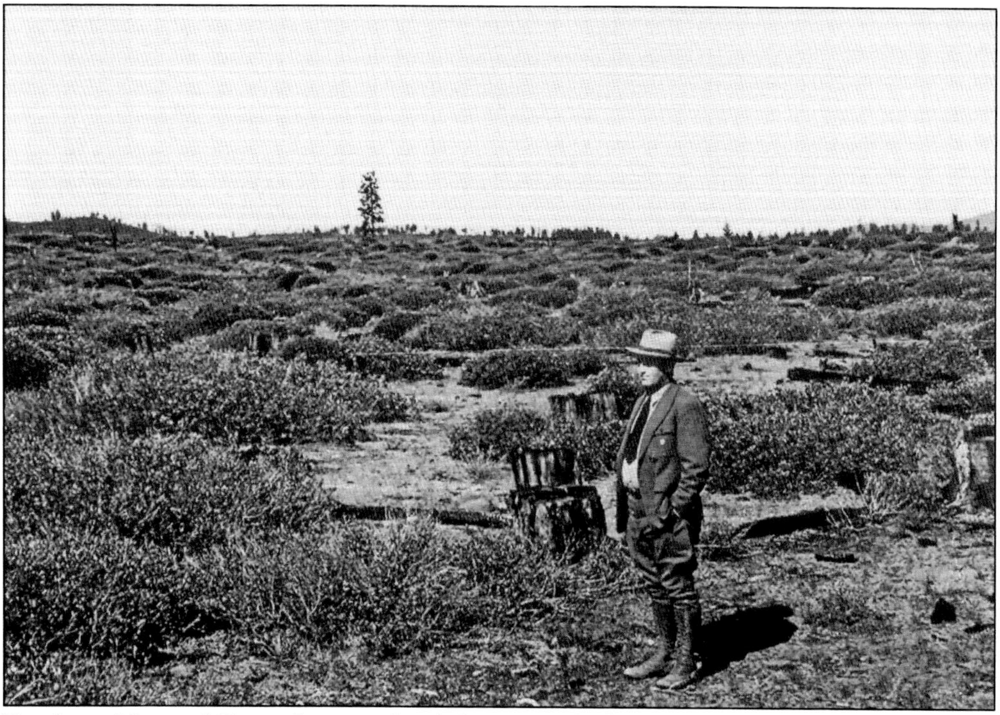

Deschutes National Forest foresters faced the major challenge of reforesting formerly private cutover timberlands added to the Deschutes National Forest under the General Exchange Act of 1922. Here, a forest officer contemplates a reforestation project in the Lava Butte area south of Bend. (Deschutes National Forest.)

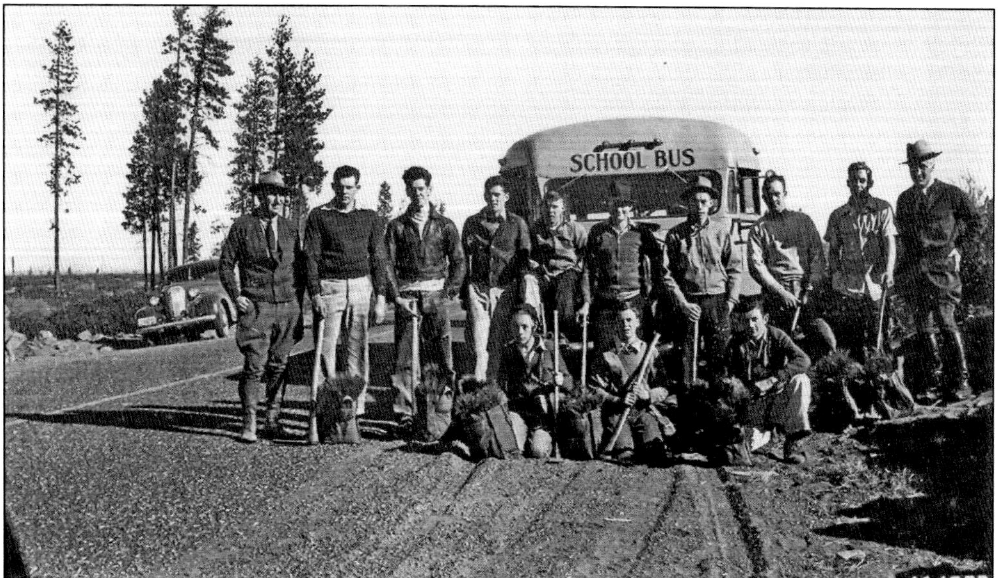

Joe Lammi (left), district ranger of the Bend Ranger District, and forester Lester McPherson (right) lead a group of Bend High School students—members of the school's Junior Sportsmen Club—on a 1940 reforestation project. The students are equipped with planting tools and supplied with packs full of ponderosa pine seedlings. (Deschutes National Forest, photograph by Merle S. Lowden.)

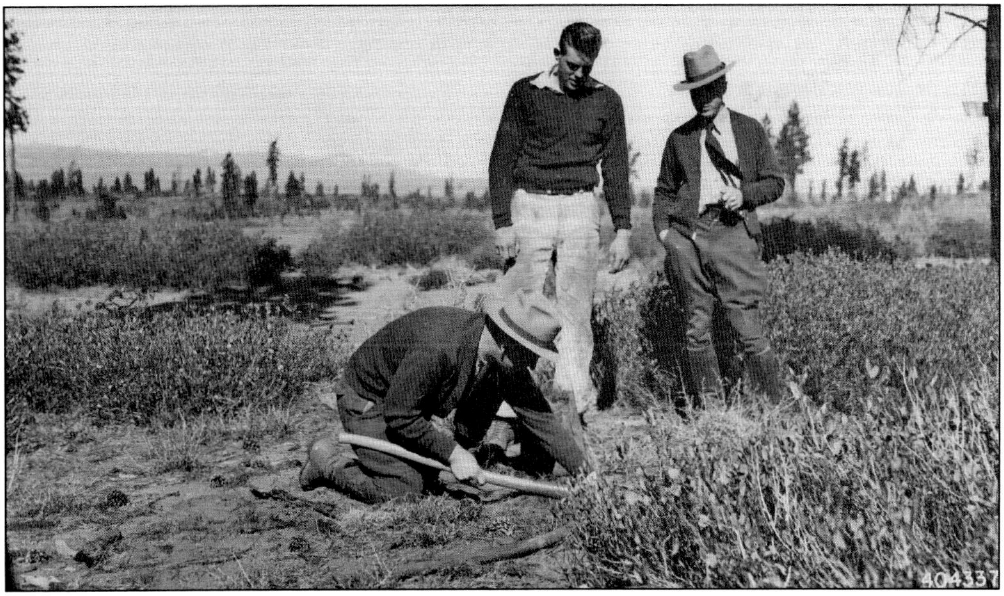

Ranger Joe Lammi and Robert Hudson, president of the Bend High School Junior Sportsmen Club, watch forester McPherson demonstrate the proper technique for planting a ponderosa pine seedling. Club members proceeded to plant the hundreds of seedlings with which they were supplied. (Deschutes National Forest, photograph by Merle S. Lowden.)

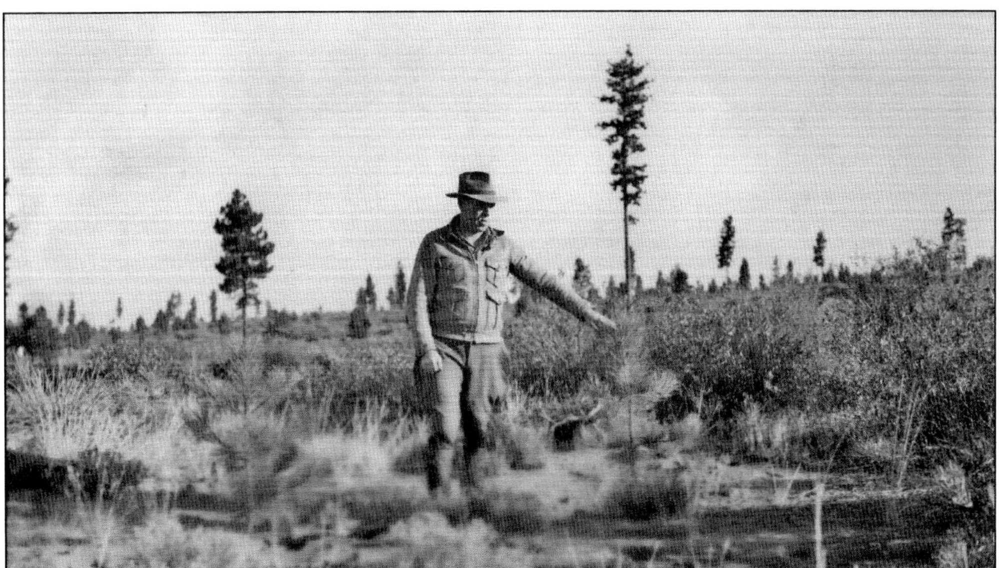

In 1944, Deschutes National Forest supervisor Ralph Crawford inspects the ponderosa pine trees planted in 1940 at the Lava Butte plantation by the Bend High School Junior Sportsmen. By then, the trees stood three to four feet high. (Deschutes National Forest.)

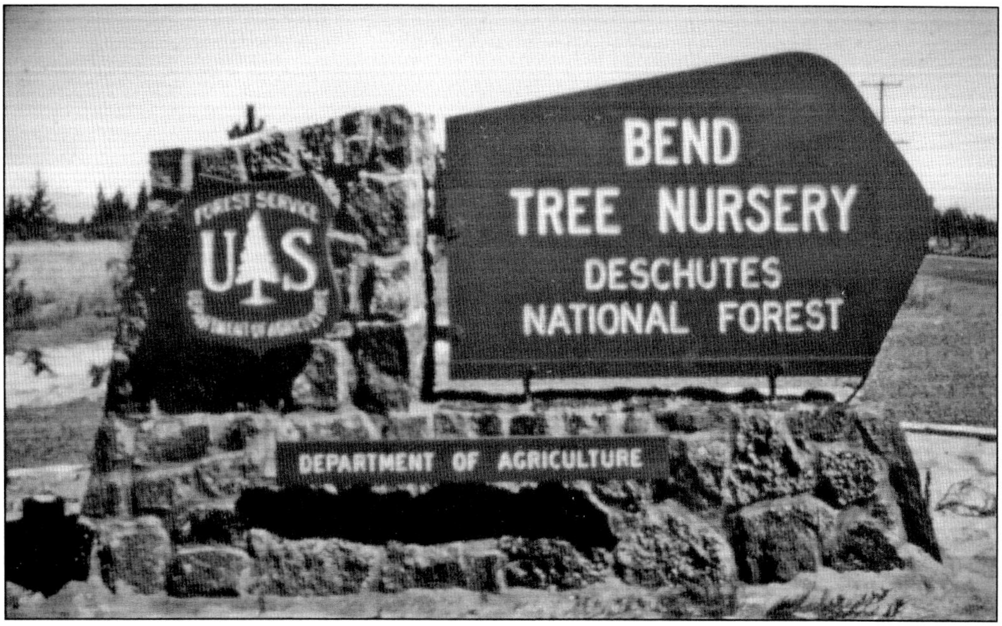

In 1948, the Deschutes National Forest established the Bend Tree Nursery—later known as the Bend Pine Nursery—on land acquired northeast of Bend. Over the next five decades, millions of ponderosa pine seedlings and seedlings of other tree and plant species were produced to reforest and restore national forest lands. (Deschutes National Forest.)

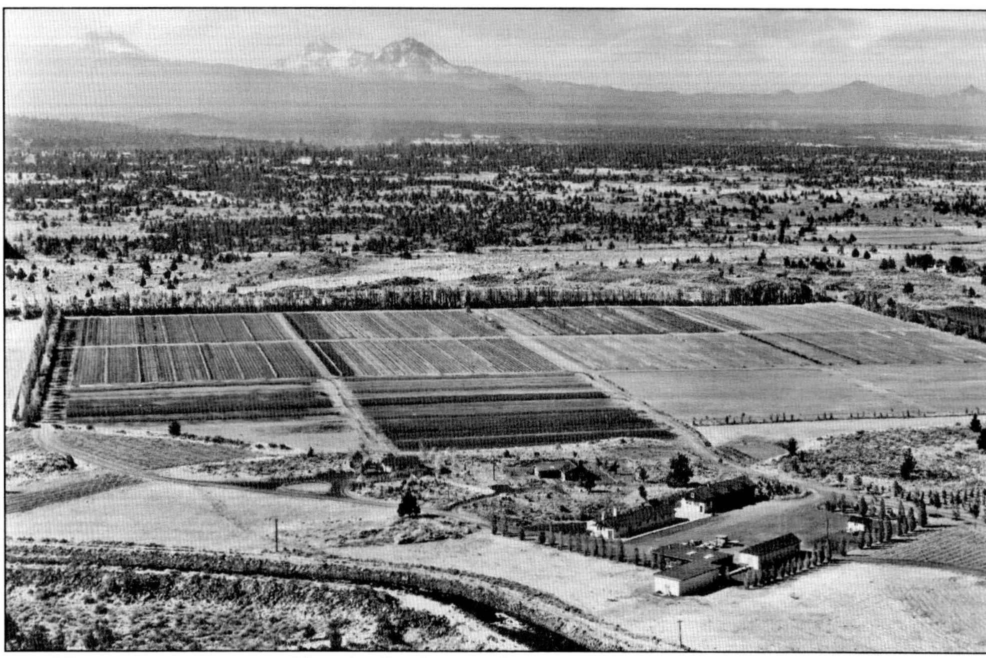

In addition to extensive seedling beds, the Bend Pine Nursery included a facility for extracting seeds from pine cones and a packing shed for packing seedlings for transportation to planting sites. A new Deschutes National Forest headquarters built on this site was occupied in 2011, and land used for growing seedlings has been developed by the Bend Parks and Recreation District as a public park. (Deschutes National Forest.)

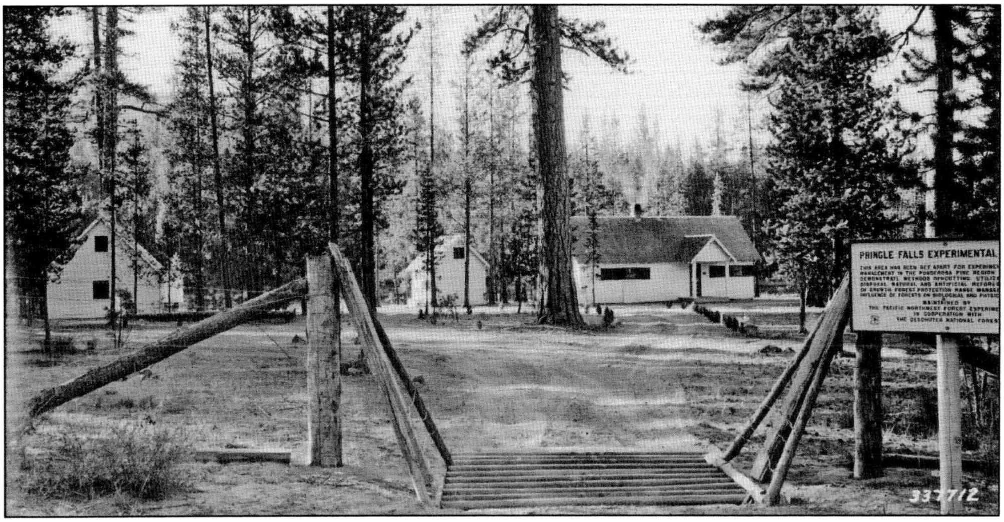

Successful forest management requires scientific knowledge. The Pringle Falls Experimental Forest was established within the Deschutes National Forest in 1931 to develop the ecologically, environmentally, and economically viable silvicultural systems that would convert stagnant old-growth ponderosa pine forests into more productive second-growth forests. Its headquarters, shown in this 1936 photograph, were on the Deschutes River about 30 miles south of Bend. (Pacific Northwest Research Station, photograph by Ernest L. Kolbe.)

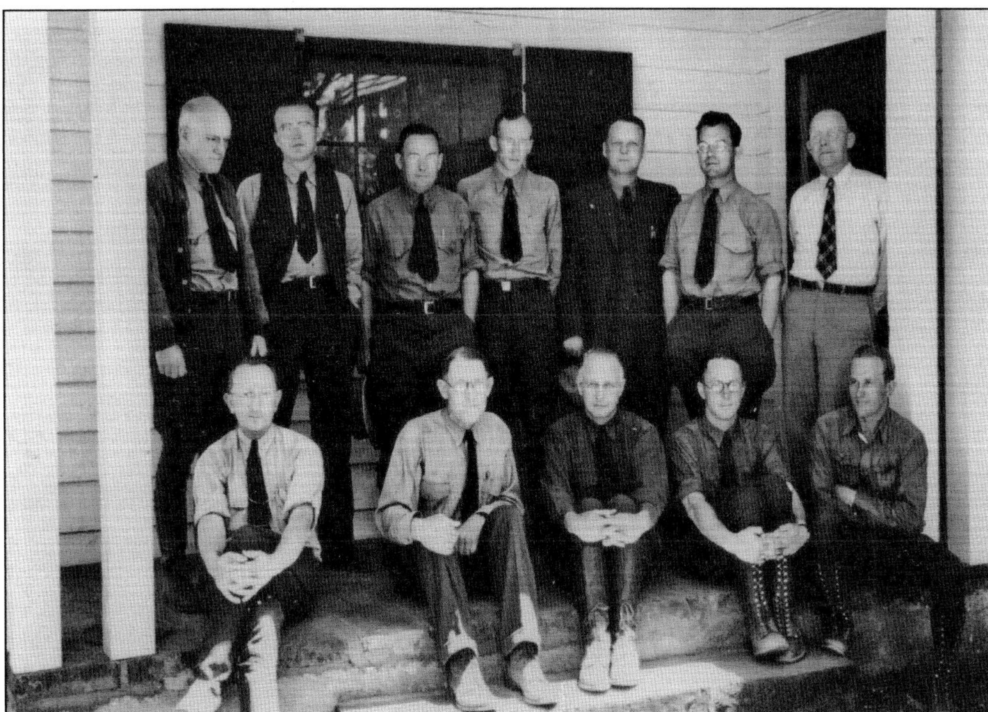

About 30 silviculturists from the US Forest Service's western regional offices and experiment stations met in June 1937 at the Pringle Falls Experimental Forest headquarters during a traveling conference on ponderosa pine silviculture. The facility remained a center of forestry research for decades. (Pacific Northwest Research Station.)

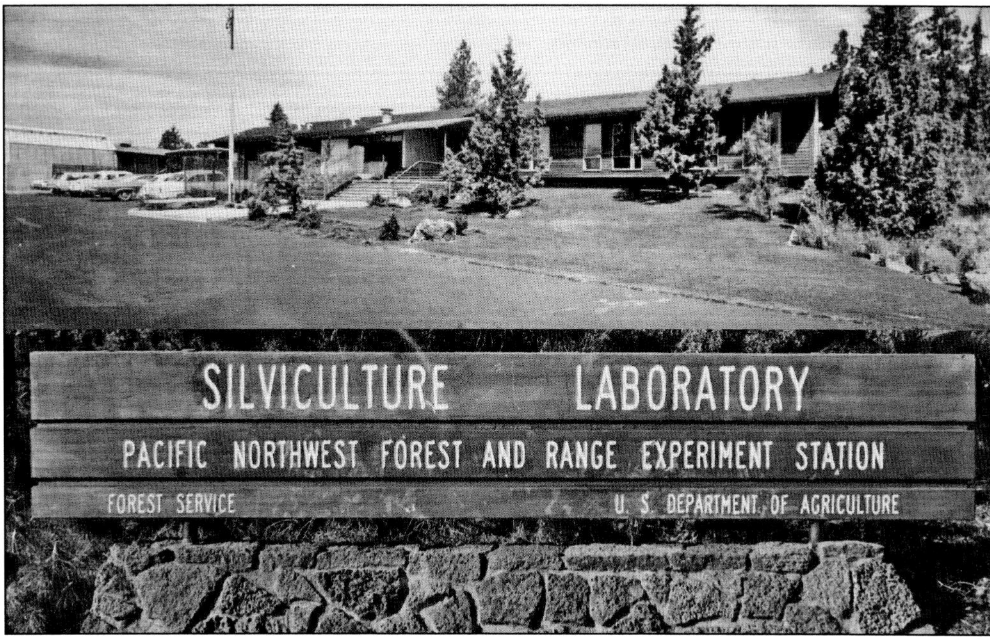

Silvicultural research moved to town in the late 1950s with the establishment by the Pacific Northwest Forest and Range Experiment Station of a small Deschutes Research Center in downtown Bend. In 1964, the larger Bend Silviculture Laboratory opened on Awbrey Butte in northwestern Bend. The laboratory complemented the continuing Pringle Falls Experimental Forest field studies until it was closed in 1996. (Pacific Northwest Research Station.)

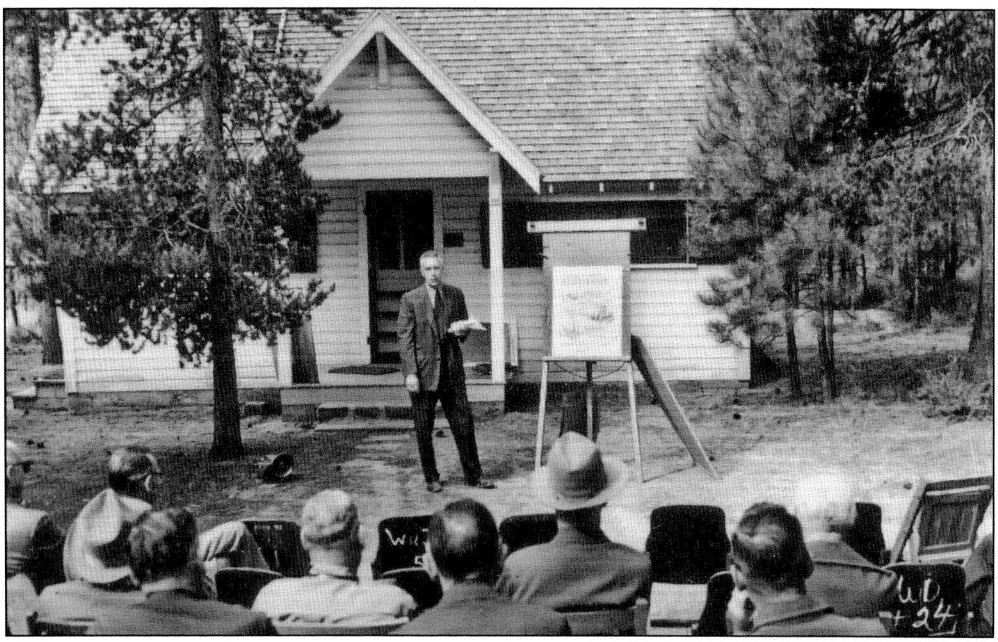

Bend Silviculture Laboratory project leader Carl Berntsen, PhD, briefs the US Forest Service's national advisory committee on the "Silviculture of Interior Conifer Types" research program at the Pringle Falls Experimental Forest during the committee's fall 1963 tour of Forest Service research facilities in the West. (Pacific Northwest Research Station.)

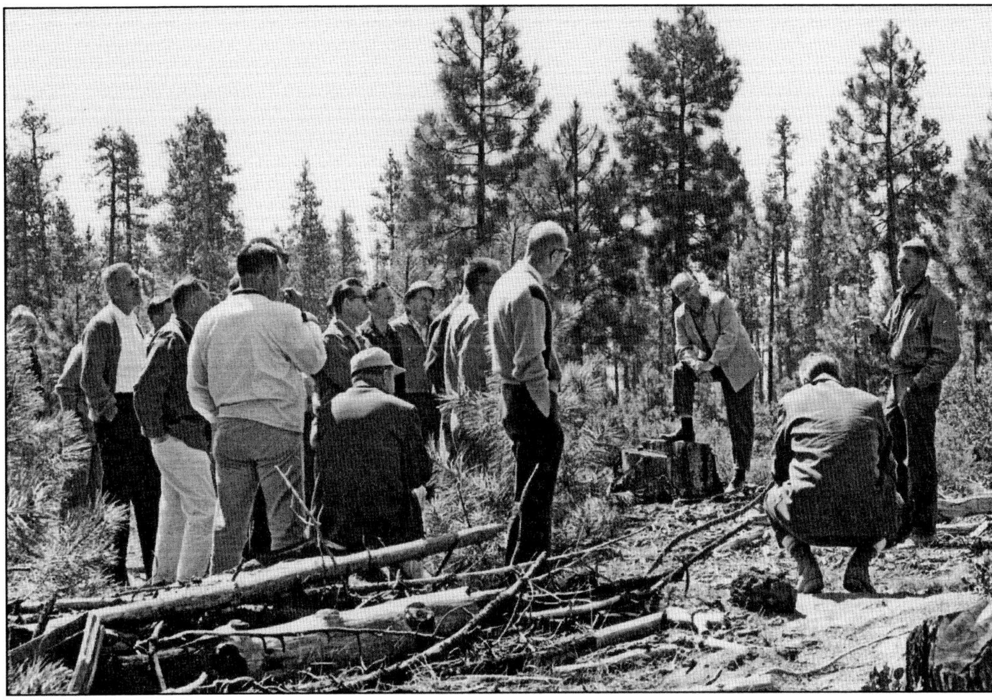

Research forester Jim Barrett explained the ponderosa pine spacing study he began at Pringle Falls Experimental Forest in 1957 and 1958 to many groups. Here, in May 1966, he briefs a group of Bureau of Indian Affairs foresters. (US Bureau of Indian Affairs, photograph by Harold Weaver.)

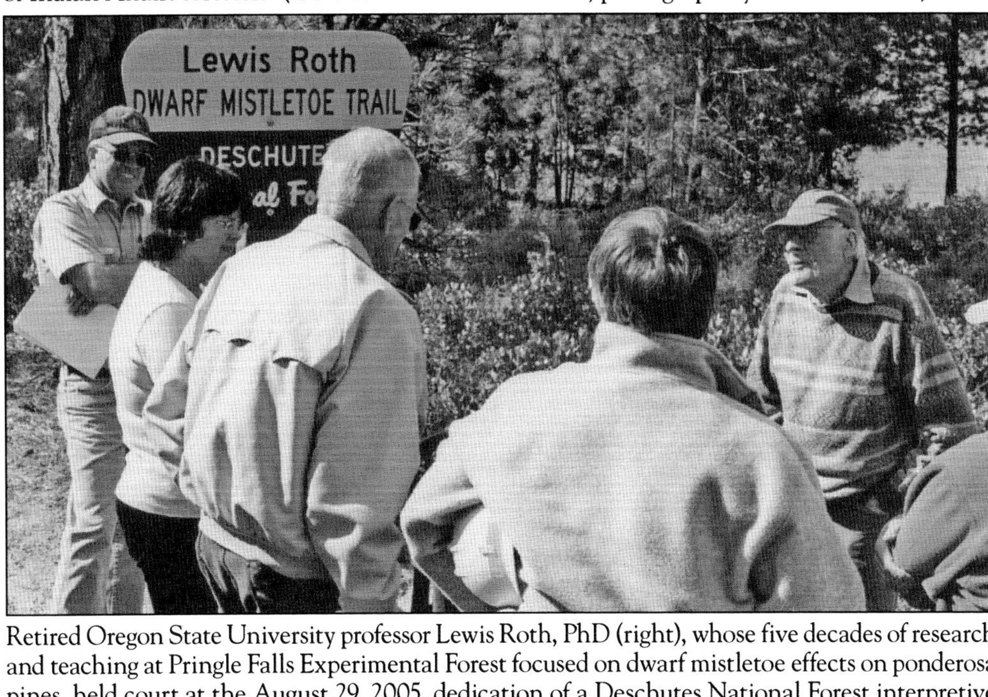

Retired Oregon State University professor Lewis Roth, PhD (right), whose five decades of research and teaching at Pringle Falls Experimental Forest focused on dwarf mistletoe effects on ponderosa pines, held court at the August 29, 2005, dedication of a Deschutes National Forest interpretive trail named for him. Longtime colleague Jim Barrett (third from left) was among many colleagues, friends, and former students in attendance. (Photograph by Chris Jensen.)

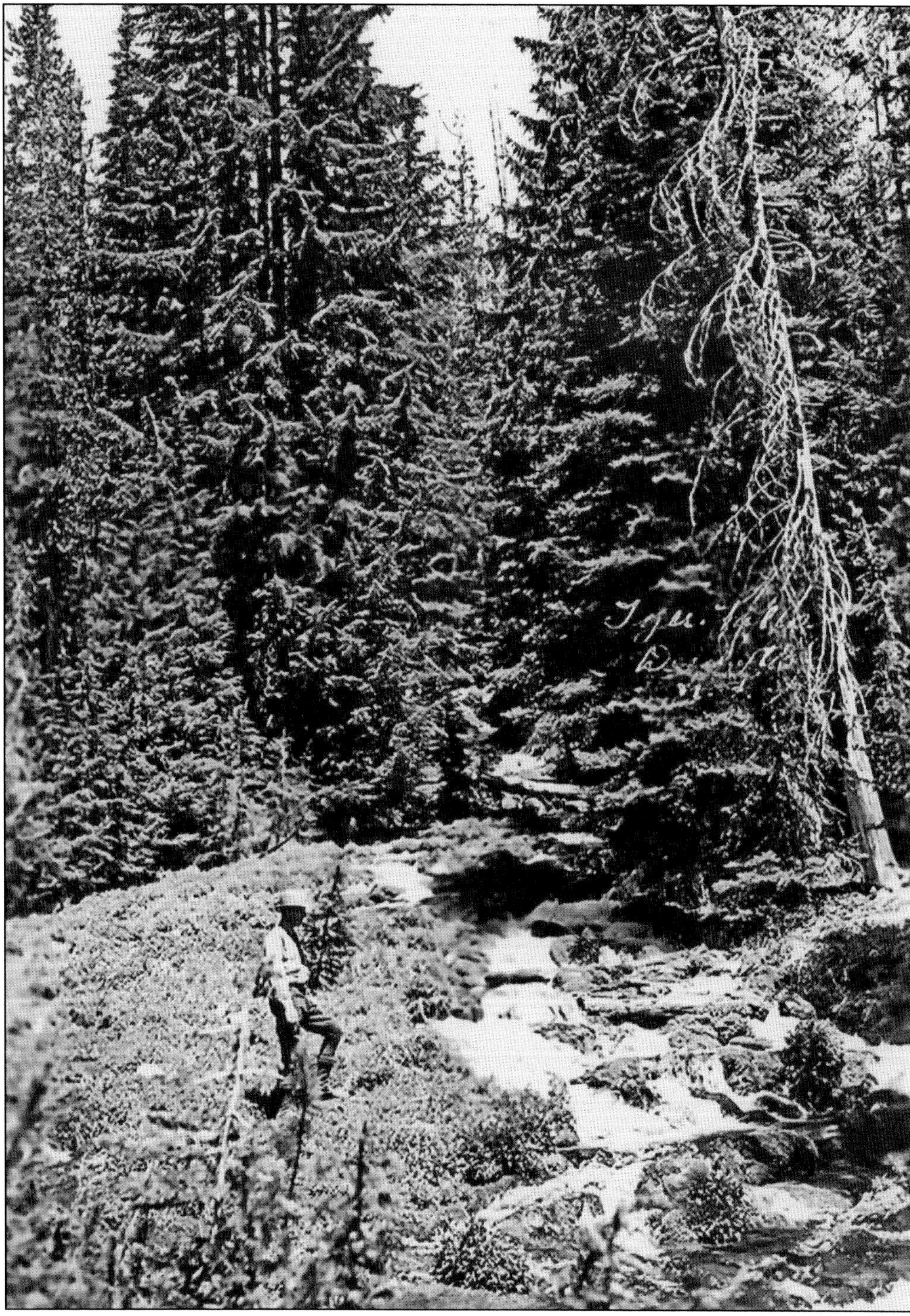

Bend district ranger Oswald Beedon checks watershed health and water flow at Tyee Creek in 1937. All natural resource management decisions made by Deschutes National Forest natural resource managers take the health and productivity of watersheds and this most vital resource into consideration. (Deschutes National Forest.)

Five

Water Resources

Water for domestic, industrial, and agricultural uses is the most precious Deschutes National Forest resource. In cooperation with federal, state, and local agencies and authorities, the US Forest Service manages all Deschutes National Forest resources and their uses to assure healthy watersheds and dependable supplies of clean water.

The upper Deschutes country's growing population has depended on Deschutes National Forest watersheds for its domestic, agricultural, and industrial water supplies for over a century. Households and industries—including Bend's booming breweries—depend on Bend's municipal water supply, derived from the Bridge Creek watershed about a dozen miles west of Bend and within the national forest. Management of this watershed allows limited recreation use (including access to beautiful Tumalo Falls), precludes uses that would adversely affect its vital water resource, and protects it against wildfires such as the major Bridge Creek Fire of July 1979.

Passage by Congress of the Carey Act of 1894 significantly changed agriculture in the upper Deschutes country from cattle and sheep ranching and some dryland wheat farming to irrigated agriculture early in the 20th century. That act authorized the federal government to contract with the states for arid land reclamation. Lured by the possibility of developing irrigation—as well as by the area's natural beauty—Bend founder Alexander M. Drake arrived in 1900 and founded the Pilot Butte Development Company in 1902 to provide water for irrigation of farmlands. The first such water, provided by a successor company, irrigated 40 acres in 1904, and the rush was on. Irrigation districts evolved, and 20 years later, the Central Oregon Irrigation District alone supplied water to irrigate 28,500 acres. Currently, six irrigation districts, which annually divert more than 650,000 acre-feet of water (the amount of water that would cover one acre to a depth of one foot) near Bend, irrigate almost 100,000 acres of cropland. One of these, the Central Oregon Irrigation District, successor of Drake's pioneering enterprise, also provides municipal water to the city of Redmond, Oregon, and neighboring subdivisions as well as to parks and schools in Bend and also produces hydroelectric power.

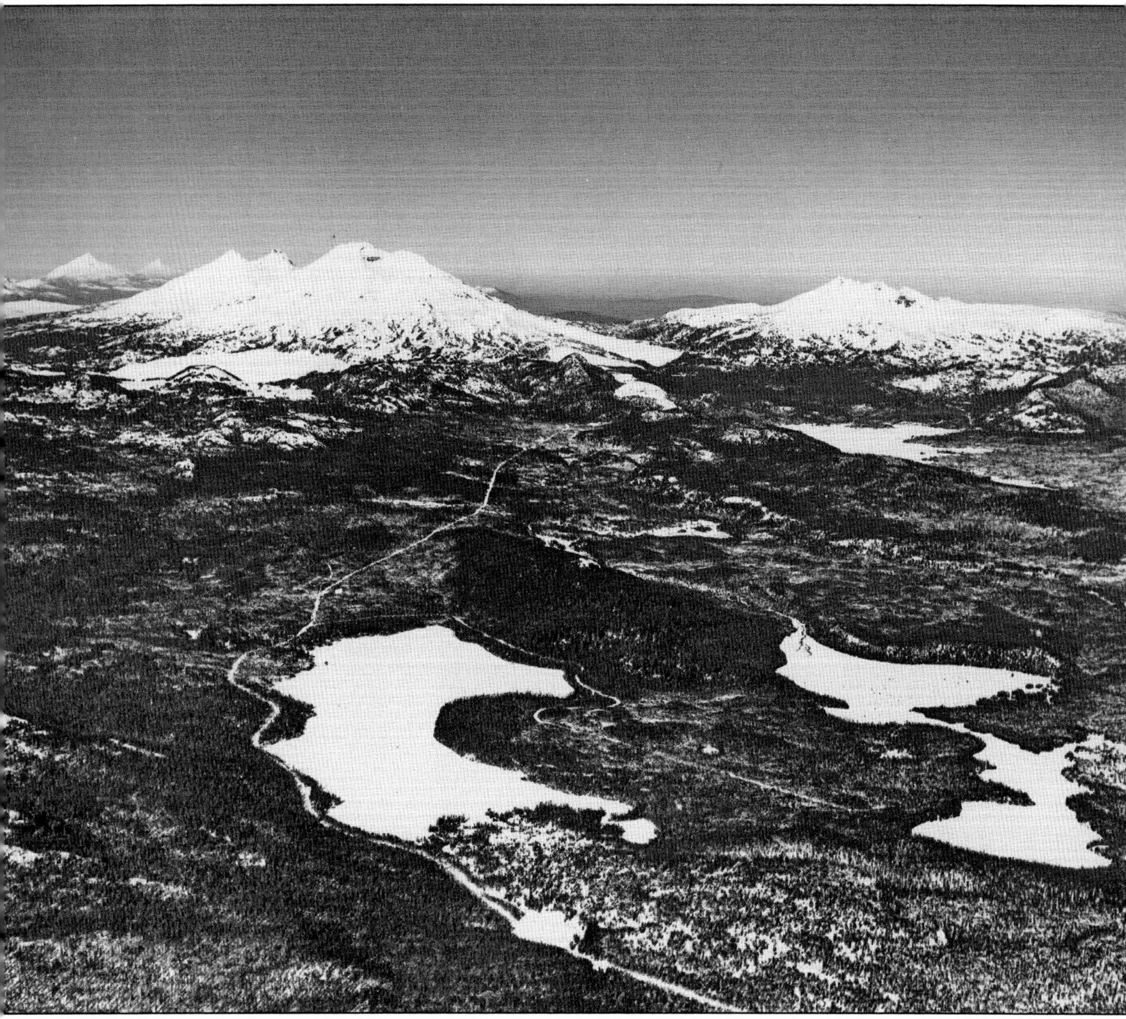

Winter snowfall stored in central Cascade Range mountains of the Deschutes National Forest melts, percolates into the region's porous volcanic watershed, surfaces in upper Deschutes country spring-fed streams and lakes, and also recharges area groundwater supplies. These waters are managed to provide for domestic, industrial, and agricultural needs as well as for stream and lake habitats for fish and wildlife and for recreation uses. Here, the Three Sisters (top left) and Broken Top (top right) and surrounding forested highlands store the winter snowpack that fills Sparks Lake (below Broken Top), Elk Lake (left), and Hosmer Lake (right). This snowmelt makes its way to the headwaters of the spring-fed Deschutes River at Little Lava Lake and into the Crane Prairie and Wickiup Reservoirs along that river. Lakes and reservoirs in other reaches of the Deschutes National Forest also are filled by Cascade Range and Paulina Mountains snowmelt. This water flows to its various users via an intricate distribution system including municipal waterworks and irrigation district canals developed since the beginning of the 20th century. (Deschutes County Historical Society.)

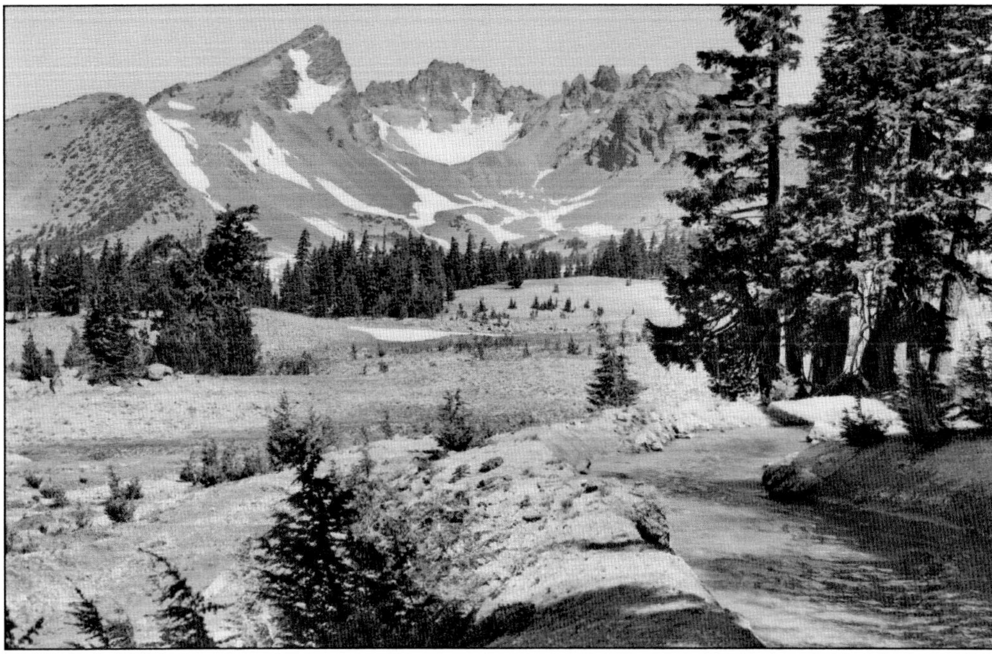

Early irrigators built extensive ditches, canals, and other facilities in the Deschutes National Forest to facilitate the flow of irrigation waters toward agricultural users. Crater Creek Ditch (above), on the eastern side of Broken Top, has long carried Cascade Range water into the Tumalo Irrigation District system. Across rugged terrain where ditches could not be dug, flumes were built to carry the water. The Central Oregon Irrigation District flume (below), constructed during the 1920s, demonstrates just how sophisticated some of those structures were and just how vital and valuable those irrigation waters were to developing the region's agriculture. (Both, Deschutes County Historical Society.)

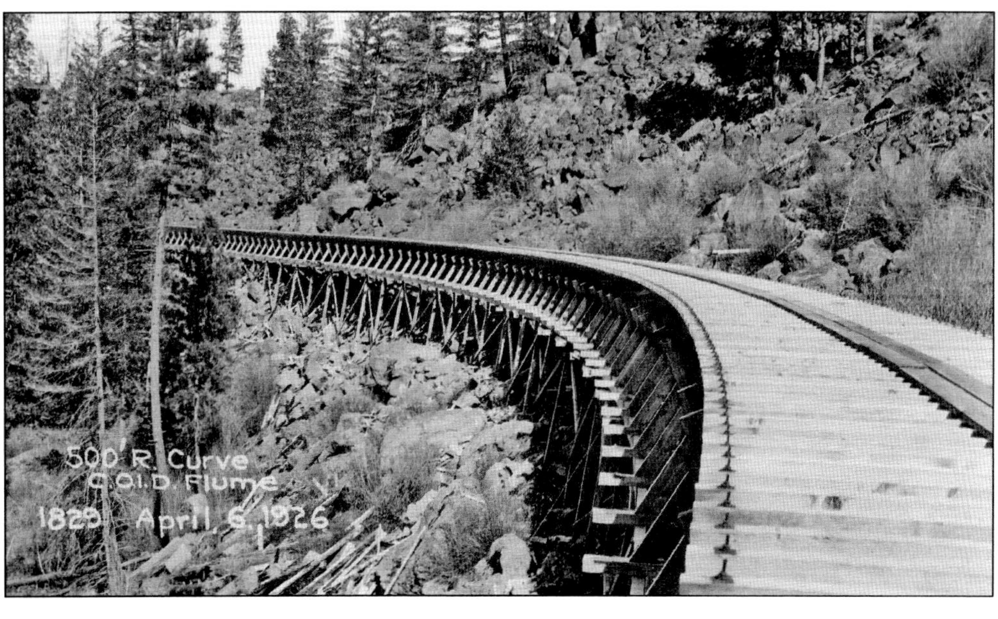

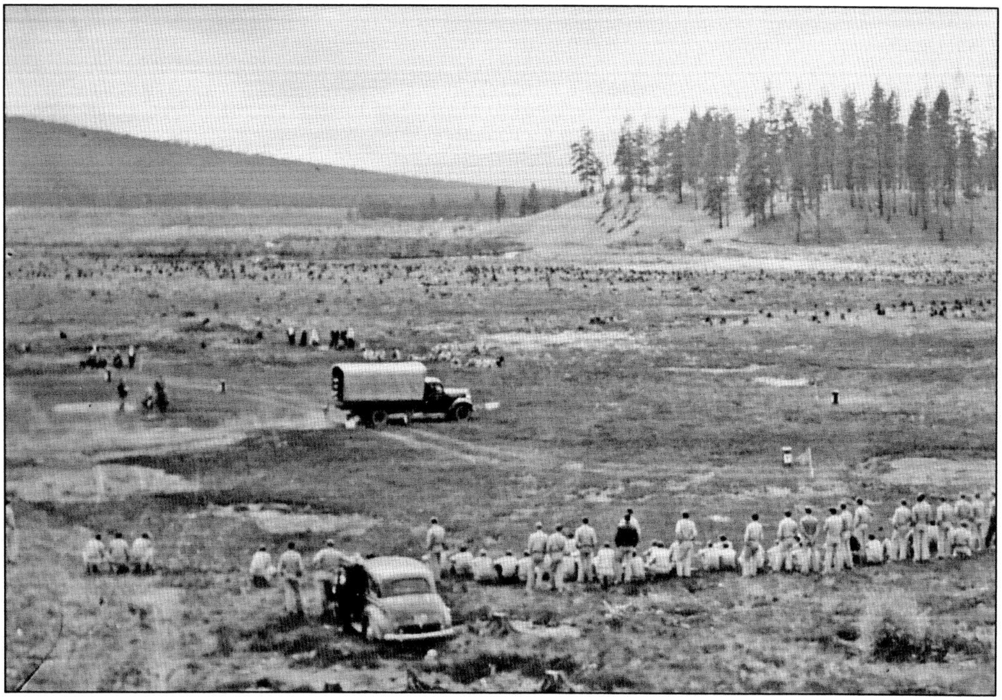

The Wickiup Dam and Wickiup Reservoir were developed within the Deschutes National Forest between 1939 and 1949 by the US Bureau of Reclamation. Much of the area to be inundated—the Wickiup Basin along the Deschutes River, where Native Americans camped to hunt and fish in the fall and left poles for their shelters called "wickiups"—was cleared by CCC enrollees, shown above apparently reviewing their work, and during World War II by conscientious objectors. The rising ground on the left is Davis Mountain. This marked the southern shoreline of the reservoir that covered the pine-studded ridge on the right with 20 feet of water once the dam (below) was completed and the reservoir filled. (Above, Deschutes County Historical Society; below, Deschutes National Forest.)

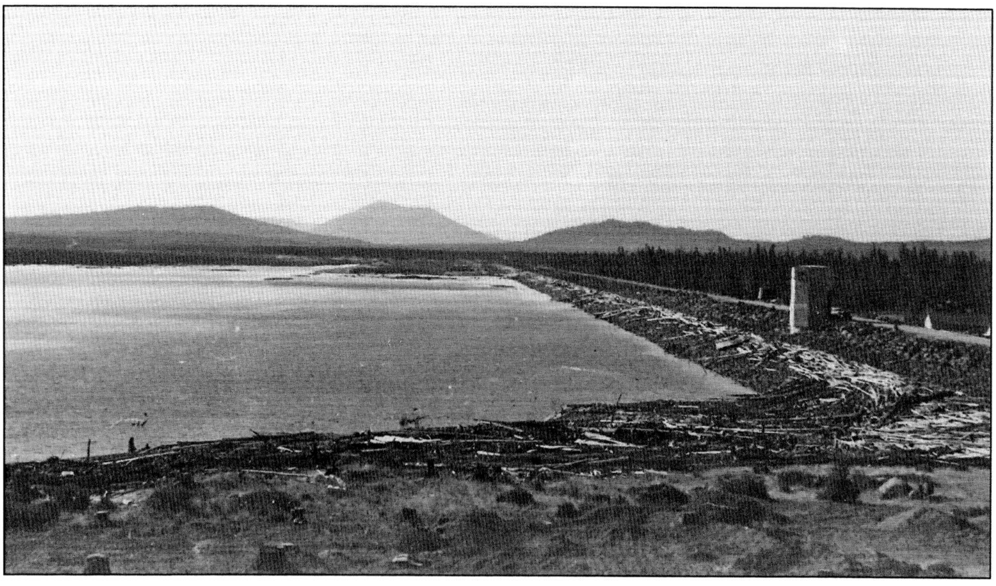

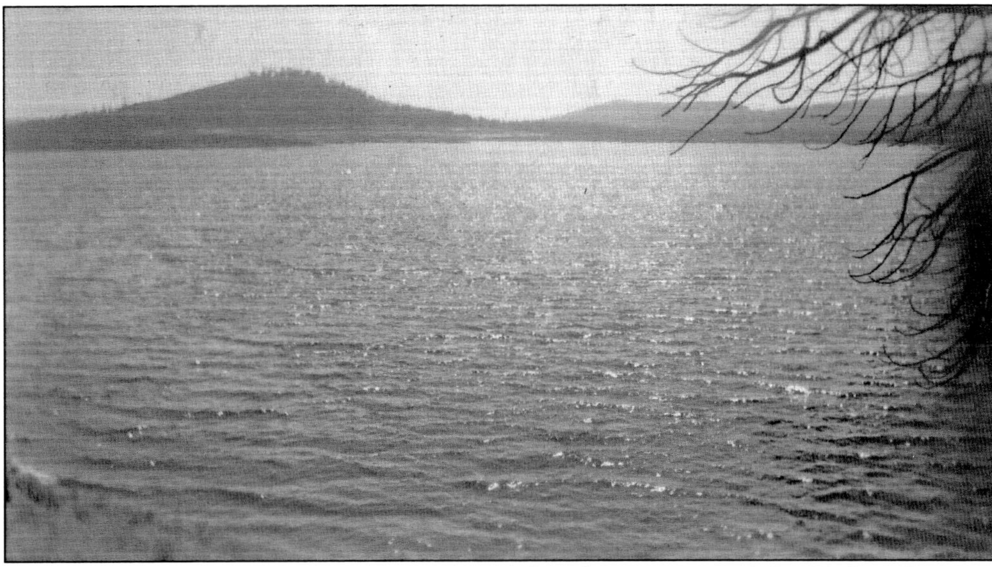

After it was completed in 1949, the US Bureau of Reclamation turned the Wickiup Dam and Wickiup Reservoir over to the North Unit Irrigation District. The reservoir's capacity is sufficient to meet the water rights held by that district to irrigate over 50,000 acres of agricultural land surrounding Madras, Oregon, about 100 miles north of the reservoir (above), and to irrigate other areas. With a surface area of 10,334 acres, the Wickiup Reservoir (below) is the largest body of water within the boundaries of the Deschutes National Forest. In addition to irrigation water, the reservoir provides sites for several national forest campgrounds and waters valued for boating and fishing. (Above, Deschutes National Forest; below, Deschutes County Historical Society.)

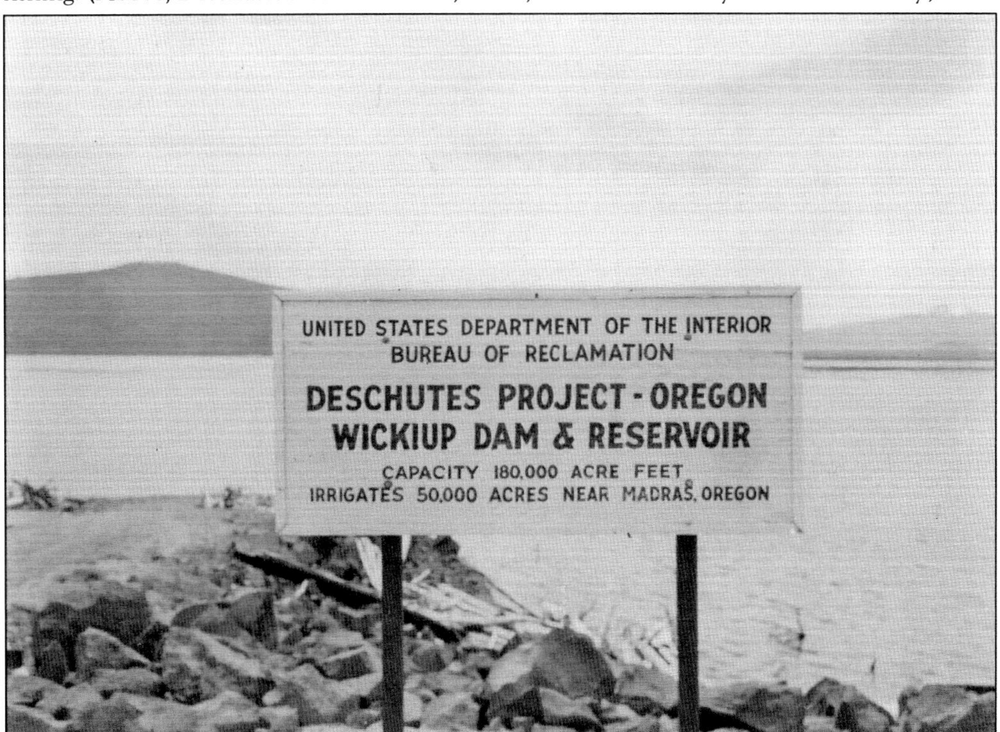

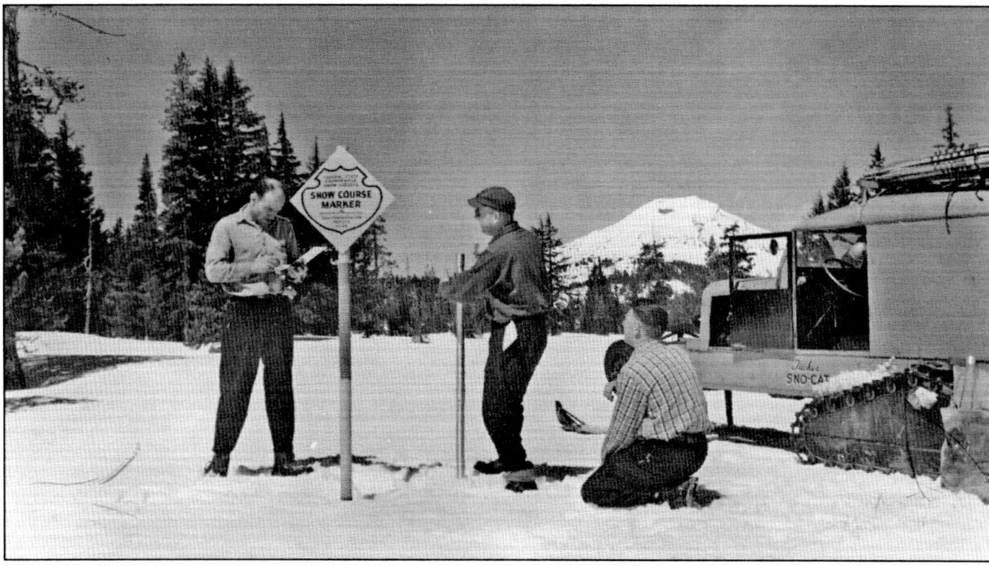

Watershed managers and consumers need to know how much water the watersheds produce so they can plan for its annual distribution and use by the entities that hold water rights for and depend on water for irrigation and other uses. To develop and provide that information, US Forest Service and other agency officials annually gather data on Deschutes National Forest snowpack water content at federal-state cooperative snow survey snow course markers. In the March 1946 photograph above, water content of 12.5 feet of snow is measured and reported to the coordinating US Department of Agriculture agency. Streamflow rates are measured at water gauging stations such as the one below, photographed in 1964 below Crescent Lake Dam on the Crescent Ranger District. (Above, Deschutes County Historical Society; below, Deschutes National Forest.)

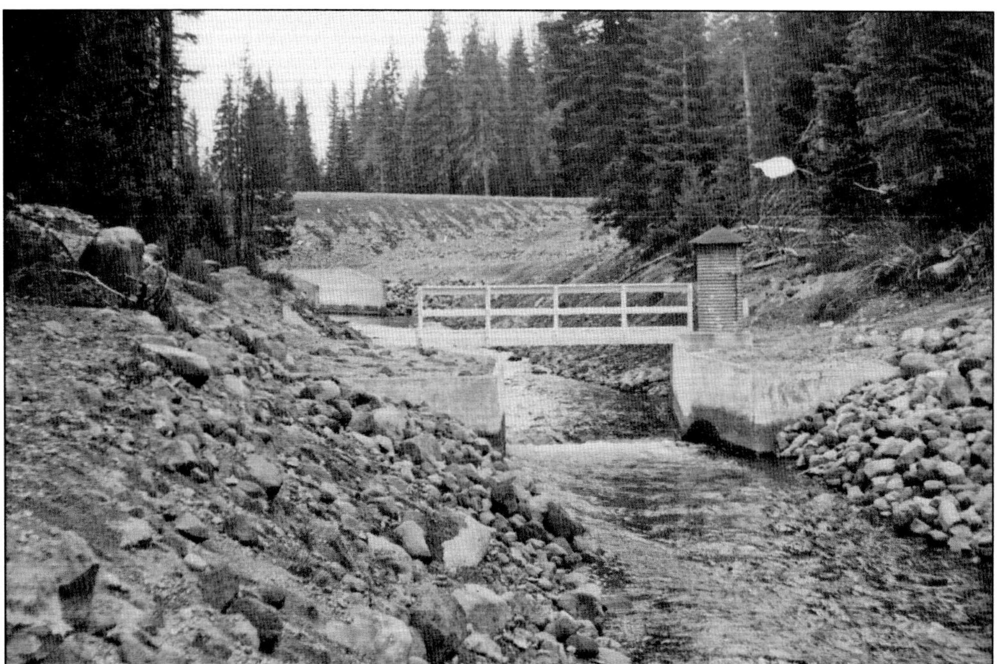

Six

Grazing Resources

Wool and beef became important Oregon products in the 1860s, and much of it was grown east of the Cascades. The first challenge the US Forest Service faced on the Deschutes National Forest involved not timber and water resources but the grazing resources exploited early and extensively before the national forest evolved from the forest reserve.

As early as the 1870s, when Oregon sheepmen needed more summer range, sheep were driven toward the alpine ranges each spring. Dozens of bands of 1,500 to 2,500 approached from the east in May or June, moved toward the alpine meadows as the snow receded, and trailed out of the high country before the winter snows. Eventually, on a smaller scale, cattle were grazed. By the 1890s, some of these ranges were seriously overgrazed, and livestock was excluded from the Cascade Range Forest Reserve from 1894 until brought under regulation in 1897. Grazing based on the carrying capacity of the range was enforced by pioneer forest rangers such as Cy Bingham. Grazing peaked in the alpine ranges of the western Deschutes National Forest about 1910, then began to fall off as a result of competing uses for the land and a decline in the livestock industry.

Early-20th-century homesteading in the Millican Valley and Fort Rock Basin increased grazing on the lower, drier rangelands of the eastern Deschutes National Forest. Forest supervisor J. Roy Harvey, who took over the national forest in 1911, had practical ranch experience, got along well with stockmen, and had a good handle on this grazing. Although grazing on Fort Rock Ranger District rangelands was limited by a lack of water, drilling of the Cabin Lake well in 1916, other water development, and water hauling increased grazing.

Grazing on the Deschutes National Forest fluctuated with the economy and the markets. In 1921, some 10,400 cattle and 23,000 sheep were authorized to graze on the forest. By 1945, the numbers permitted were 2,243 cattle and 30,180 sheep. In 1981, the forest was authorized to permit 4,600 cattle and 6,000 sheep, but 3,818 cattle and 3,782 sheep actually grazed. Grazing on the national forest continues but at much lower intensity.

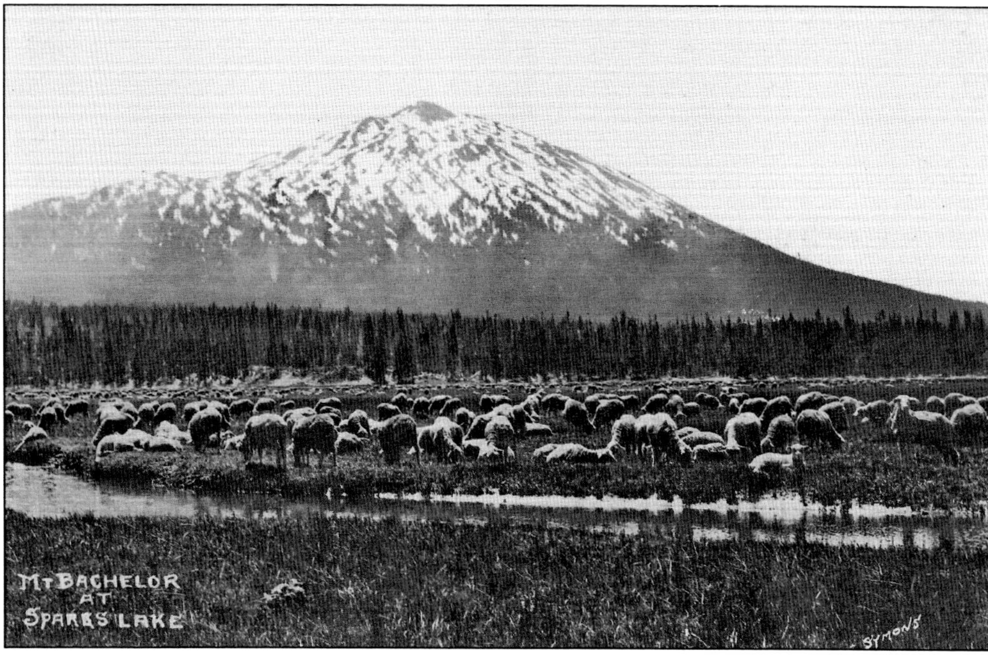

Sheep wintered on the sagebrush steppes of Central Oregon and grazed the lush high meadows of the Deschutes National Forest during the summers. These sheep graze on the northeast side of Sparks Lake Meadow, about 25 miles west of Bend near Bachelor Butte. (Deschutes County Historical Society.)

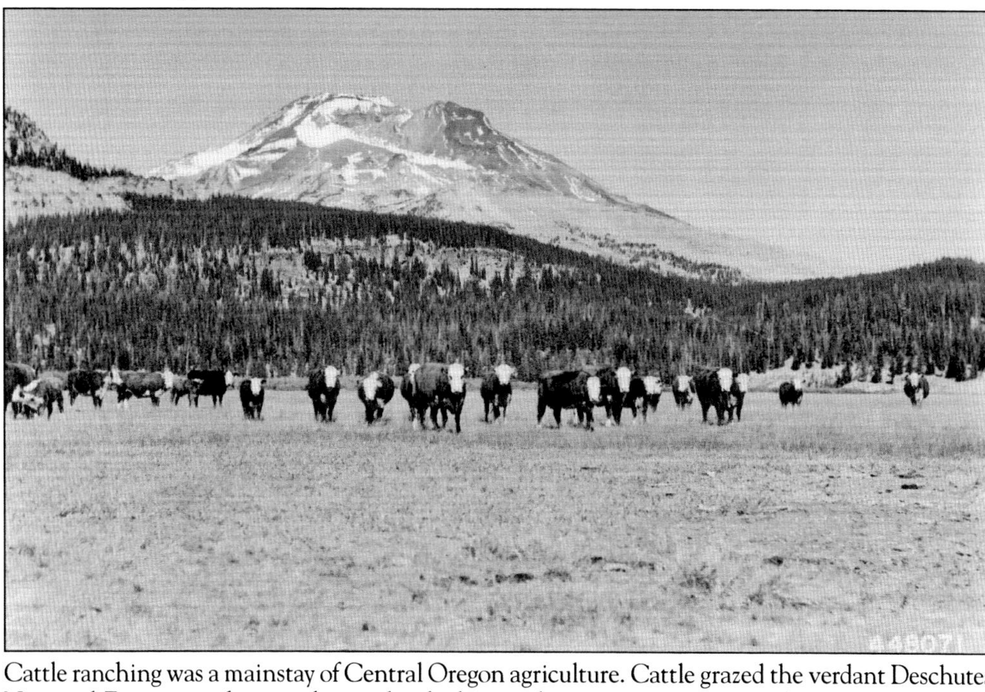

Cattle ranching was a mainstay of Central Oregon agriculture. Cattle grazed the verdant Deschutes National Forest meadows and rangelands during the summers. In 1947, these cattle grazed a Sparks Lake Meadow allotment south of South Sister. (Deschutes National Forest, photograph by Leland J. Prater.)

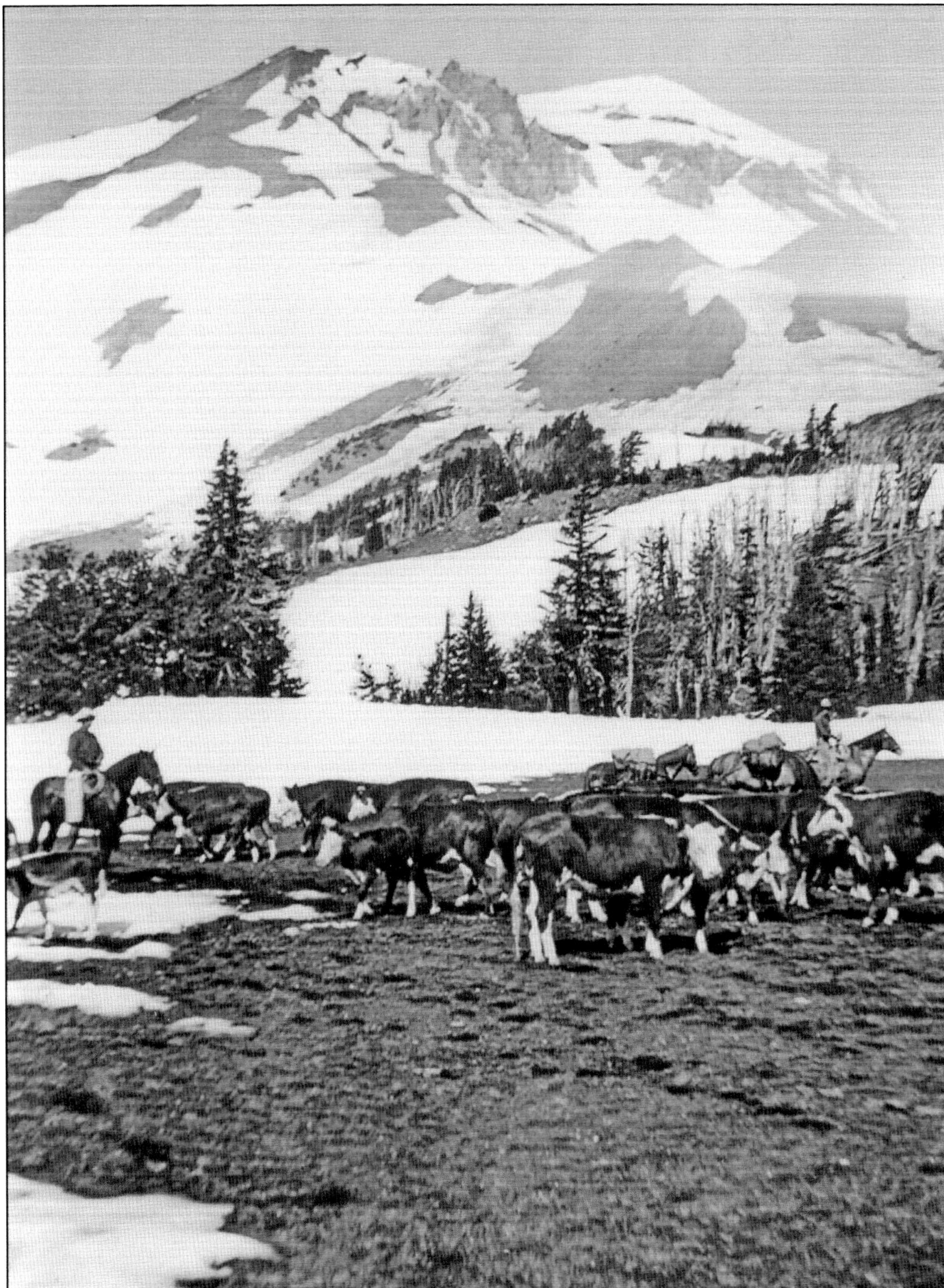

To reach that Sparks Lake Meadow grazing allotment, cattle ranchers Walt McCoin and Priday Holmes drove their cattle from their ranches south of Culver, past the town of Sisters, up the Squaw Creek (now Wychus Creek) drainage, past the Green Lakes and South Sister, and down the Fall Creek stock drive. After 1949, they trucked the cattle to the allotment and, according to one participant, "all the glamor went out of it." (Deschutes National Forest, photograph by Hazel McCoin.)

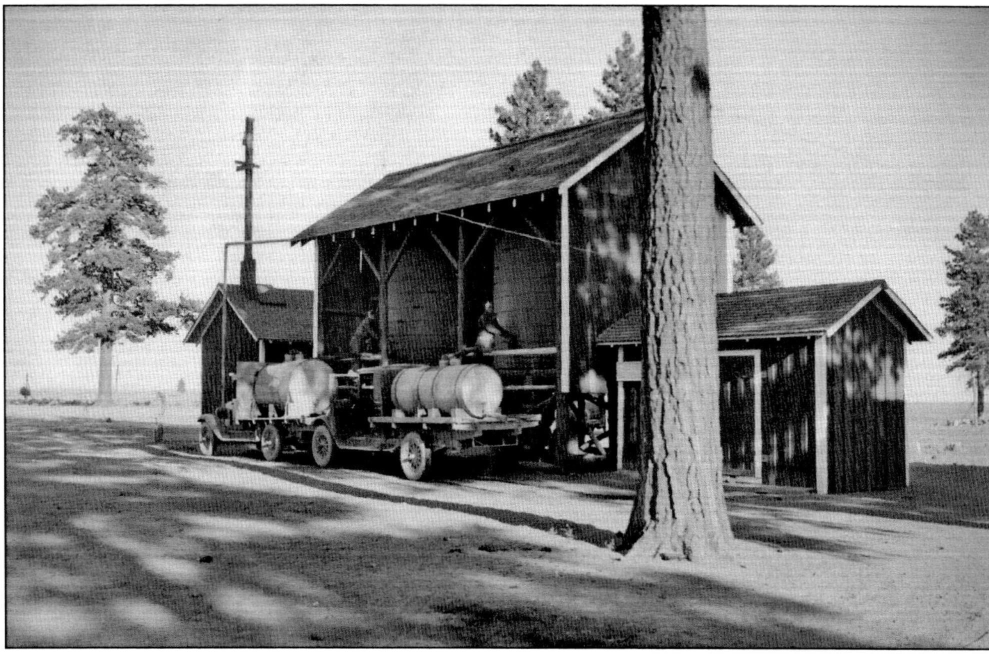

Livestock grazing on the dryer eastern Deschutes National Forest rangelands was enhanced beginning in 1916 by hauling water from wells. Here, water trucks are filled at the Cabin Lake Well in 1929. (Deschutes National Forest, photograph by D.C. Ingram.)

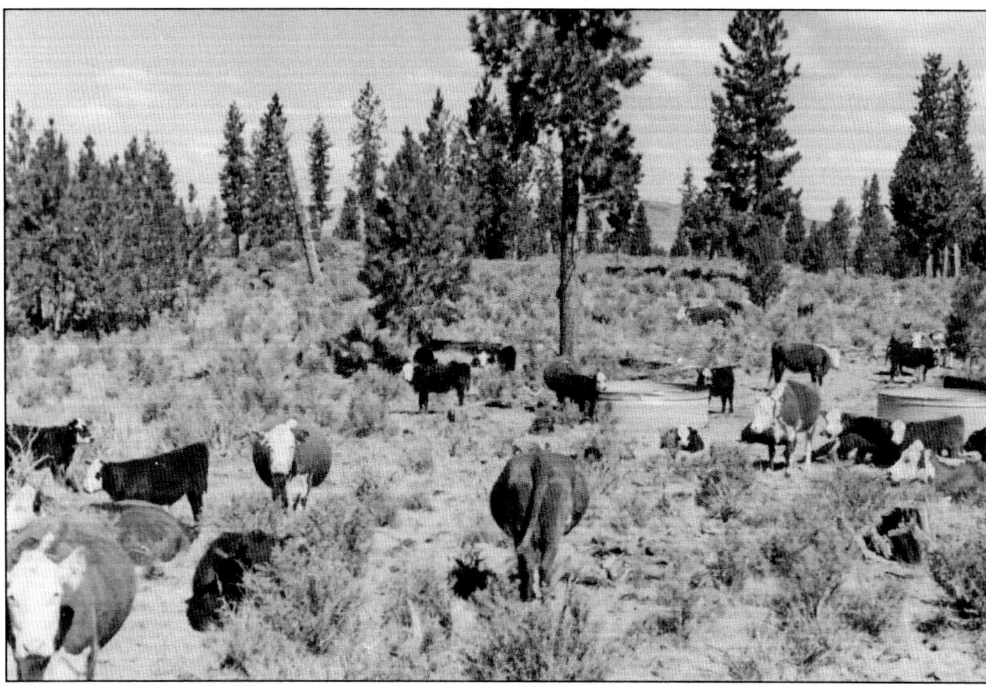

Hauled water filled stock watering tanks such as these at a range water development on a grazing allotment in the dry ponderosa pine woodlands of the Fort Rock Ranger District. Livestock grazing helped reduce wildfire in those grazed woodlands by reducing finer fuels such as grass and brush. (Deschutes National Forest.)

Seven

Fish and Wildlife Resources

Management and conservation of fish and wildlife on national forests, a state's right under the US Constitution, involves complex interaction and cooperation between federal and state agencies. After 1905, the US Forest Service managed the land and the fish and wildlife habitat on the forest reserves—called national forests since 1907—and the US Biological Survey, a forerunner of the US Fish and Wildlife Service, accomplished wildlife research and some predator control. As the Deschutes National Forest evolved, so did its management relationship with Oregon fish and wildlife authorities, now the Oregon Department of Fish and Wildlife, whose operating professionals serve the appointed Oregon Fish and Wildlife Commission.

Although trapping fur-bearing animals for pelts and hunting predators for bounties are things of the past, recreational hunting and fishing in accordance with Oregon fish and wildlife laws and regulations remain important uses of the Deschutes National Forest. Visitors who do not hunt or fish appreciate viewing, photographing, and studying wildlife.

Cooperation began early. Forest Service rangers were appointed as deputy state game wardens with authority to enforce state fish and game laws. As early as 1912, the state game commission enlisted the help of Forest Service rangers and packers in stocking Deschutes National Forest lakes and streams with trout to promote sportfishing. In 1913 and 1929, the state established two game refuges within the Deschutes National Forest. Beginning in the 1920s, the Forest Service and the Biological Survey conducted an annual game census on the Deschutes National Forest that benefitted state management. In 1929 and 1947, the state established fish hatcheries within the Deschutes National Forest at Fall River and Wizard Falls.

As the science of wildlife management evolved, techniques such as predator control and game refuges intended to produce large deer and elk herds gave way to more enlightened methods that emphasized habitat management for sustainable populations. Now, Deschutes National Forest fish and wildlife biologists cooperate closely with other federal and state agencies, university scientists, and national and local fish and wildlife groups to balance wildlife and other values.

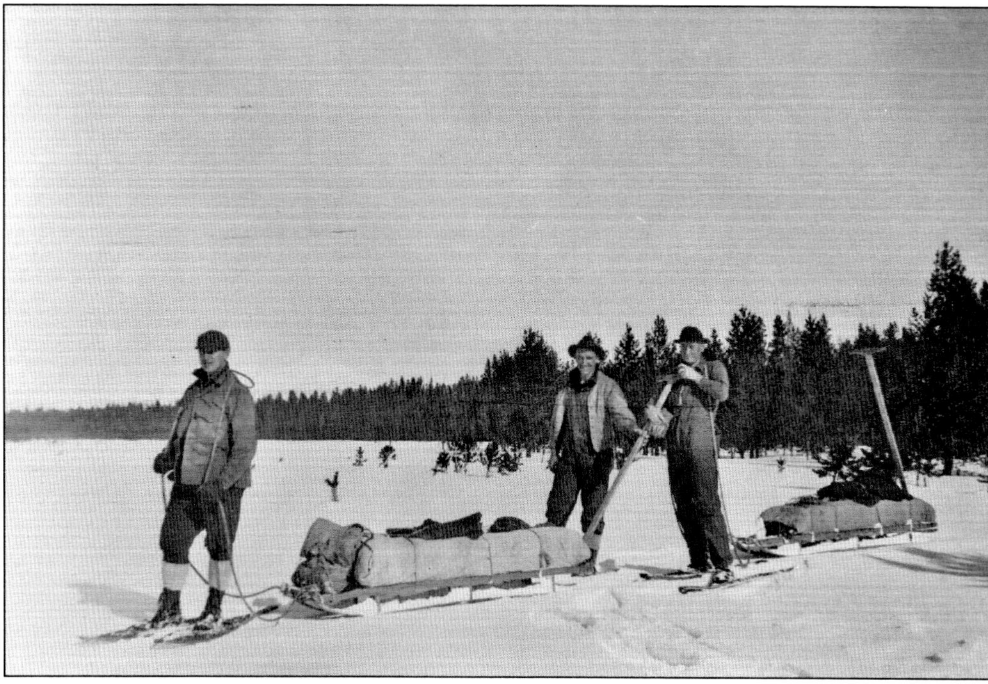

Early efforts to raise fish for planting in Deschutes National Forest streams and lakes included collecting fish eggs. In January 1919, some 350,000 eastern brook trout eggs were gathered at Elk Lake, taken to Bend by sled, and transported by automobile to the state's Bonneville fish hatchery. Development of the Deschutes National Forest sportfishing resource benefitted significantly from this and other efforts. (Both, Deschutes County Historical Society.)

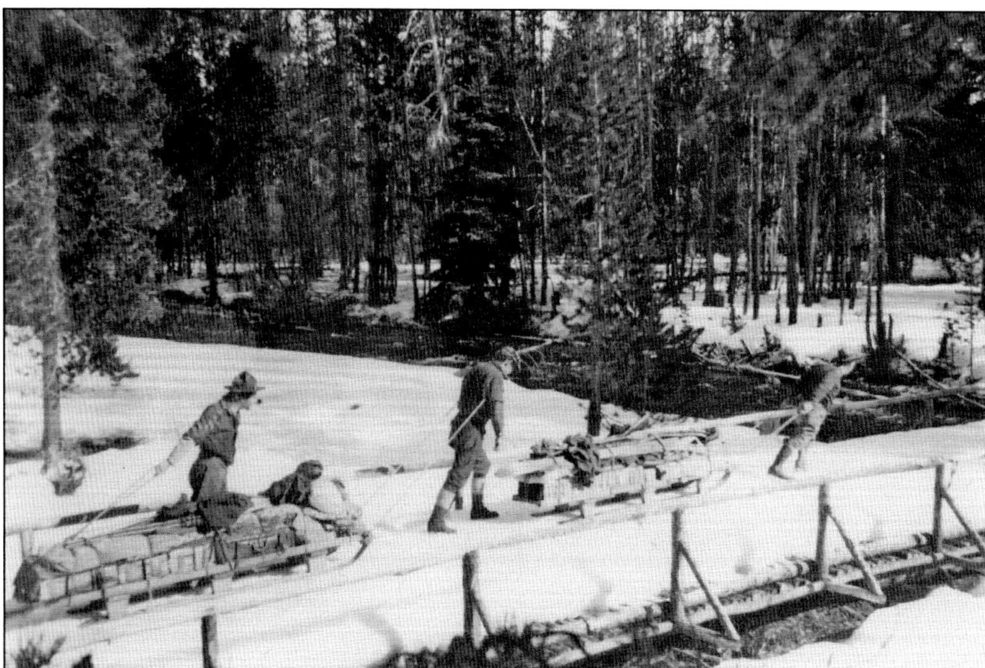

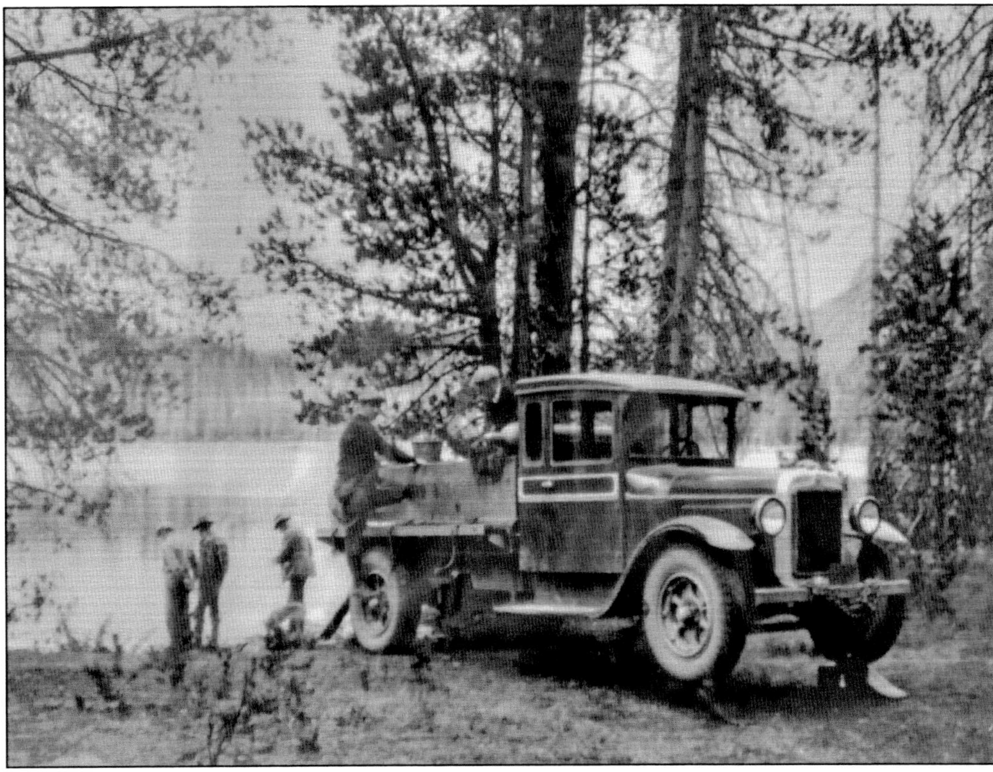

Fish raised in early hatcheries were used to stock Deschutes National Forest streams and lakes beginning early in the 20th century. This photograph shows fish being planted by cooperating federal and state personnel at East Lake in the Newberry Caldera. (Deschutes National Forest.)

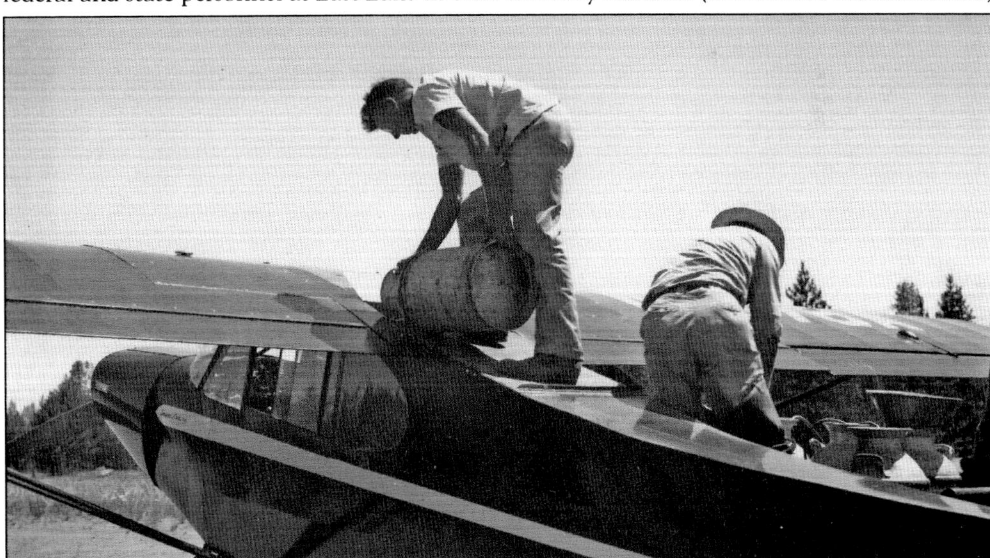

Aircraft—as well as pack animals—were used to stock remote mountain lakes with fish. In July 1953, trout raised at the state's Fall River Fish Hatchery within the Deschutes National Forest were poured into fish planting plane tanks at the airstrip adjacent to the hatchery. (Deschutes National Forest, photograph by E.J. Parker.)

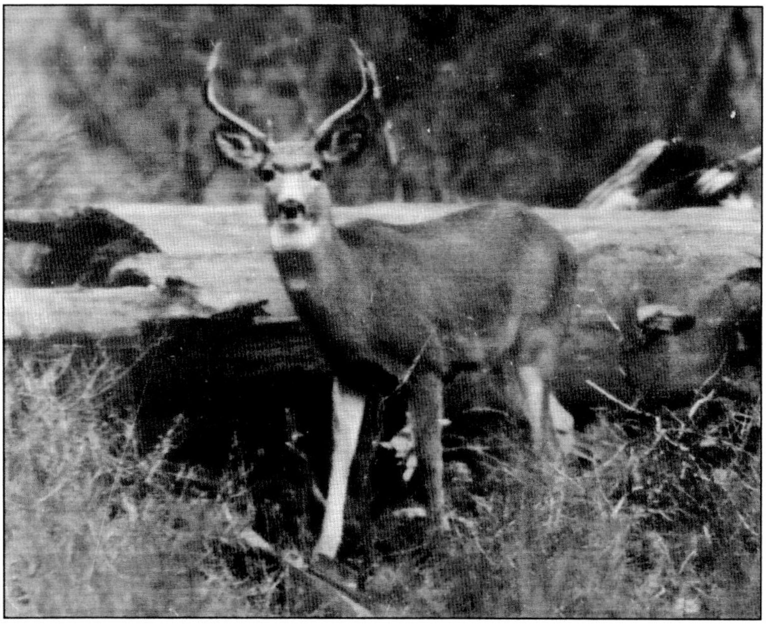

Mule deer are important game animals east of the Cascade Range. Within the Deschutes National Forest, they once ranged eastward into sagebrush steppe habitat. They now inhabit mainly open forests and mountain meadows and in winter descend to lower valleys. (Deschutes National Forest, photograph by Ralph Crawford.)

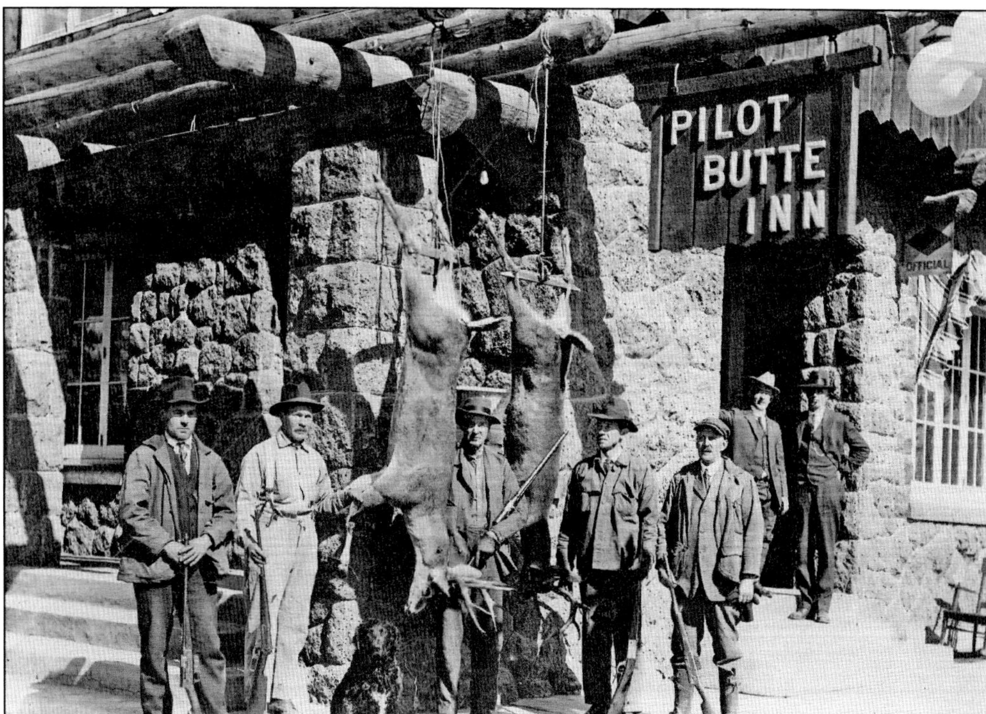

These early-20th-century hunters hung mule deer bucks taken on the Deschutes National Forest pursuant to state hunting regulations in front of Bend's fashionable Pilot Butte Inn. Good forest management includes maintaining good deer habitat. (Deschutes County Historical Society.)

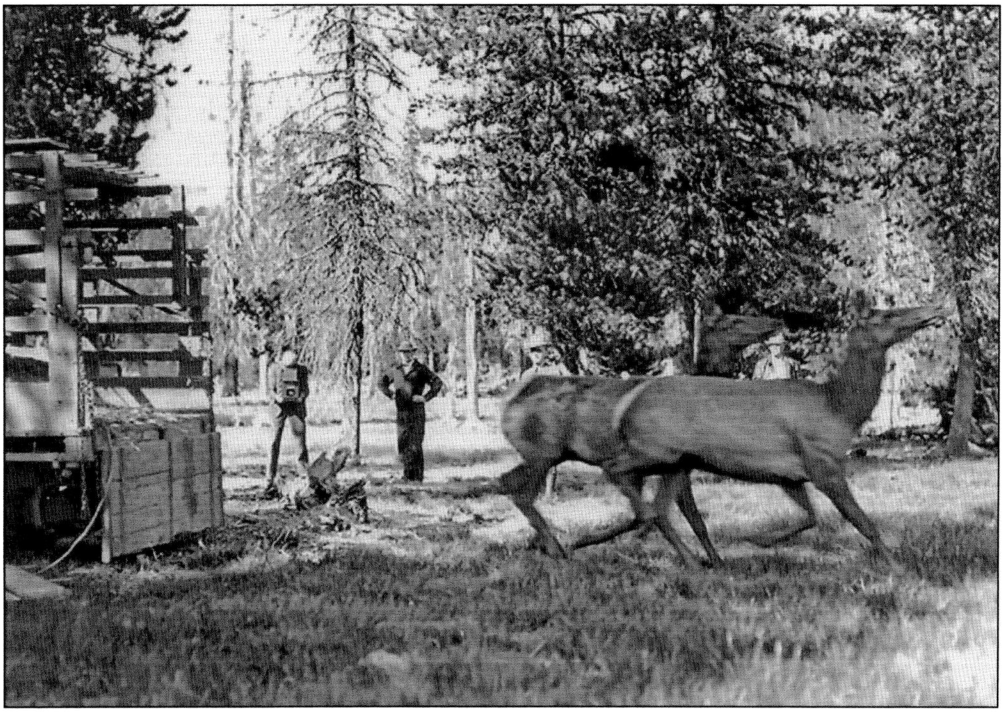

Elk, the second-largest member of the deer family, are grazing animals found in the forests and meadows of the Deschutes National Forest. Reduced in numbers by early settlers, they have been reintroduced throughout their ranges. These elk were released by the Oregon Game Commission and the US Forest Service (above) at Sparks Lake Meadow (below) in 1934. (Both, Deschutes National Forest.)

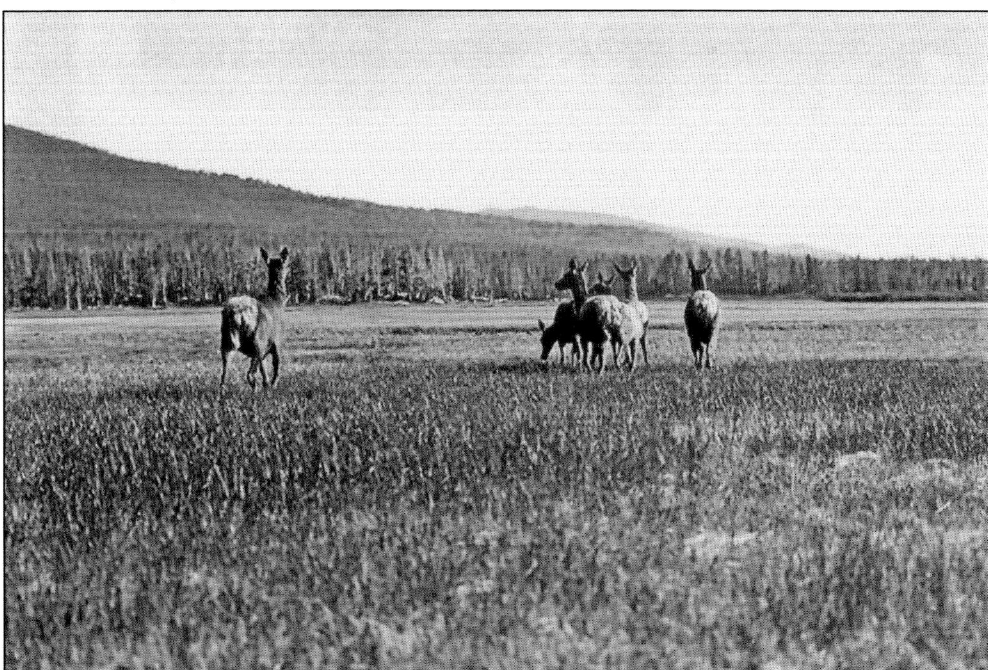

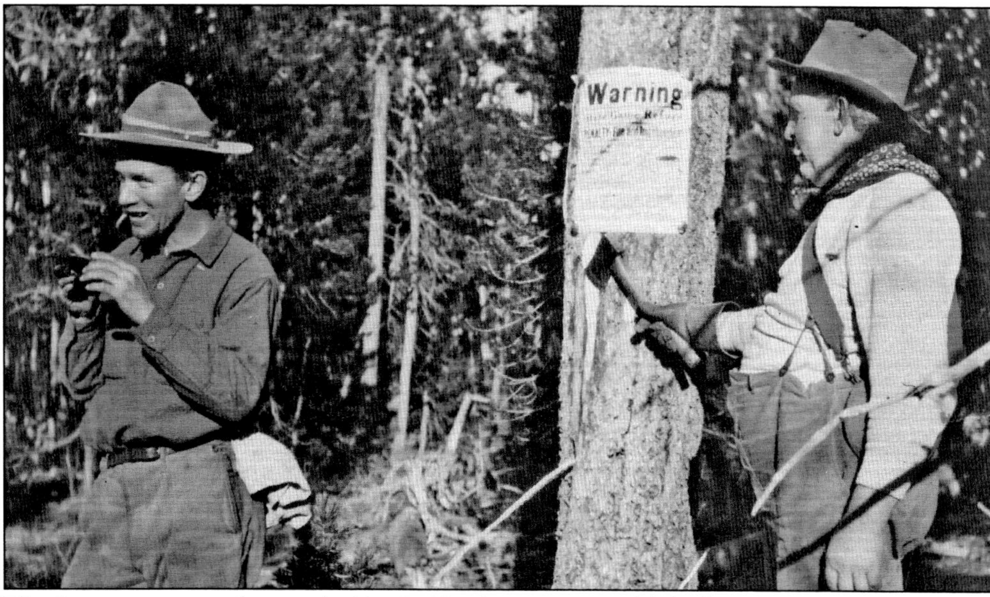

The first state game refuge in the Pacific Northwest was established on the Deschutes National Forest. After he resigned from the US Forest Service in 1913, John Riis (left) was appointed a deputy state game warden to help post the boundaries of the 36-square-mile Paulina Game Refuge, established that year to protect mule deer and antelope. The area was reopened to hunting in 1949. (John Riis Group.)

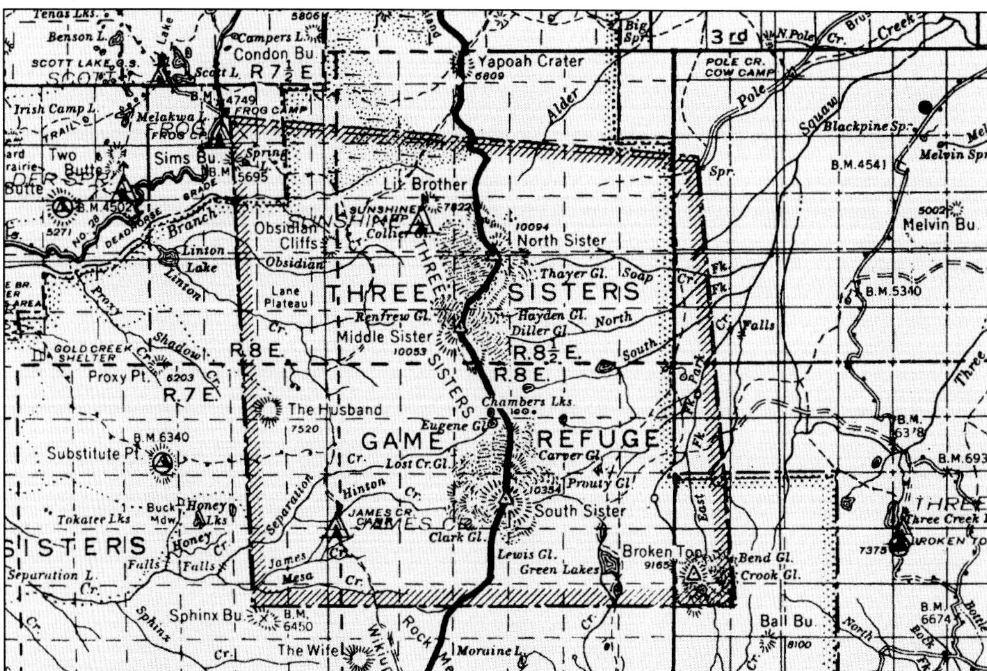

The second state game refuge on the Deschutes National Forest was the 56-square-mile Three Sisters Game Refuge, which included the Three Sisters, Broken Top, and surroundings from 1929 until 1955. Unlike most game refuges, it was designated largely at the request of recreationists who objected to random shooting. (US Forest Service.)

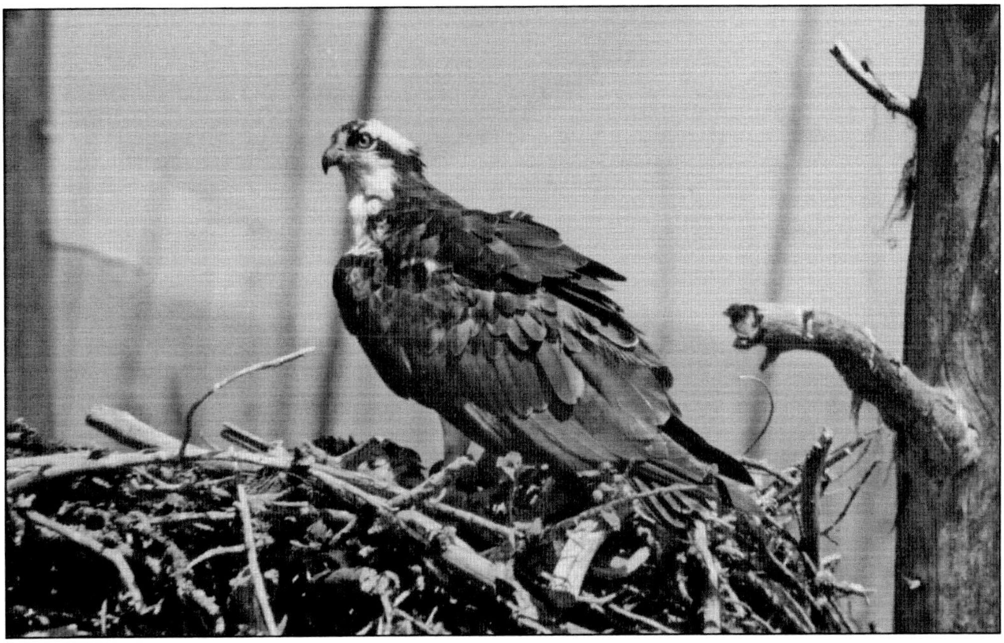

Ospreys winter in South America and breed in North America. Snags in the Crane Prairie Reservoir on the Deschutes National Forest provide nesting places for the largest nesting colony of this large bird in the Pacific Northwest. (Deschutes National Forest, photograph by Milt Griffith.)

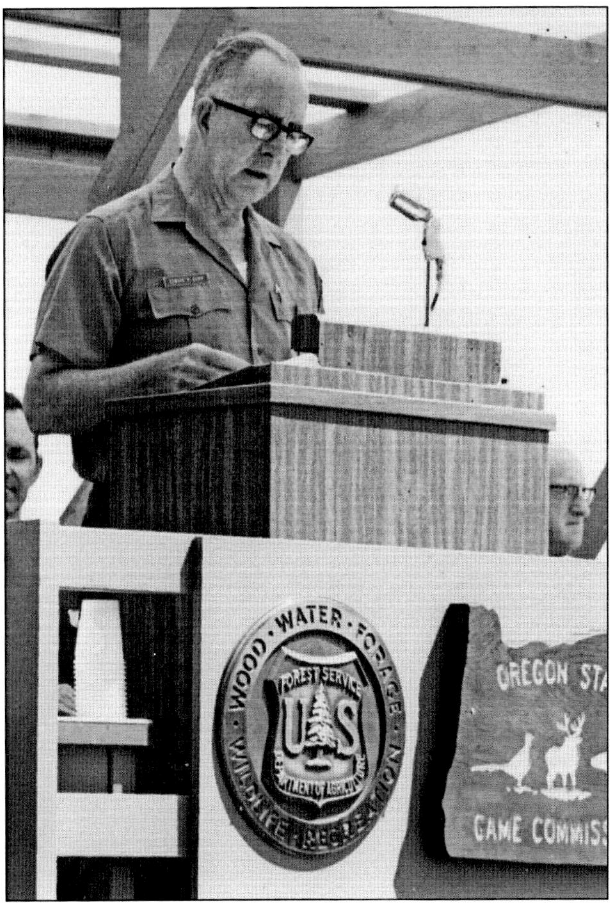

Chief of the US Forest Service Edward P. Cliff speaks at the 1970 dedication of the Osprey Management Area at Crane Prairie Reservoir. State and federal agencies cooperate in the management of this 10,600-acre area, which protects the osprey nesting colony on the Deschutes National Forest. (Deschutes National Forest.)

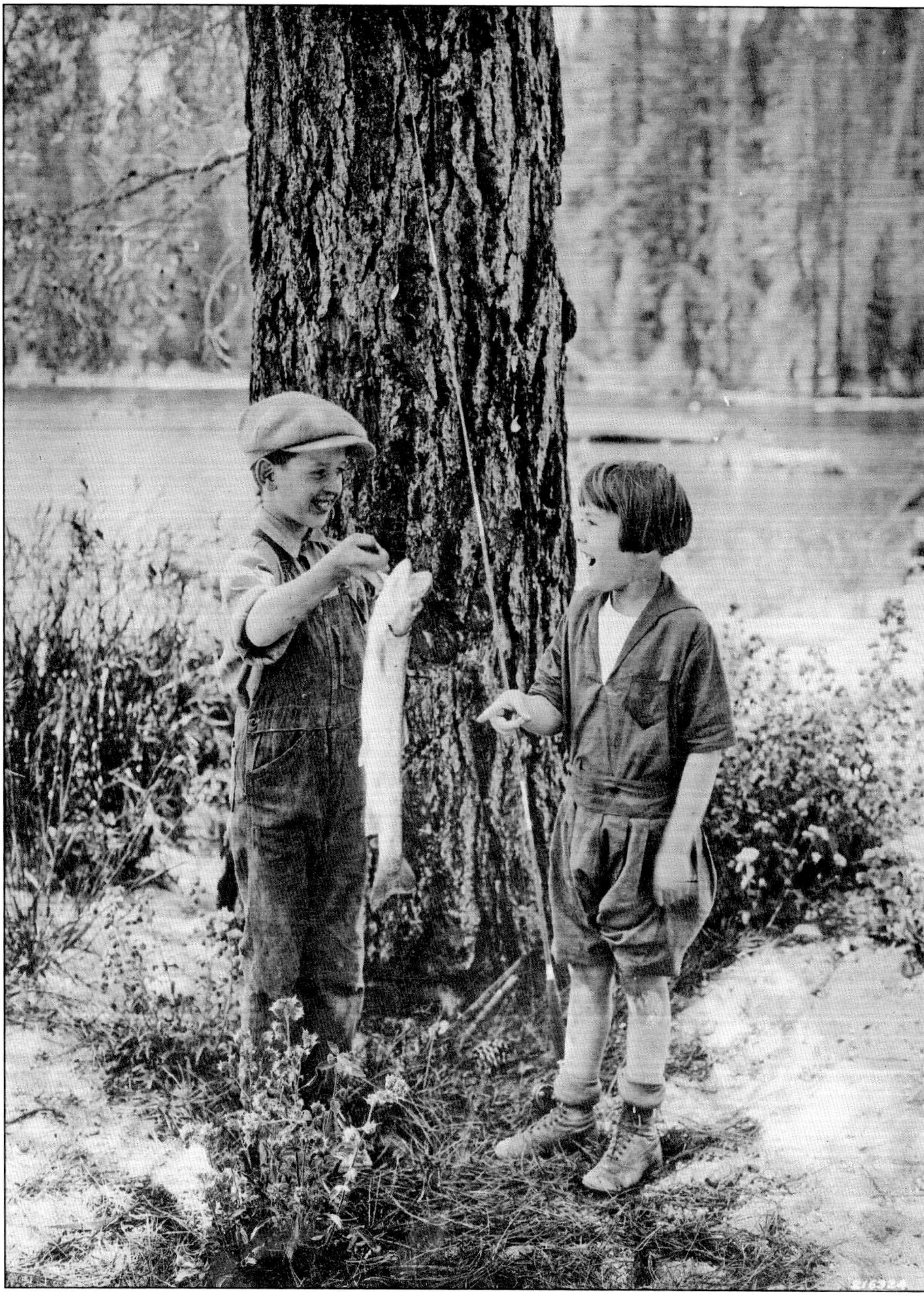

Sportfishing has long been a primary Deschutes National Forest recreation attraction. This little girl in the 1920s seems pleased with her friend's catch. (Deschutes National Forest.)

Eight

Recreation and Heritage Resources

In addition to valuable commodity resources such as water, timber, forage, and wildlife, the Deschutes National Forest affords extensive amenity resources such as recreational fishing, hunting, camping, hiking, and water sports as well as a full range of winter sports opportunities. These amenities were enjoyed by early settlers—once they felt secure on their farms and ranches and in their towns and had leisure time—and have been enjoyed ever since by the many visitors the area has attracted for more than a century.

Many in the upper Deschutes country saw development of recreation resources as an economic boon to their communities and for decades proposed national park status for the High Cascades and Newberry Caldera. National parks were not established, but Deschutes National Forest recreation resources—which run the gamut from extensive visitor accommodations and facilities to wilderness solitude—evolved.

Access was provided by roads into the Newberry Caldera as early as 1912 and as far as Elk Lake by 1921. Permits to build a dozen lodges and hundreds of summer homes on lakes and along rivers were issued beginning in the second decade of the 20th century, and national forest campgrounds soon followed. Pack trips were popular, and pack stations outfitted and guided trail trips to backcountry destinations for several decades. Wilderness trails were built and maintained for hikers and backpackers. Later in the 20th century, off-road motorized sports were permitted in appropriate areas.

Winter sports were accommodated on the Deschutes National Forest when the Skyliners' first ski development west of Bend was opened for use in the mid-1930s and a permit to develop a Bachelor Butte ski area was issued in 1957. Mount Bachelor became Oregon's largest winter sports area. Nordic skiing trails and snowmobiling routes were developed as demand grew.

A modern visitor center and a new welcome station introduce Deschutes National Forest opportunities. Heritage resources that reflect the forest's evolution are preserved and interpreted. Some historic Forest Service administrative facilities were converted to recreation uses. The national forest's sublime scenery was protected as recreation facilities were planned and developed to contribute to the area's environmental and economic viability.

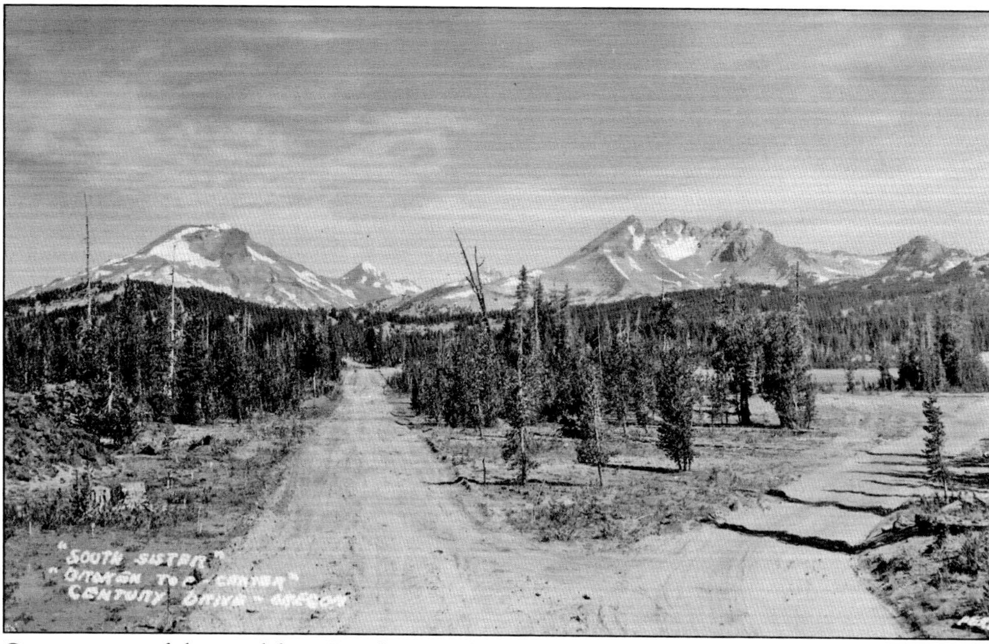

Construction of this road from Bend to Sparks Lake and beyond began in 1920 and stimulated recreation development at Elk Lake and other lakes. Soon called Cascade Lakes Highway and now designated Cascade Lakes National Scenic Byway, this 66-mile part of a hundred-mile circuit called Century Drive was paved with red cinders in the 1950s. The Three Sisters and Broken Top dominate the skyline. (Deschutes County Historical Society.)

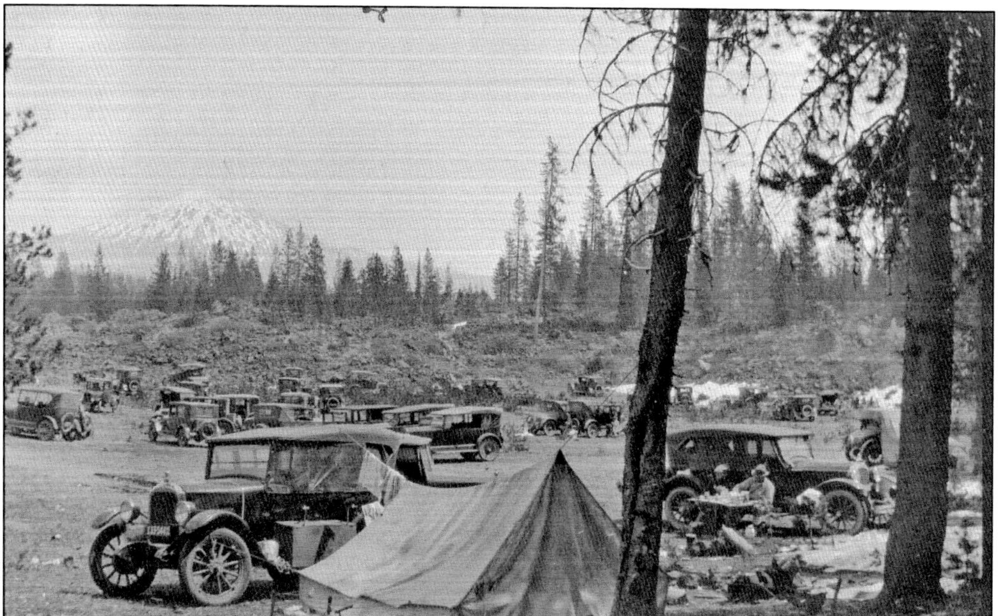

Automobile access brought summer visitors to picnic and camp at Elk Lake as well as Todd Lake, Sparks Lake, the Lava Lakes, Cultus Lake, and the Twin Lakes. The Deschutes National Forest eventually developed campgrounds at all of these lakes and permitted construction of summer homes and resorts at some of them. (Deschutes County Historical Society.)

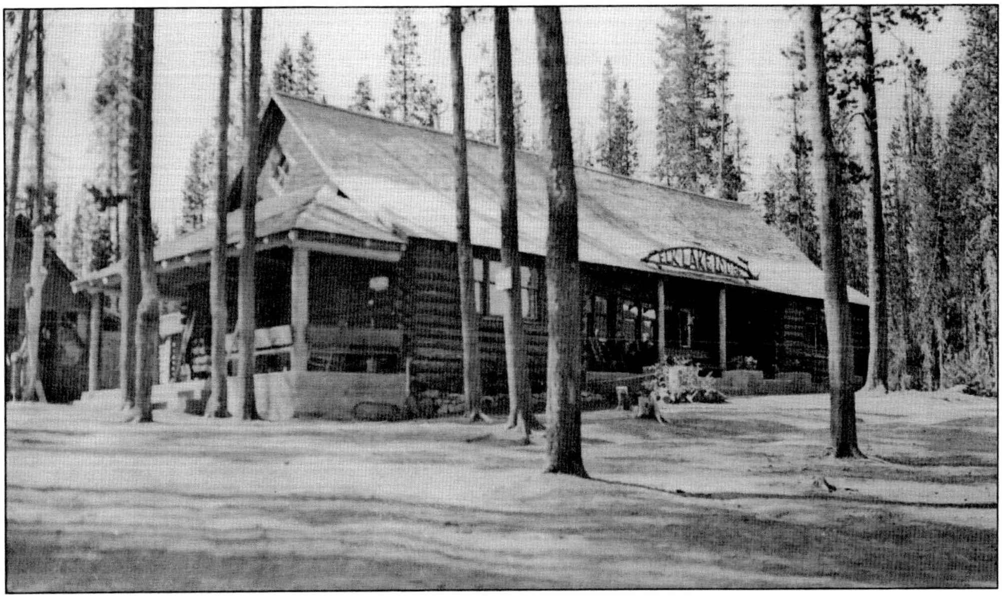

About 1920, while he built trails for the Deschutes National Forest, Allen Wilcoxen and his wife were stationed in a tent cabin camp on the shores of Elk Lake. Experiences feeding hungry fishermen convinced the Wilcoxens that a lodge serving Elk Lake visitors would succeed. With the necessary permit from the US Forest Service, the Wilcoxens began building Elk Lake Lodge in 1921. After the winding, dusty road from Bend via Sparks Lake had been completed, the Wilcoxens were in business. The log lodge (above), which also rented tent cabins and log cabins (below), had its own post office from 1924 to 1954. Elk Lake Resort, along the paved Cascade Lakes National Scenic Byway, remains a hub of Deschutes National Forest recreation and offers more modern facilities. (Above, Deschutes National Forest; below, Deschutes County Historical Society.)

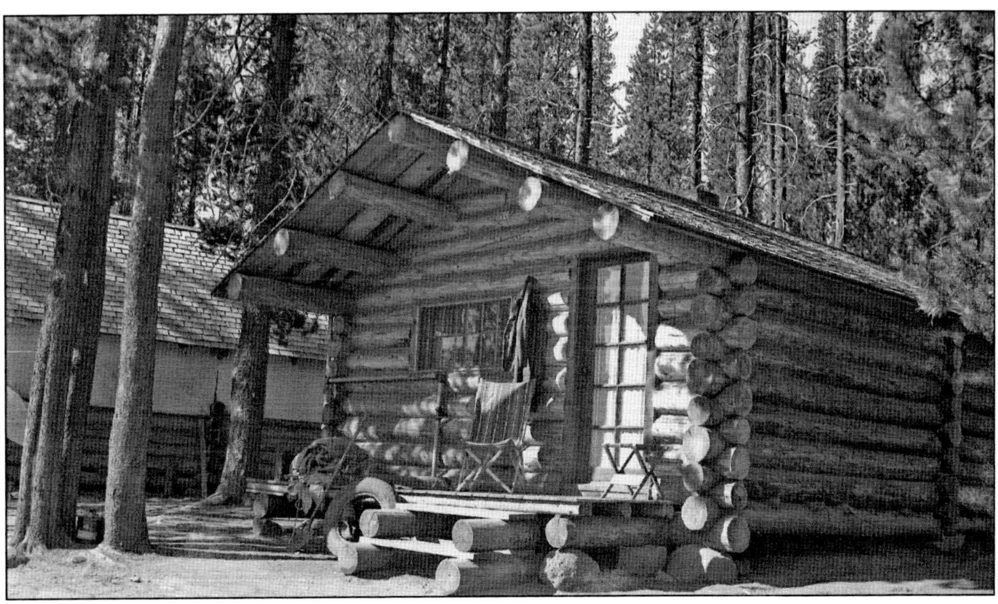

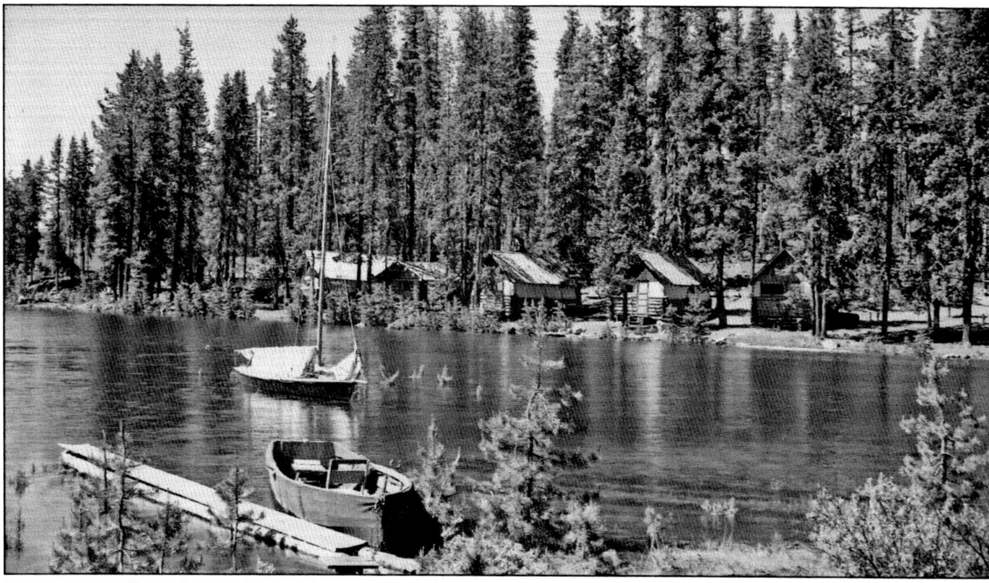

Visitors to Elk Lake Lodge and its cabins, users of its marina, owners of Elk Lake summer homes, and campers at Elk Lake campgrounds—and, at one time, summer camps—enjoyed a full range of aquatic sports including swimming, sailing, and, of course, fishing. Trail travel into the Cascades high country was by foot or on horses available from a nearby pack station. (Deschutes County Historical Society.)

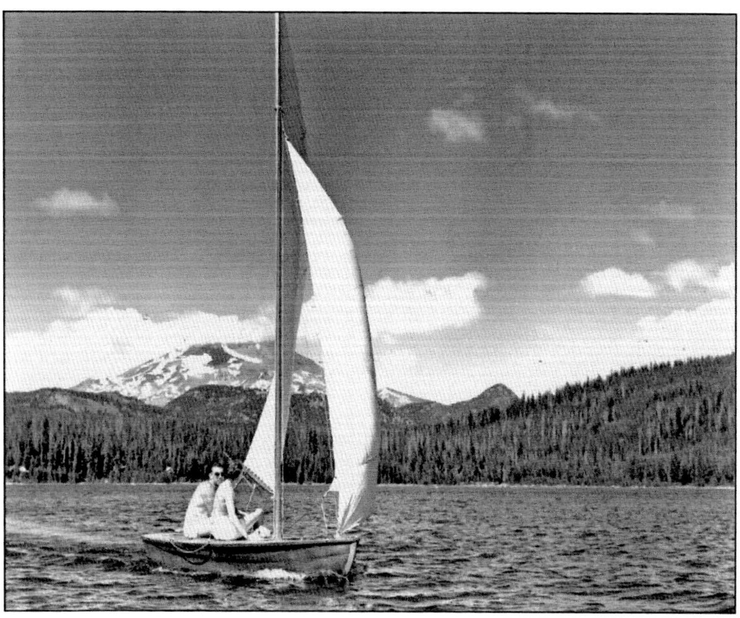

Sailing became an especially popular activity at Elk Lake, noted for its excellent sailing conditions that included a wide expanse of water and afternoon breezes. Citizens from Bend formed an Elk Lake sailing club and competed in races from the Fourth of July until Labor Day. A cloud-capped South Sister looms behind these early sailors. (Deschutes County Historical Society.)

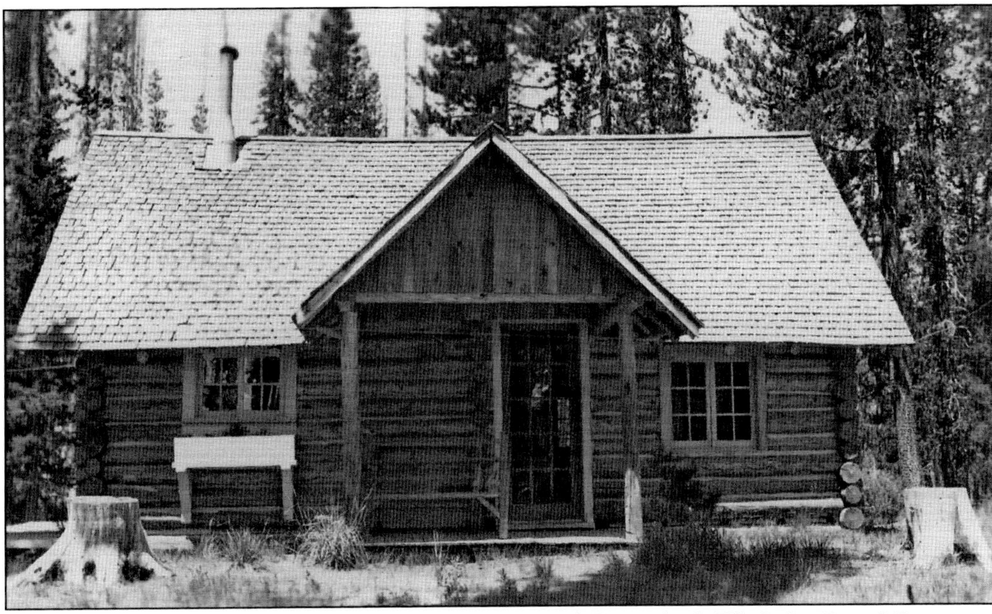

As recreational use increased, the Deschutes National Forest built Elk Lake Guard Station in 1929 for a forest guard to help the district ranger administer and protect the area. During some 1930s summers, when funds were scarce and no guard was employed, forest supervisor Carl Neal's wife and their daughter Shirley stayed at the station cabin. Forest guards and later recreation technicians were based there through 1993. (Deschutes National Forest.)

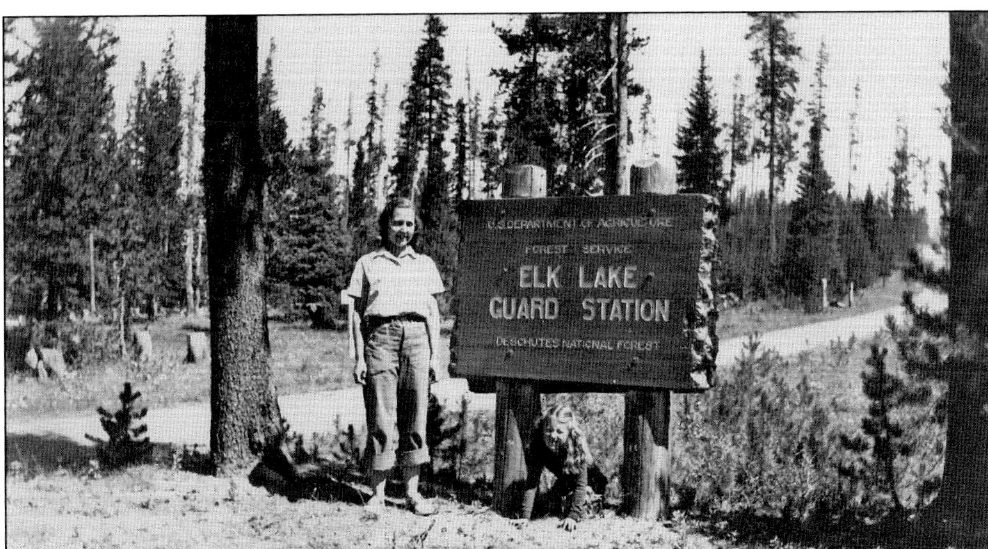

During the 1947 and 1948 summers, the Elk Lake forest guard was Clifford Wynkoop, a teacher from Sherwood, Oregon. His wife, Marjorie, and their daughter Fran, shown at the sign that marked Elk Lake Guard Station along the road, lived with him at the guard station. (Fran Lattin.)

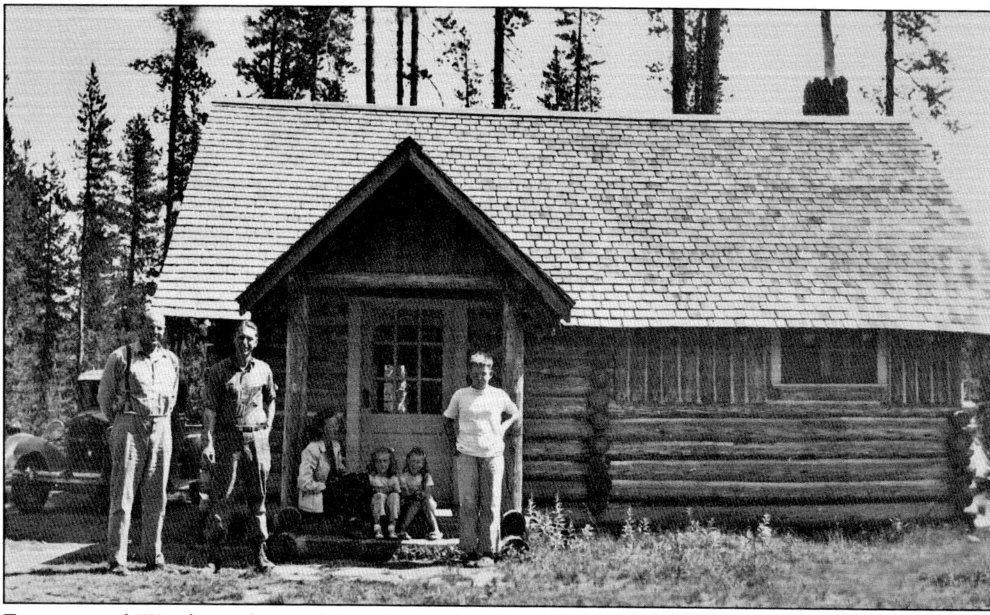

Forest guard Wynkoop (second from left) provided information and assistance to visitors to Elk Lake Guard Station and to visitors he met as he worked in the field. In the tradition of Forest Service ranger's wives for decades, Marjorie Wynkoop filled in for her husband at the station when he was working in the field. (Fran Lattin.)

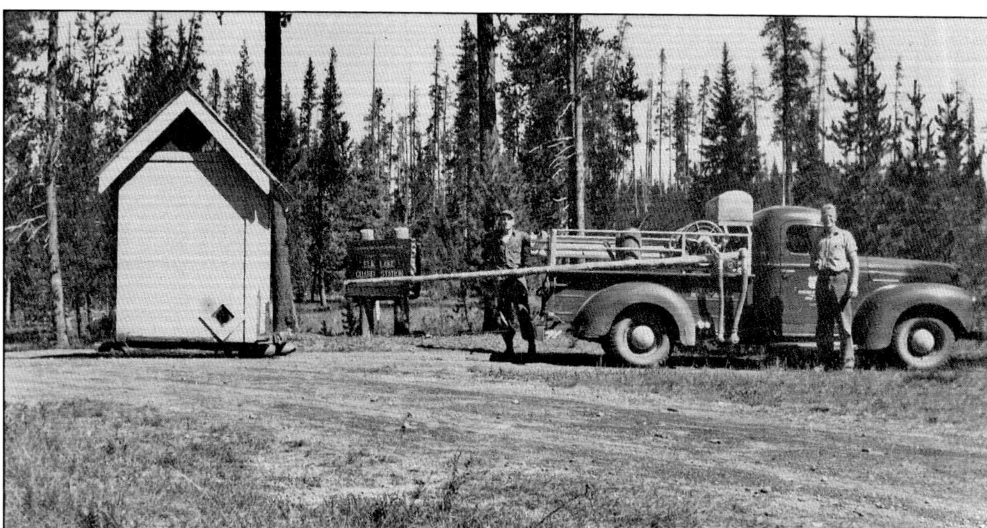

During one of the summers the Wynkoops served at Elk Lake Guard Station, the Forest Service delivered and installed a new outhouse. The restored historic guard station cabin and the outhouse remain at what since 2002 has been an operating visitor information station and interpretive heritage site called Historic Elk Lake Guard Station. (Fran Lattin.)

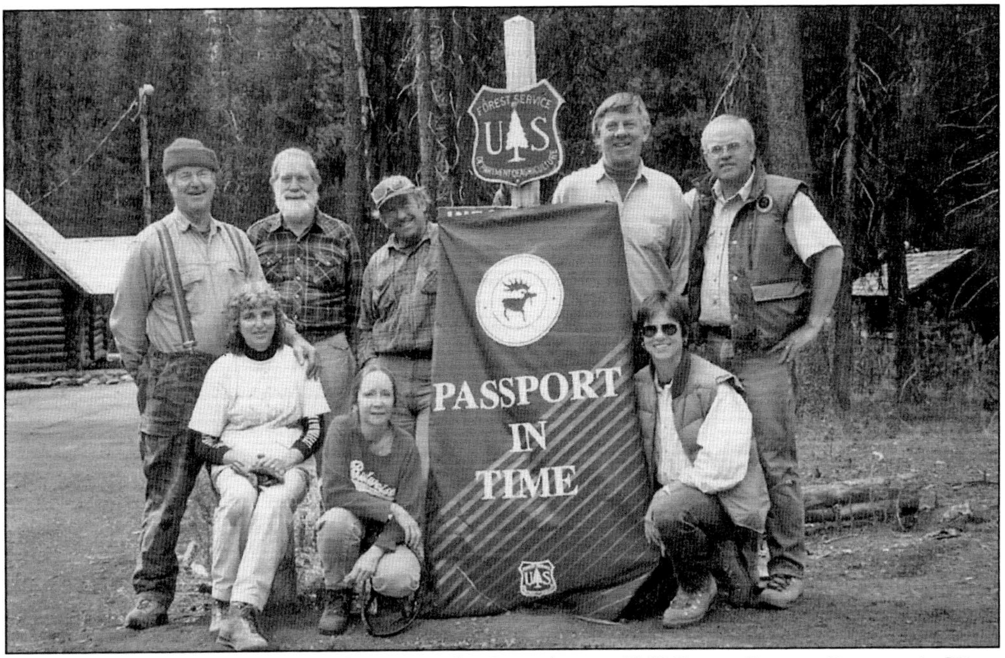

In late September and early October 1998, the first of several US Forest Service Passport in Time (PIT) volunteer crews began four years of restoration projects at what became Historic Elk Lake Guard Station. By summer 2001, Forest Service personnel and PIT volunteers had restored the log cabin and rehabilitated the station grounds. (Photograph by PIT volunteer Bud LaFortune.)

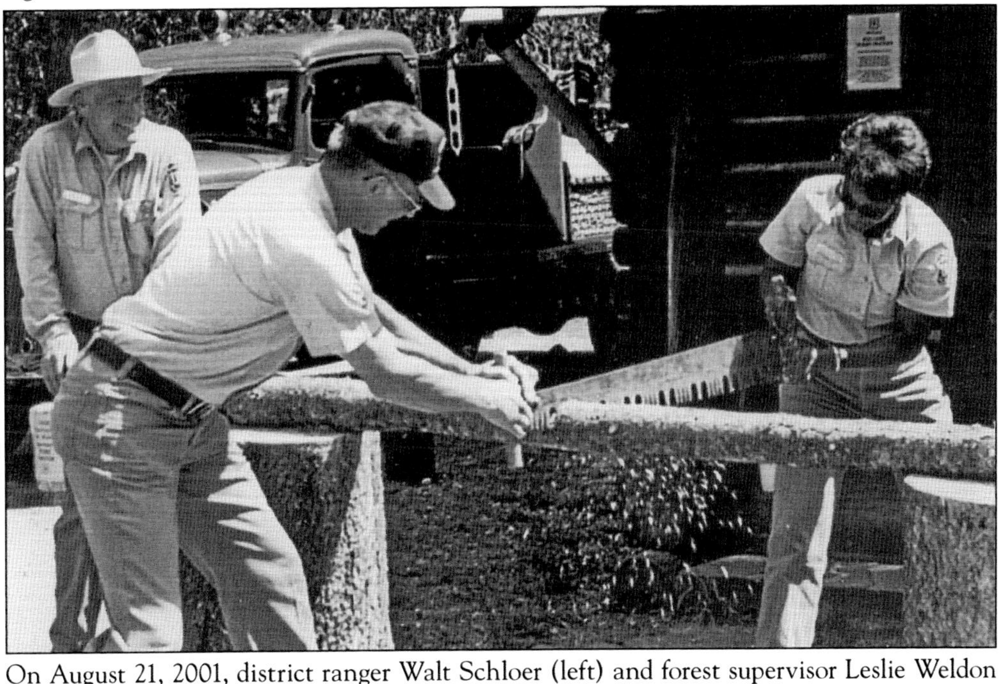

On August 21, 2001, district ranger Walt Schloer (left) and forest supervisor Leslie Weldon (right) saw a log with a misery whip to open Historic Elk Lake Guard Station as a summer visitor information station and interpretive heritage site. Wilderness ranger Jim Leep steadies the log as a cheering crowd looks on. (Photograph by the author.)

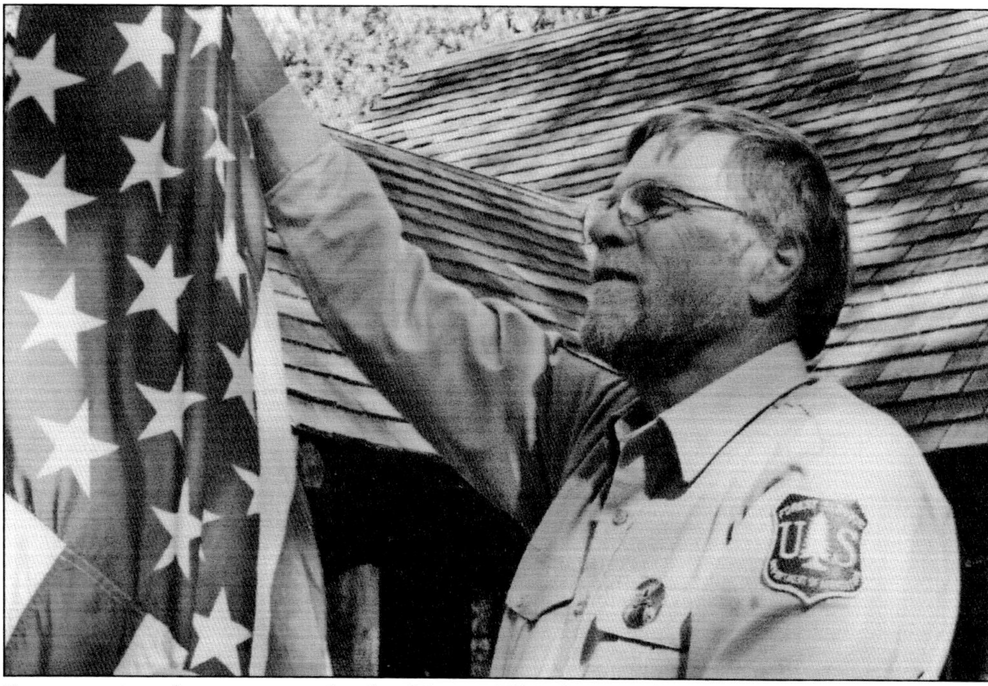

Every morning of every summer day that Historic Elk Lake Guard Station serves the public, a Forest Service volunteer raises the flag to open the station. Here, Jeff Nelson of Yakima, Washington, who with his wife, Carol, served 10 seven-day summer sessions at the station, proudly performs that duty. (Photograph by the author.)

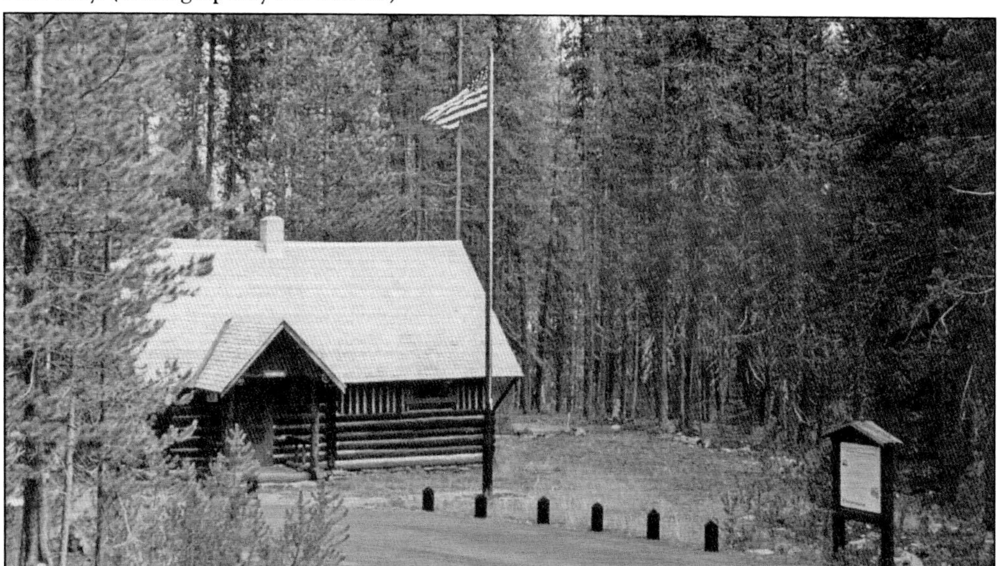

Historic Elk Lake Guard Station simultaneously preserves a heritage resource and serves as a recreation resource at which Deschutes National Forest visitors see how forest guards lived and worked as they receive information and assistance. Other historic Forest Service structures, such as the historic Fall River Guard Station, available for visitors to rent, achieve that same adaptive reuse goal. (Photograph by the author.)

Thousands of Deschutes National Forest visitors annually enjoy this view of South Sister reflecting in Sparks Lake from the Ray Atkeson Memorial Interpretive Trail. Atkeson, who lived from 1907 to 1990, was appreciated in Oregon and throughout the United States for his images of wild and noble landscapes worthy of preservation for future generations. (Photograph by the author.)

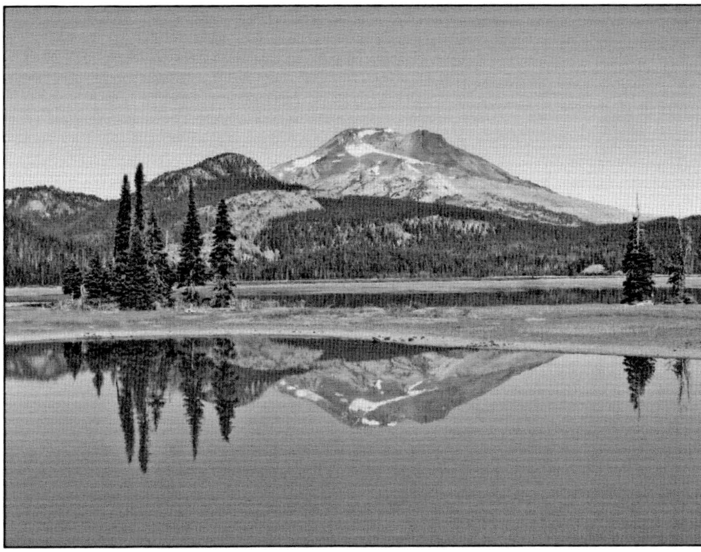

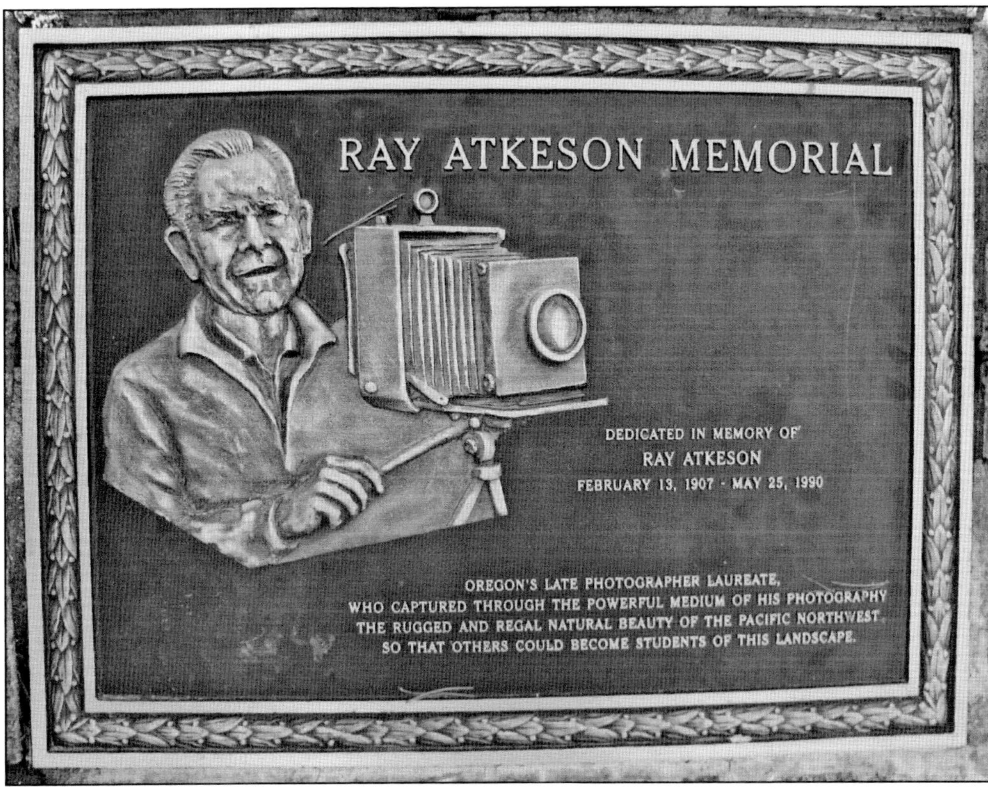

A legend in his own time as a pioneer of large-format color photography that captured the light and beauty of western landscapes, Ray Atkeson was named Oregon's first and only photographer laureate in 1987. Atkeson considered the view seen in the preceding photograph the most stunning in the state. He and his contribution to landscape photography are commemorated by this plaque along the trail. (Photograph by the author.)

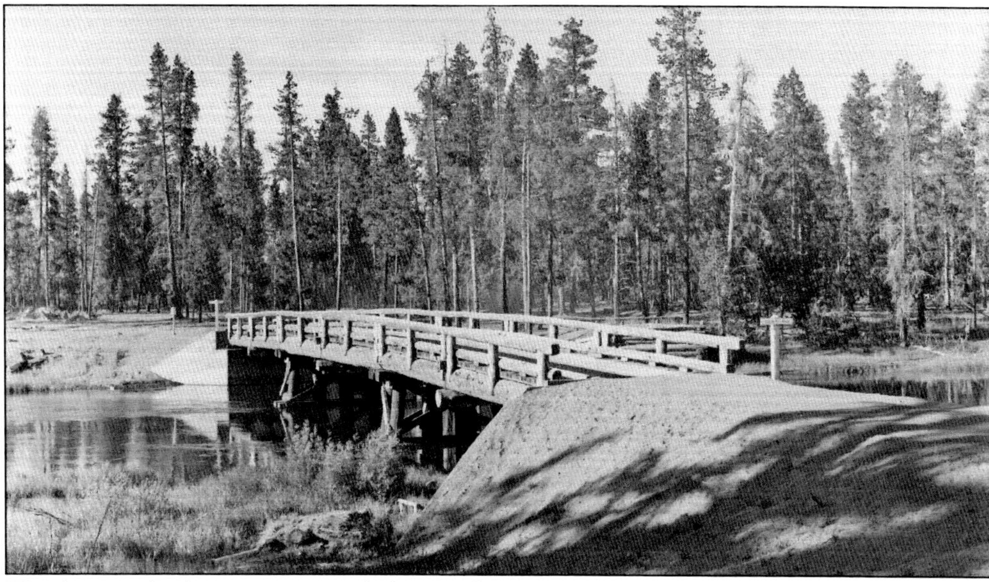

This historic bridge once spanned the Deschutes River near the site of the former Big River Ranger Station. Begun by US Forest Service personnel, it was completed by US Army combat engineers training at Camp Abbot during World War II. It was named General Patch Bridge for Gen. Alexander M. Patch, who conducted the 1943 Oregon Maneuvers in Central Oregon to train soldiers he led in combat in Europe. (US Forest Service.)

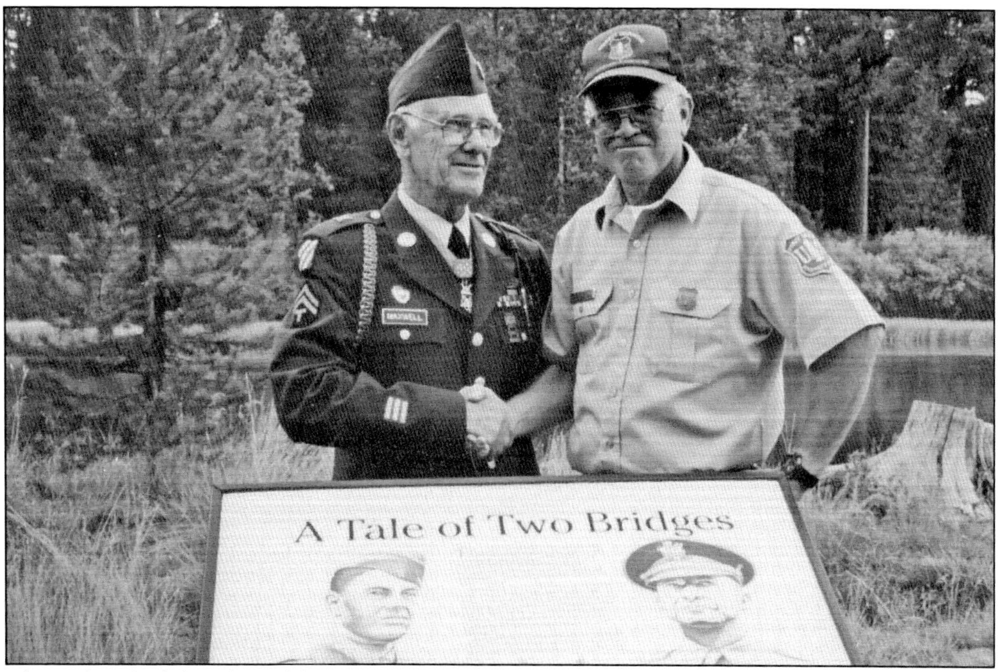

The author (right) and World War II Medal of Honor recipient Robert D. "Bob" Maxwell of Bend (left) shake hands at the September 11, 2004, dedication of the Robert D. Maxwell Veterans Memorial Bridge, which eventually replaced the General Patch Bridge. The sign explains that General Patch signed Maxwell's nomination for the nation's highest award for valor in combat action in France under the general's command. (Photograph by Robin Gyorgyfalvy.)

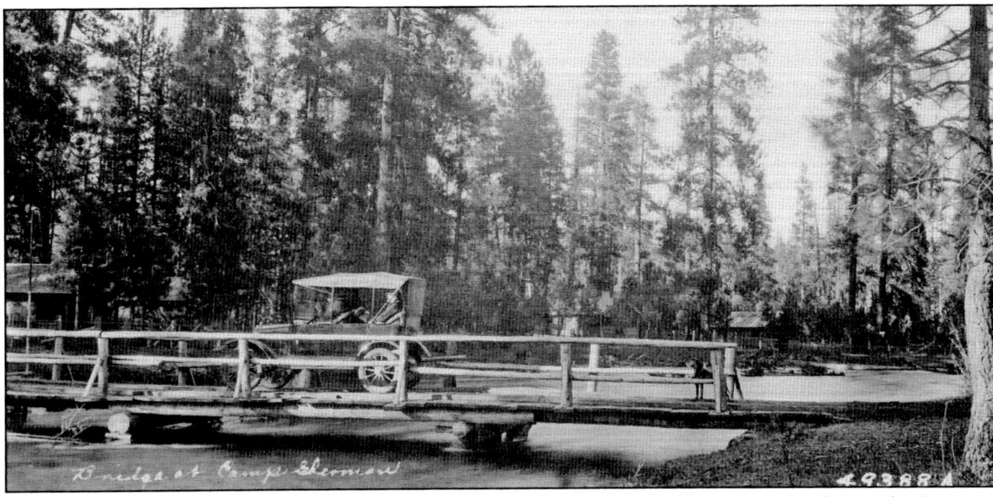

The first summer homes in the Deschutes National Forest—indeed, in the North Pacific District, now the Pacific Northwest Region, of the National Forest System—were built on the Sisters Ranger District on the Metolius River at Camp Sherman in 1916. These were built by wheat ranchers from Moro, Sherman County, Oregon. This second bridge across the Metolius River was built by the Forest Service before 1920. (Deschutes National Forest.)

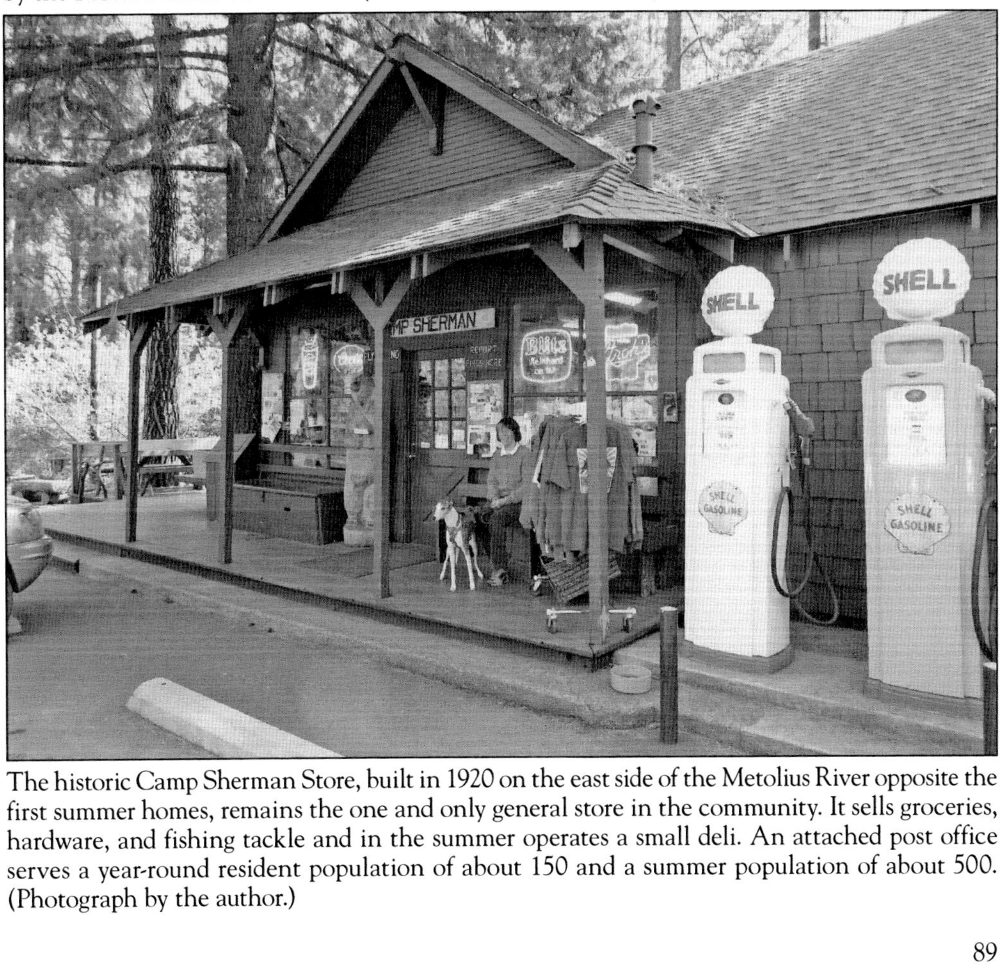

The historic Camp Sherman Store, built in 1920 on the east side of the Metolius River opposite the first summer homes, remains the one and only general store in the community. It sells groceries, hardware, and fishing tackle and in the summer operates a small deli. An attached post office serves a year-round resident population of about 150 and a summer population of about 500. (Photograph by the author.)

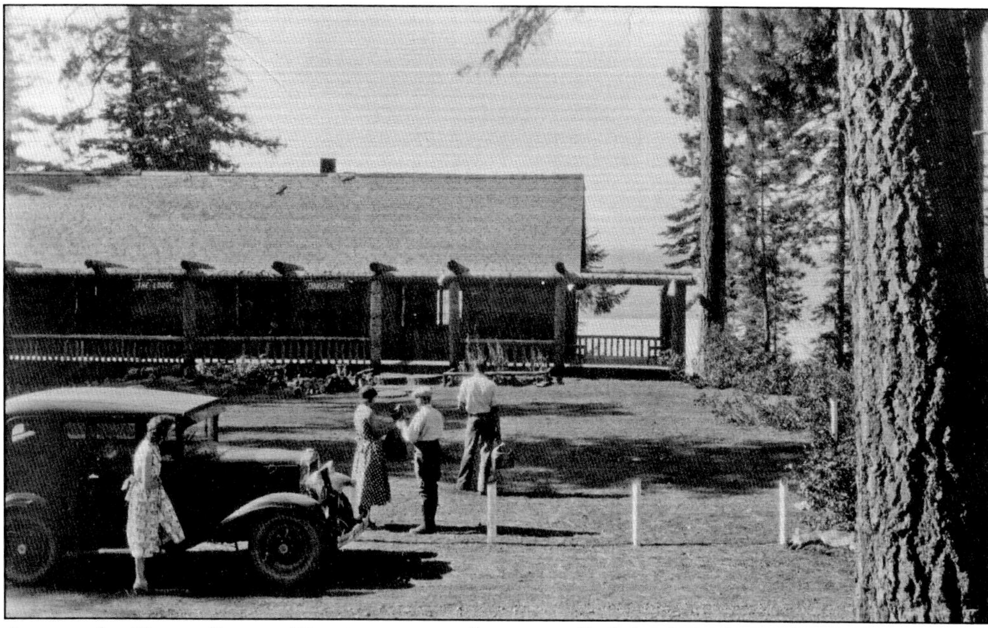

Among the Sisters Ranger District resorts, the one called Suttle Lake Lodge and Suttle Lake Resort over the years stands out as one of the finer ones, but it was beset by problems. The first Suttle Lake Lodge, opened in 1925, was destroyed by fire in September 1929. The second (above) burned down in August 1939. A new lodge, one of the finest in the Pacific Northwest national forests, opened in March 1942 and was sold and resold several times before it burned to the ground in May 1974. The resort has had several incarnations and owners and openings since, most recently as the Lodge at Suttle Lake. Purchased in 2015 by Portland, Oregon, investors, it reopened as Suttle Lodge in 2016. Pioneer US Forest Service recreation officer Fred W. Cleator photographed "Rustic cottage construction at Suttle Lake resort" (below) in October 1925. (Both, Deschutes National Forest.)

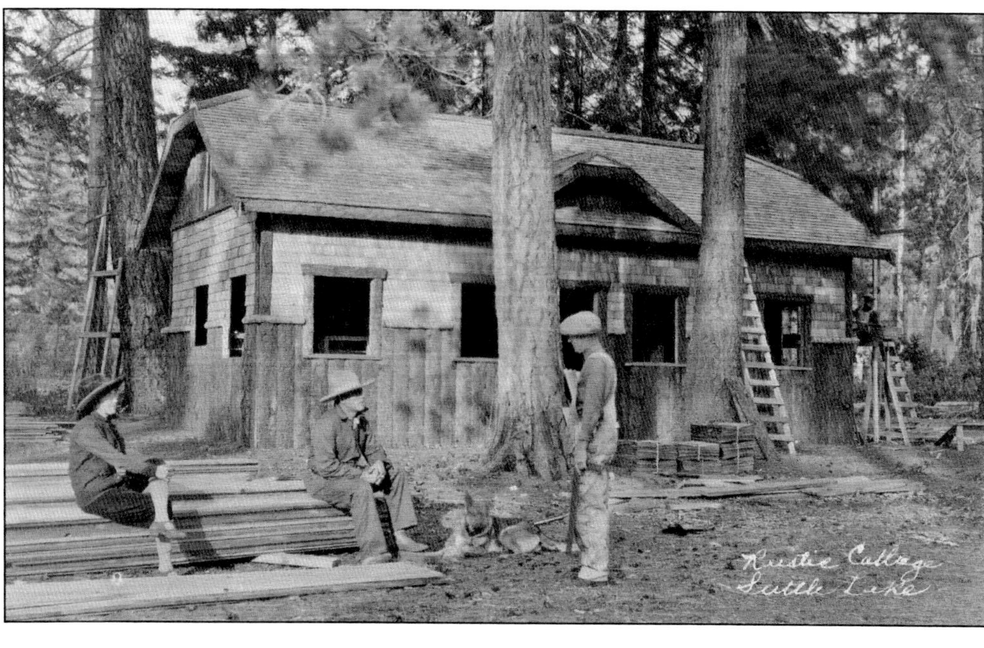

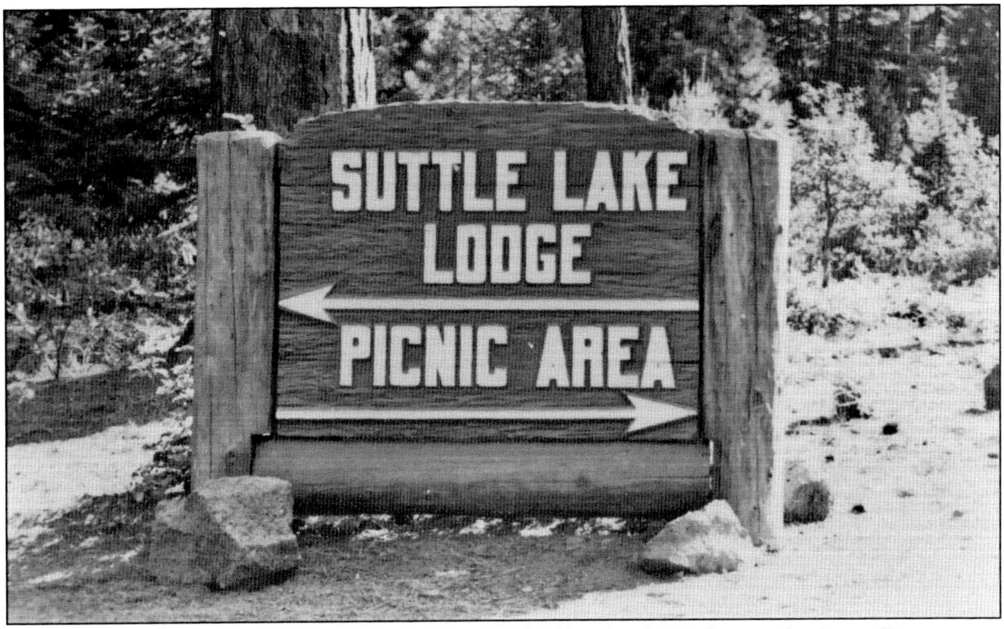

This rustic US Forest Service sign, of the type crafted by the CCC during the Great Depression, directed Deschutes National Forest visitors to Suttle Lake Lodge and to the Suttle Lake Picnic Area during the late 1930s. (Deschutes National Forest.)

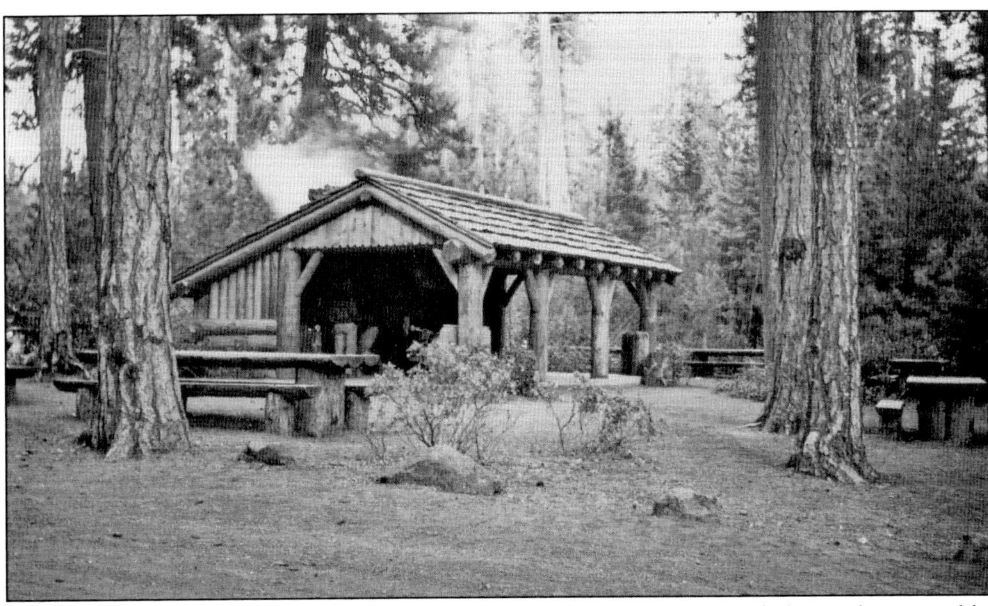

Constructed by the CCC during the 1930s, the Suttle Lake Picnic Area shelter and picnic tables showcase the beautifully rugged log construction work for which that New Deal conservation work employment program became well known. This picnic shelter, which still stands, has served Deschutes National Forest visitors for many decades. (Deschutes National Forest.)

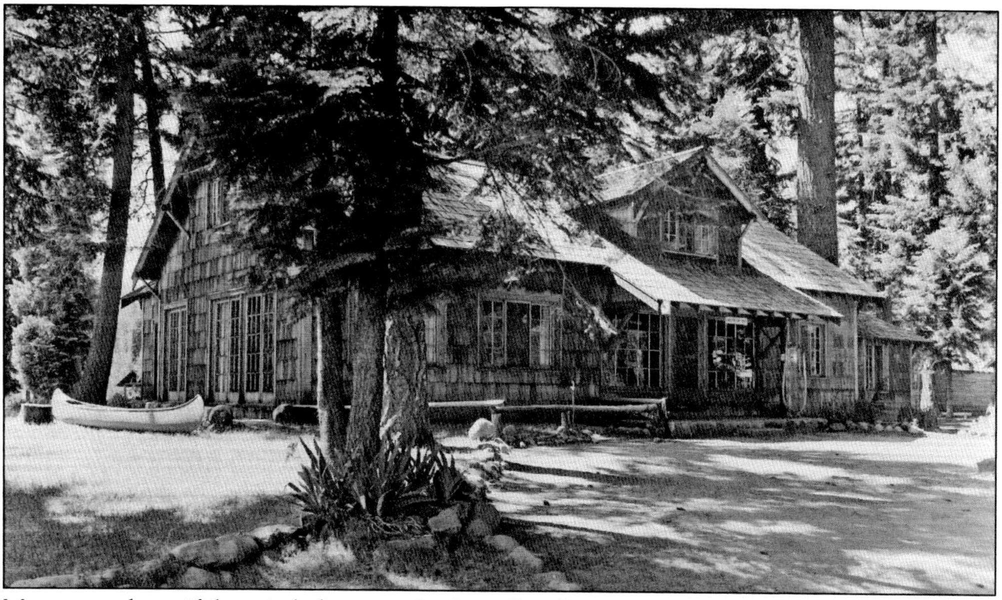

Many more beautiful rustic lodges were built on Deschutes National Forest lands by permittees during the 1930s and 1940s. Crescent Lake Lodge, on the lake of the same name, was built on the Crescent Ranger District and remains in operation. (Deschutes National Forest.)

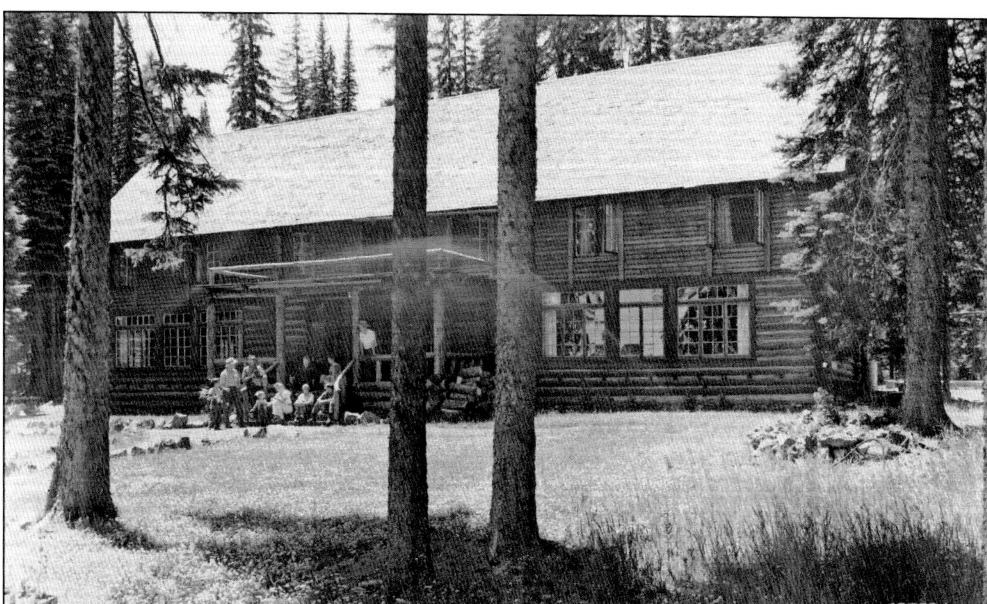

Also on the Crescent Ranger District, Summit Lodge was built at Odell Lake. (Deschutes National Forest, photograph by Ray M. Filloon.)

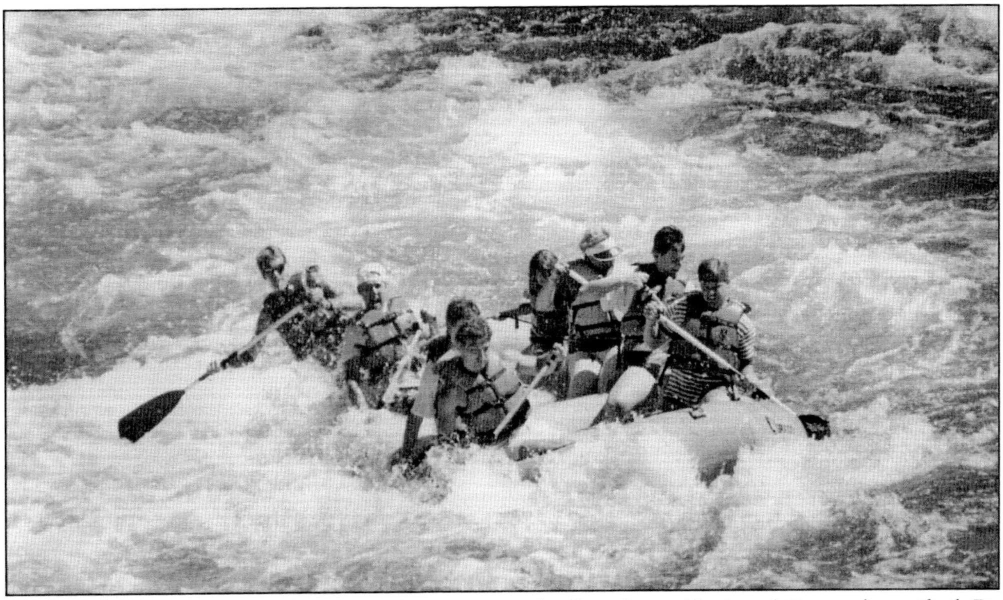

As the years passed, forest recreation activities on the Deschutes National Forest diversified. By the 1980s, several upper Deschutes country white-water rafting companies had outfitter-guide permits to offer recreationists thrilling raft rides on the Deschutes River. (Deschutes County Historical Society.)

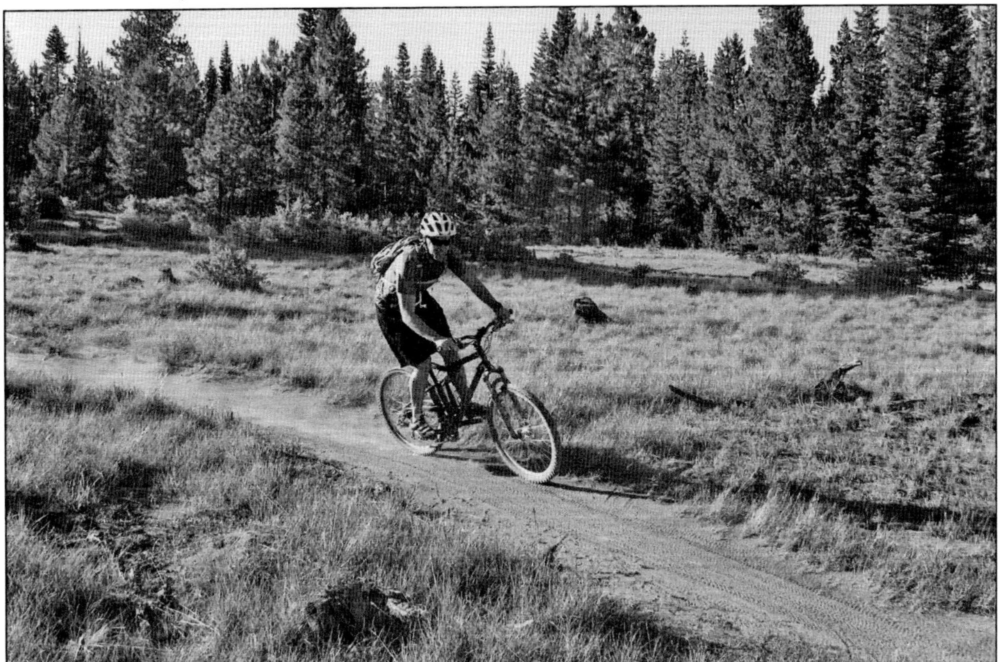

As the sport of mountain biking grew, the Deschutes National Forest became nationally known for scenic mountain biking. Working with local bicycle organizations and trail partners, the Forest Service has developed an extensive network of mountain biking trails—all of them outside congressionally designated wilderness, where mechanized forms of transportation are prohibited—for devotees of the sport. (Photograph by Wendy Joslin.)

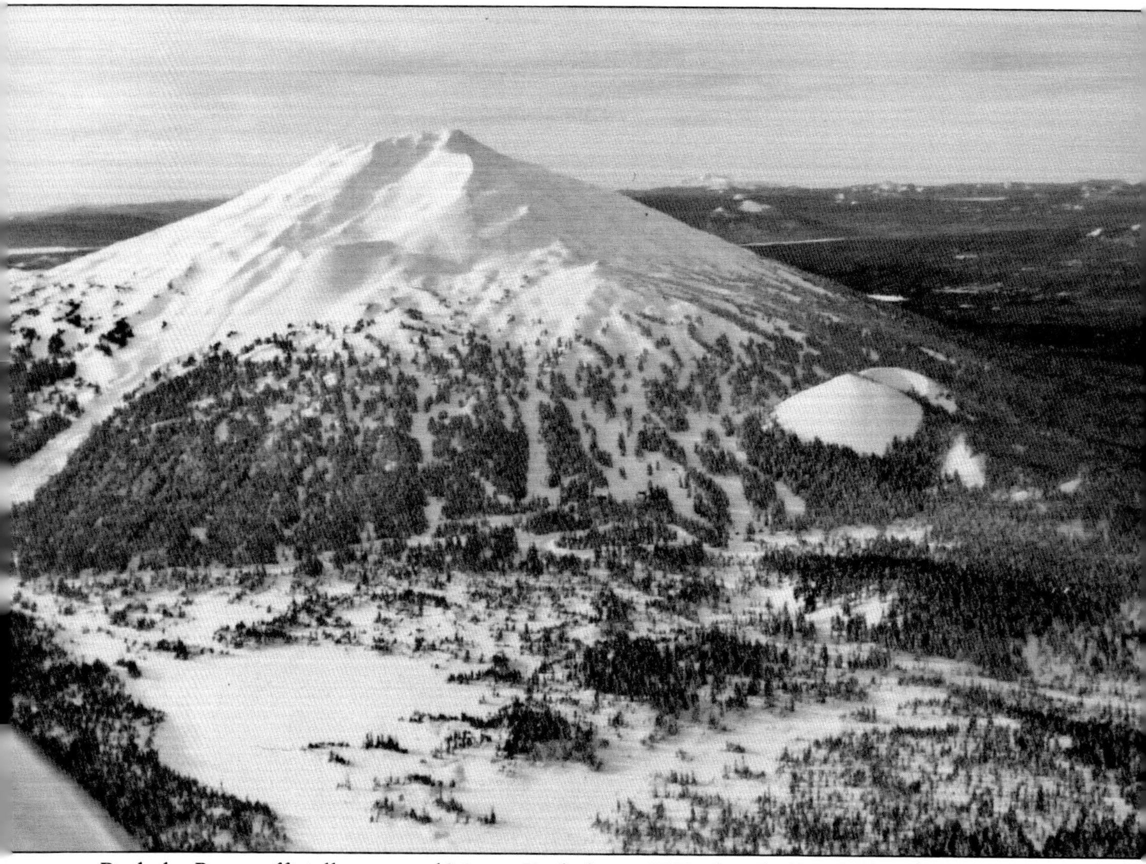

Bachelor Butte, officially renamed Mount Bachelor in 1983 after the Bend Chamber of Commerce persuaded state and federal officials to adopt the more attractive and descriptive term "mountain," is Oregon's ninth-highest peak at 9,065 feet. About 22 miles west of Bend and within the Deschutes National Forest, this ski area, founded by former World War II 10th Mountain Division ski trooper Bill Healy and developed under US Forest Service permit by local entrepreneurs, opened as Bachelor Butte for the 1958–1959 season. During that season, an estimated 10,000 people bought $3 lift tickets to access its ski hill by rope tow and a platter lift. It was the start of something big for Deschutes National Forest recreation and Bend and Central Oregon's economic growth. Development continued, and Mount Bachelor has become Oregon's largest ski area and the sixth-largest ski resort in the United States. Several ski seasons have seen over half a million skier visits. Nordic skiing and snowboarding are also popular there, and snowmobiling is enjoyed on nearby designated snowmobile trails. (Deschutes National Forest.)

Bachelor Butte's early success as a ski area created the need for a day lodge. Egan Memorial Lodge was constructed near the foot of the ski hill and honors forest supervisor James A. Egan of the Deschutes National Forest, who actively supported the ski area's development before he died in office in 1958. Mount Bachelor now boasts much larger and more modern visitor facilities. (Deschutes County Historical Society.)

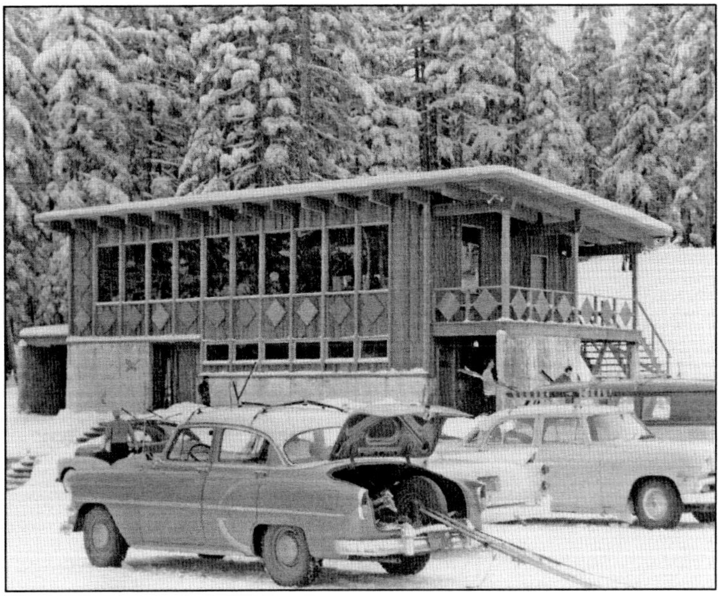

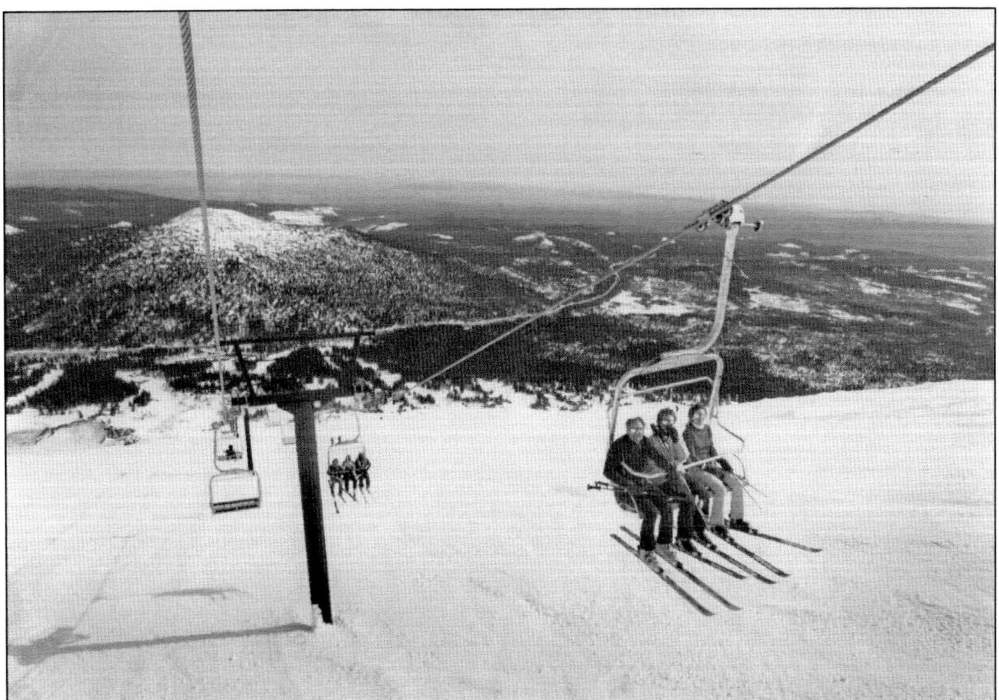

As the 1968–1969 ski season began, three chairlifts, a pomalift, and two rope tows met the demands of more than 150,000 skiers. The area continued to grow, adding many more chairlifts and runs that added to its skier capacity, to its national stature as a ski area, and to the Deschutes National Forest's stature as a year-round recreation resource. (Deschutes County Historical Society.)

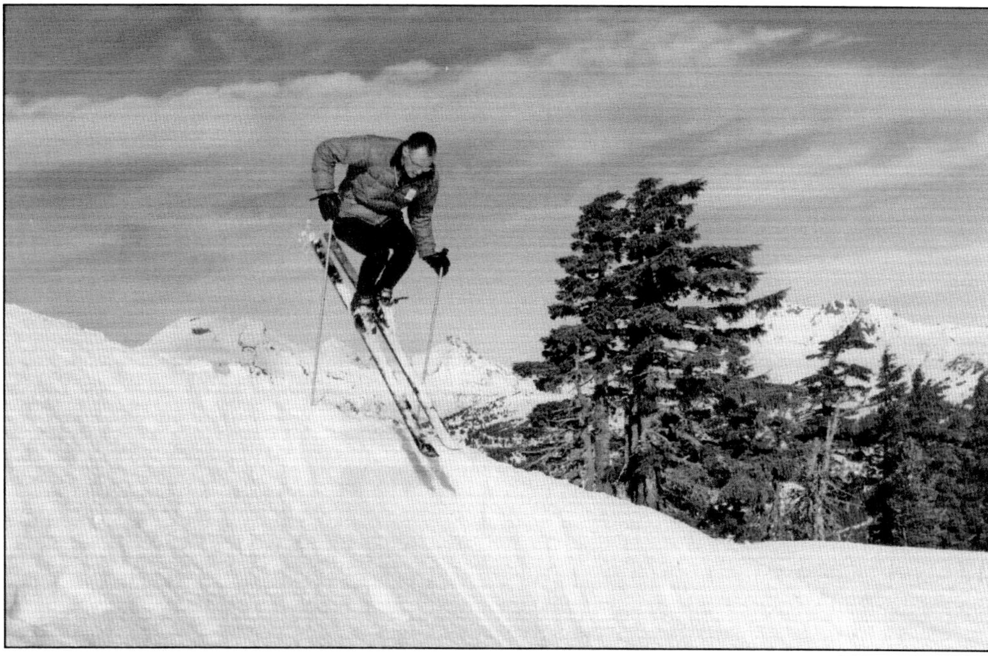

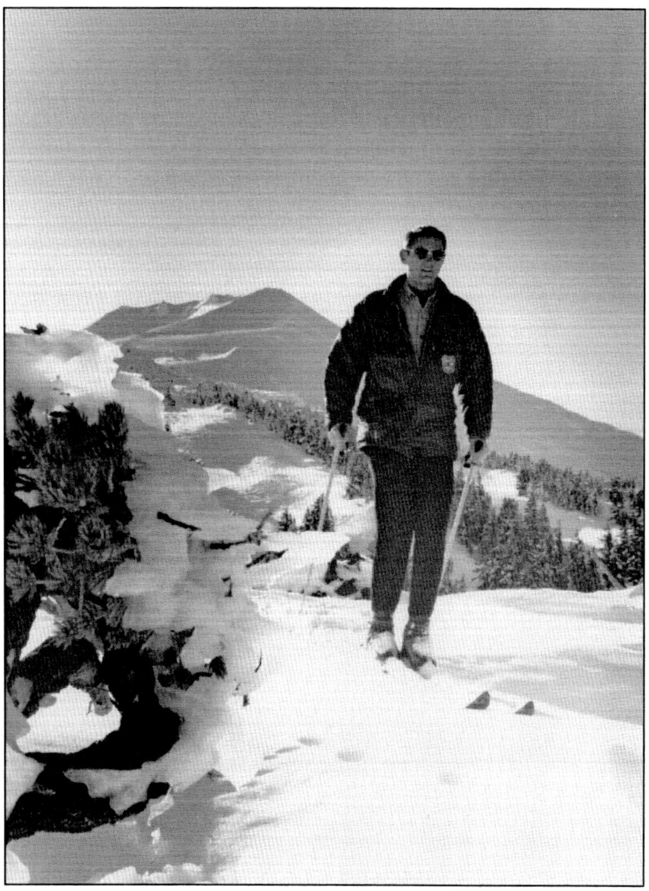

The magnificent Three Sisters provide a scenic backdrop for alpine skiers and, more recently, snowboarders at Mount Bachelor. A long ski season and powder snow are keys to the area's popularity for a full range of winter sports and recreation. (Deschutes National Forest.)

Dave Rasmussen, photographed in January 1965, was the first US Forest Service snow ranger at Bachelor Butte. Beginning in the 1940s—more than a decade before Bachelor Butte opened to skiers—snow rangers mitigated avalanches and provided safe winter sports experiences for national forest visitors. (Deschutes National Forest, photograph by W.H. Meyer.)

Nine

Wilderness Resources

Just over 10 percent of the Deschutes National Forest's almost 1.6 million acres of National Forest System land is part of five National Wilderness Preservation System units within the national forest set aside by Congress under the Wilderness Act of 1964 "to secure for the American people of present and future generations the benefits of an enduring resource of wilderness." Astride the Cascade Crest, each of these five wildernesses is within two or three national forests.

The largest of the Deschutes National Forest's wilderness lands is the 94,370-acre eastern third of the 286,708-acre Three Sisters Wilderness, the most visited and second-largest wilderness in Oregon. The western two thirds of this wilderness are within the adjacent Willamette National Forest.

The rest of the Deschutes National Forest's wilderness acreage includes 34,413 acres of the 54,185-acre Diamond Peak Wilderness and 14,116 acres of the 52,738-acre Mount Washington Wilderness, also shared with the Willamette National Forest; 32,734 acres of the 107,008-acre Mount Jefferson Wilderness, shared with the Willamette and Mount Hood National Forests; and 7,107 acres of the 54,267-acre Mount Thielsen Wilderness, shared with the Umpqua and Fremont-Winema National Forests.

Under the Wilderness Act, these and all other National Wilderness Preservation System units are managed for their intrinsic value as wilderness as well as for amenity resource values such as the "solitude or a primitive or unconfined recreation experience" emphasized in the act. Congressionally designated wilderness lands also serve as healthy watersheds that produce that most vital of commodities, water. Management for other commodity resources such as timber, minerals, and forage was either excluded or de-emphasized by the act. Wilderness visitors travel along trails or across country on foot or horseback only; mechanized and motorized travel is prohibited. Development is generally limited to trails, bridges, and necessary signs.

Wilderness must be saved twice. First, it must be saved from those who would develop or exploit it. Then, it must be saved from—as well as for—those who would "love it to death." Wilderness management, as practiced by the US Forest Service on the Deschutes National Forest, is essentially the management of human use and influences to preserve naturalness and solitude.

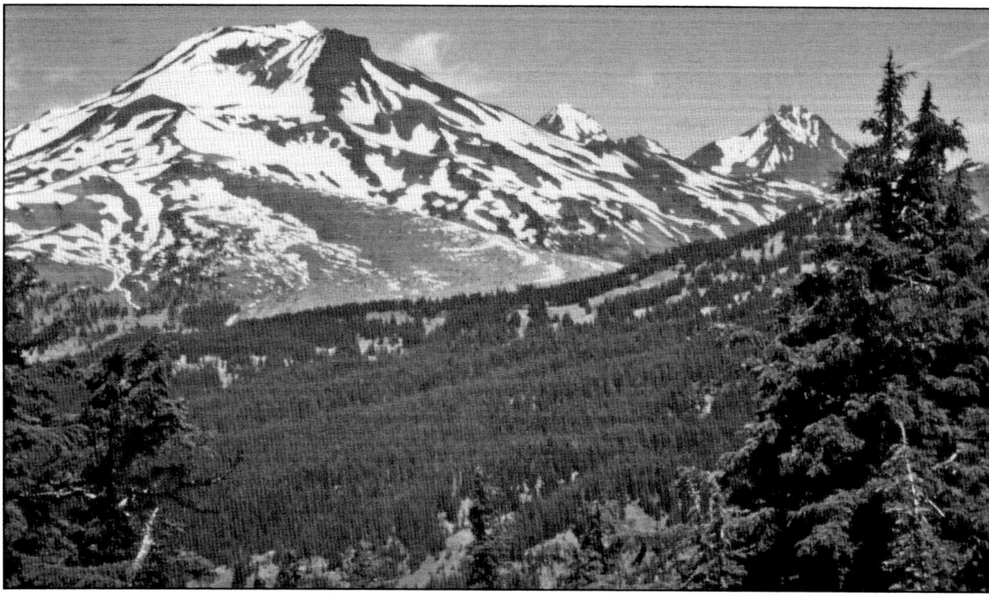

The magnificent Three Sisters—from left to right, South Sister, Middle Sister, and North Sister—are unique in the Cascade Range as a closely grouped cluster of major volcanoes. They dominate not only the Three Sisters Wilderness, established when Congress passed the Wilderness Act of 1964, but also the western skyline of the upper Deschutes country. (Photograph by the author.)

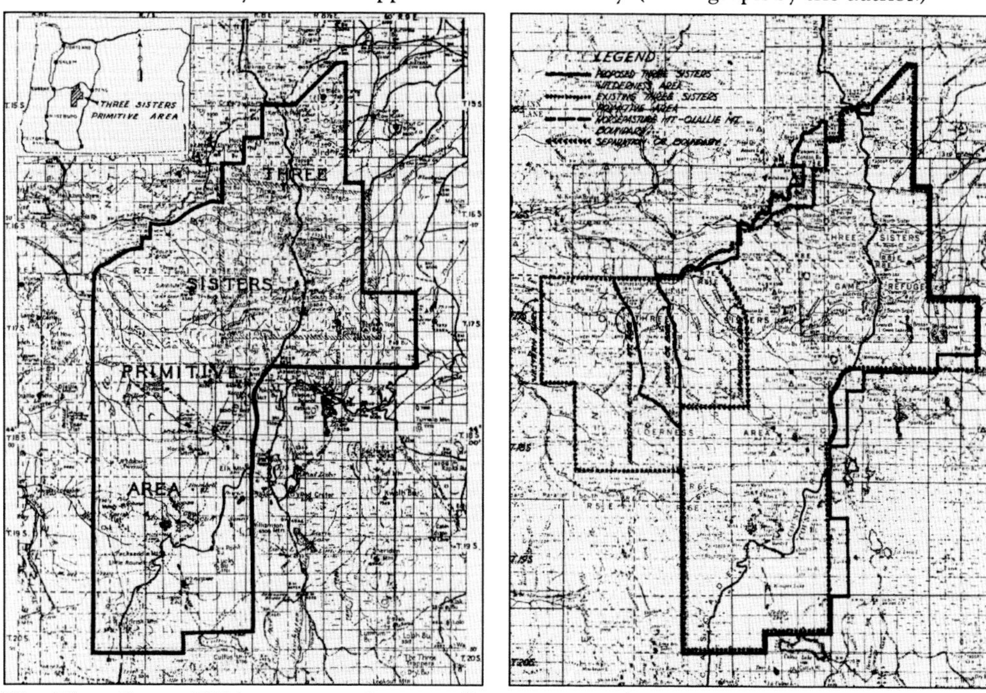

The Three Sisters Wilderness grew from smaller areas set aside to protect their wilderness values. The 191,108-acre Three Sisters Primitive Area (left) was designated by US Forest Service chief Ferdinand A. Silcox in 1937 under the L-30 Regulation of 1929. Lands were added and subtracted until the 196,640-acre Three Sisters Wilderness Area was designated by Secretary of Agriculture Ezra Taft Benson in 1957 under the U Regulations of 1939. (Both, US Forest Service.)

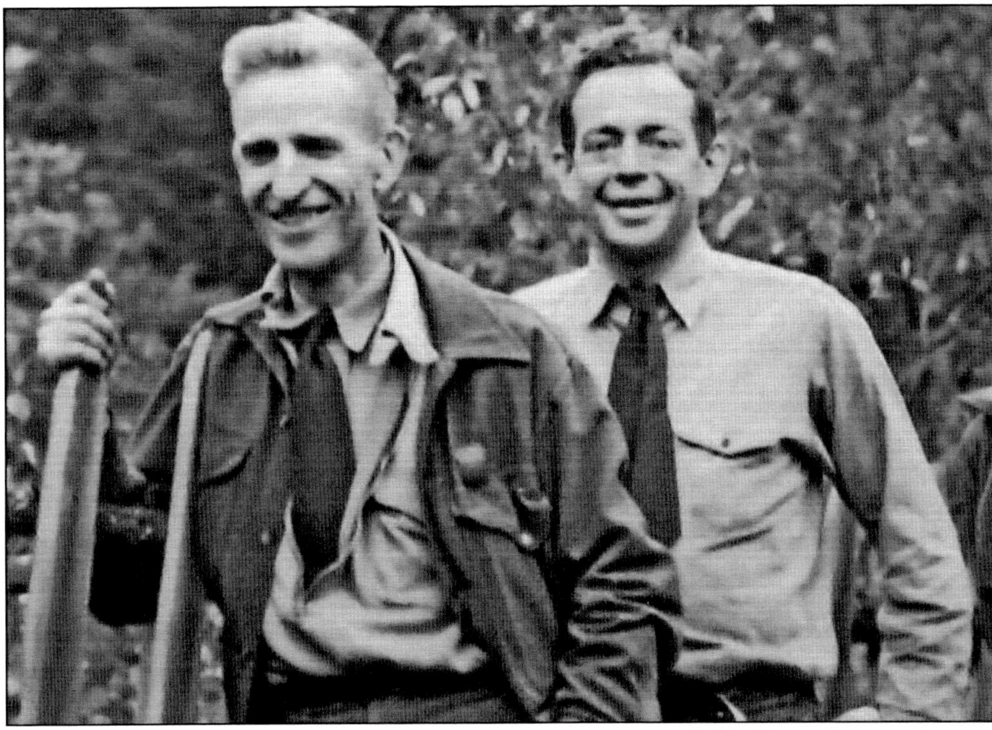

Visionary US Forest Service recreation officer Fred W. Cleator (left), shown here with Forest Service wilderness advocate Bob Marshall, was responsible for planning and developing recreation resources in Pacific Northwest national forests. In 1920, Cleator moved on proposals to build an Oregon Skyline road and trail along the Cascade Crest from Mount Hood through the Deschutes National Forest high country to Crater Lake. (US Forest Service.)

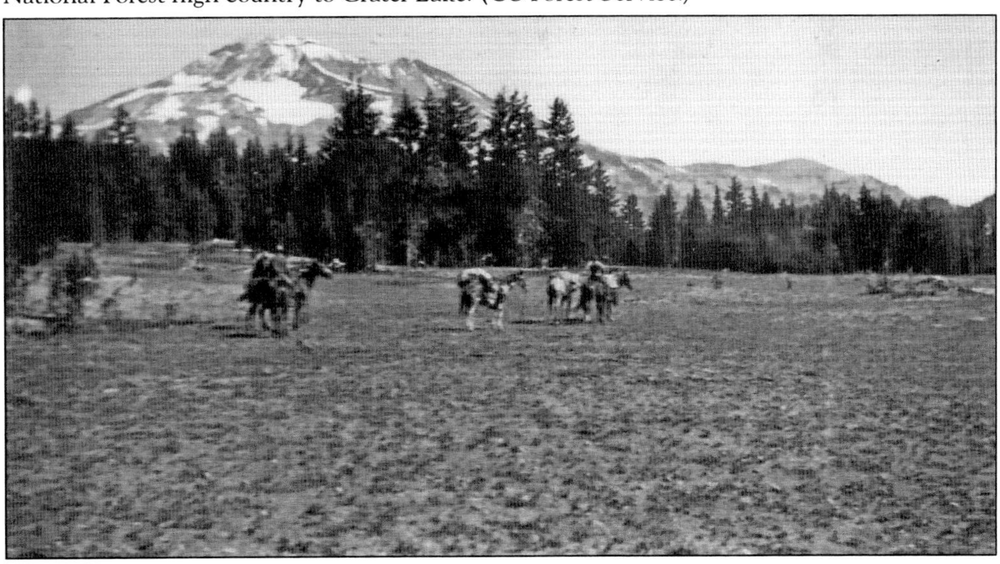

Cleator and his party scouted the proposed route for an Oregon Skyline road and trail during a summer 1920 pack trip. En route, the party crossed the Wickiup Plain along the boundary of the Deschutes National Forest and the Cascade National Forest (combined with the Santiam National Forest to form the Willamette National Forest in 1933). (US Forest Service.)

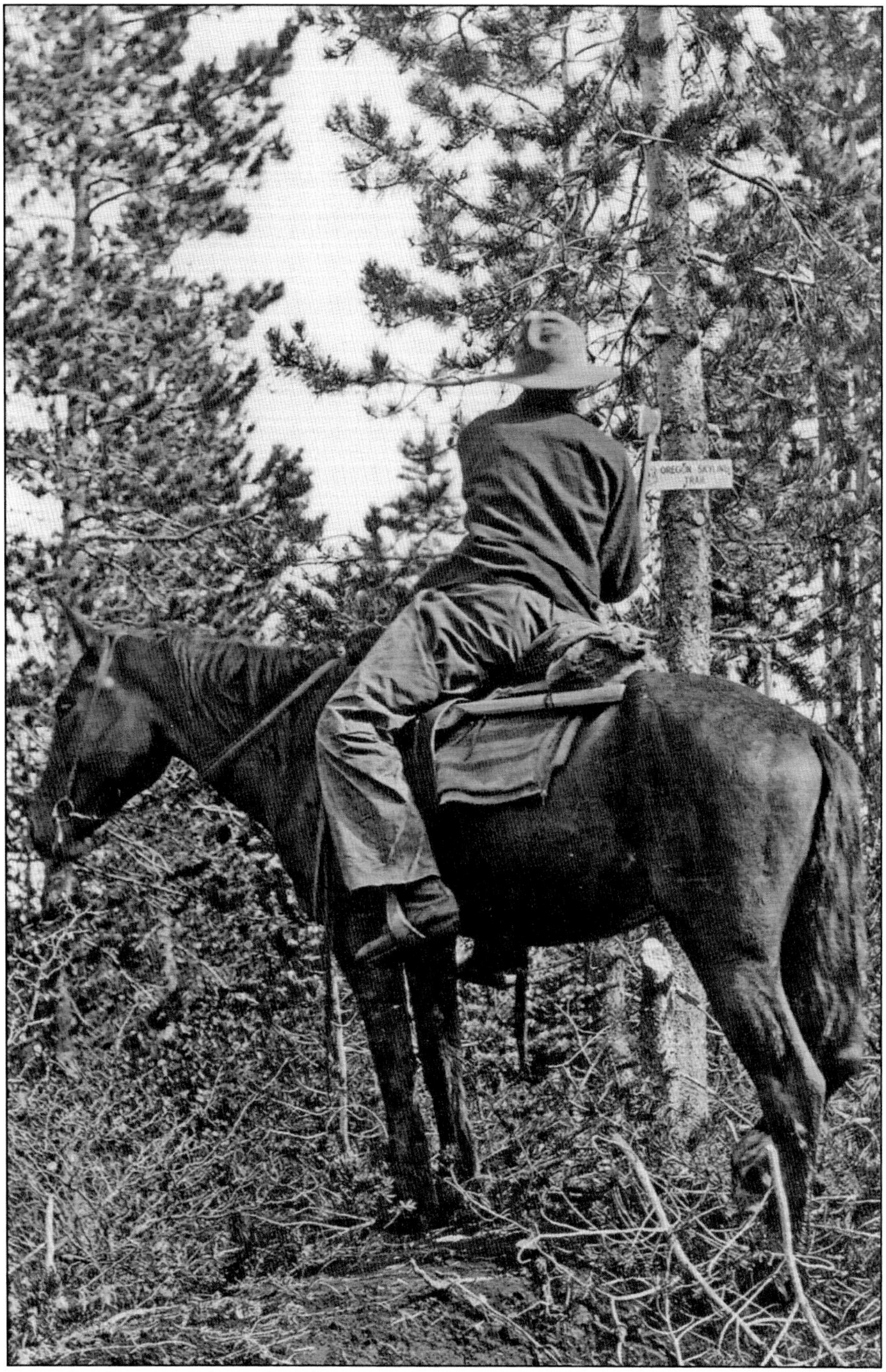

Cleator took a large number of trail markers and signs on that trip. When he posted them, the Oregon Skyline Trail was officially born. Later incorporated into the Pacific Crest Trail (PCT), it was designated the Pacific Crest National Scenic Trail (PCNST) with passage by Congress of the National Trails System Act of 1968. That trail passes through all five congressionally designated wildernesses on the Deschutes National Forest along its 2,650-mile route from Mexico to Canada. The proposed Oregon Skyline Road was never built. (US Forest Service.)

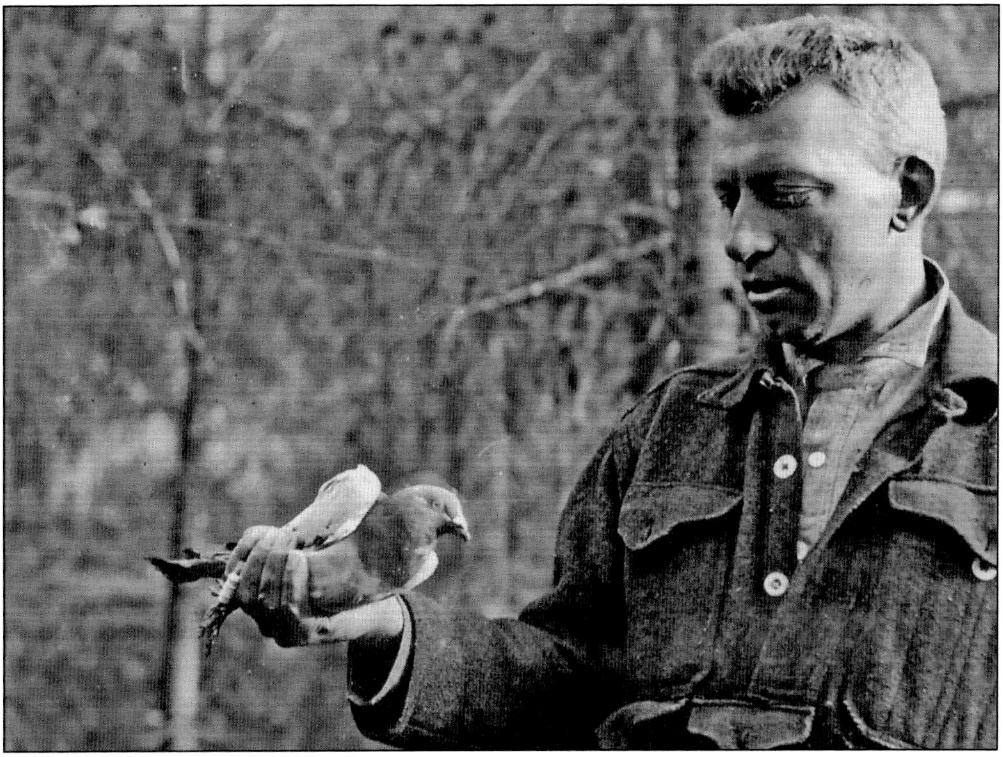

Although telephone communication between ranger stations and fire lookouts had been established, no modern communications were available to Cleator's party in the remote wilderness it traveled. His party used carrier pigeons (above) to communicate its progress along the crest of the Cascade Range to the various forest supervisors' offices. The carrier pigeon below was launched from the top of 10,358-foot South Sister. Middle Sister and North Sister appear in the distance. (Both, US Forest Service.)

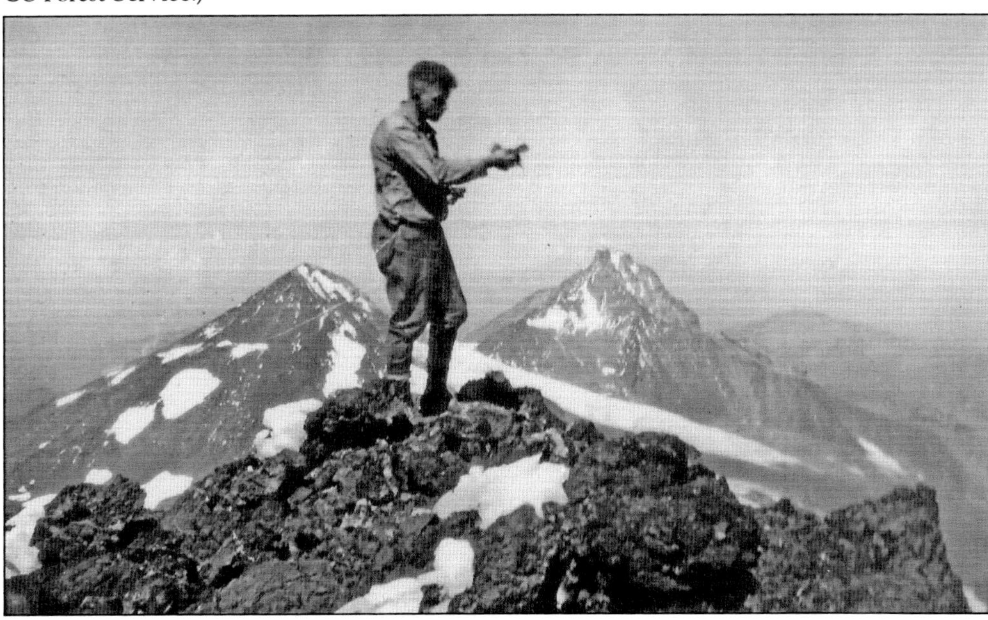

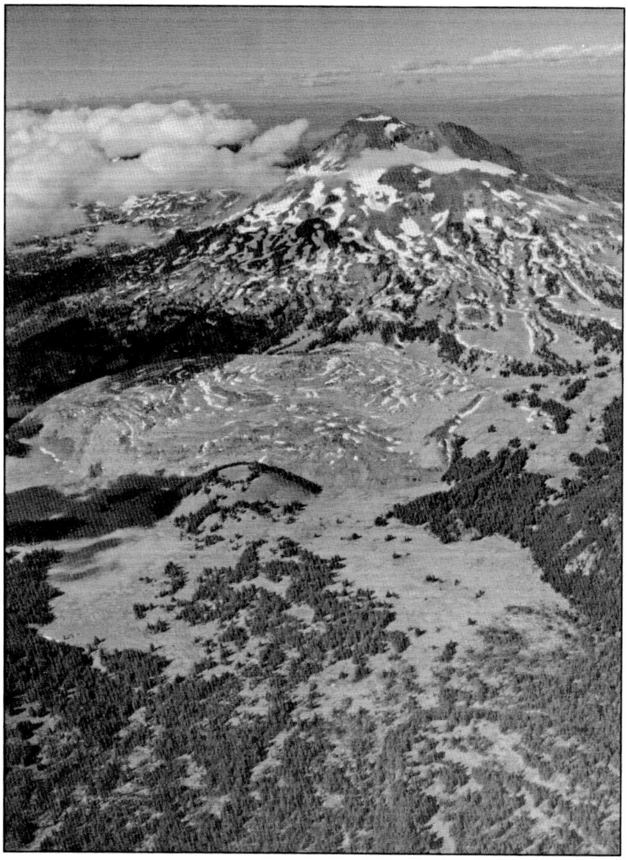

South Sister, an about-2,000-year-old lava flow called Rock Mesa, and a cinder cone named Le Conte Crater dominate the undulating, pumice-strewn Wickiup Plain to the south, all within the Three Sisters Wilderness. (US Geological Survey, photograph by Austin Post.)

About 50 miles of the Pacific Crest National Scenic Trail traverse the Three Sisters Wilderness and roughly approximate the Deschutes National Forest–Willamette National Forest boundary. These trekkers, south of a heavily glaciated volcano named the Husband, approach the Wickiup Plain, crossed by Cleator's party decades before. (Photograph by the author.)

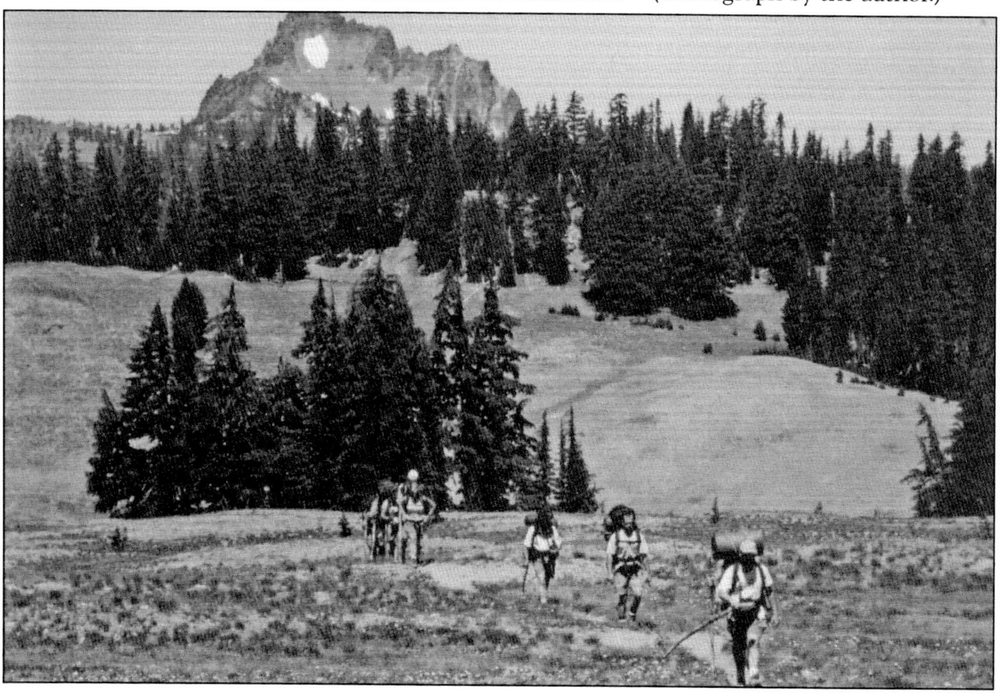

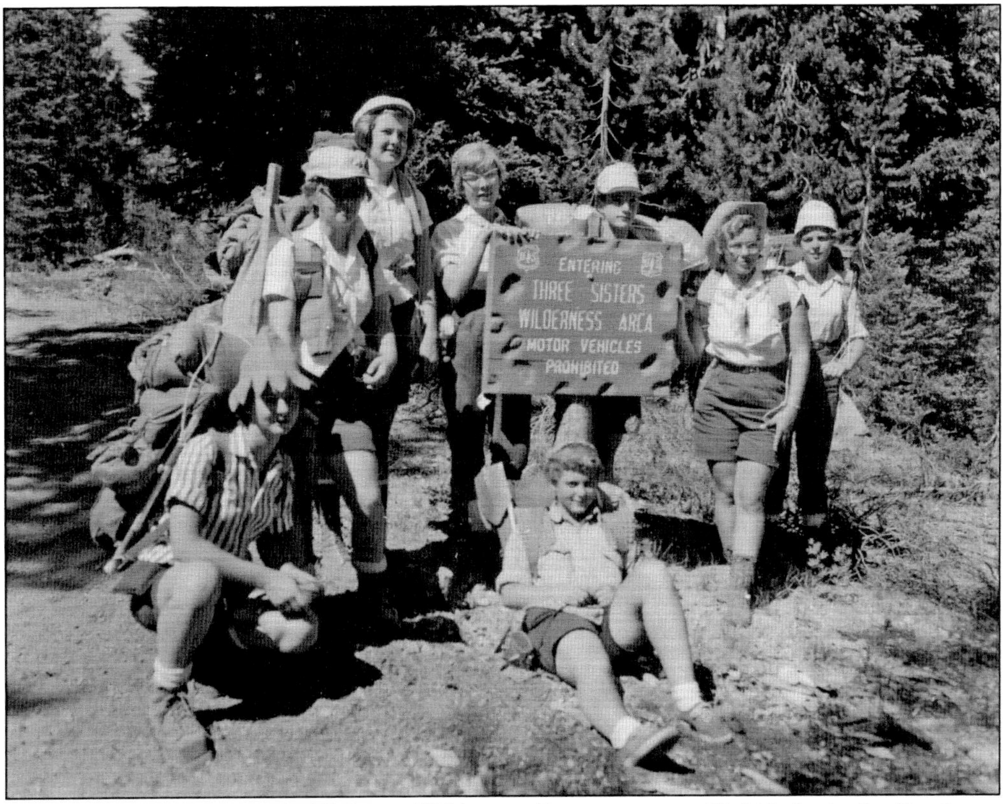

In August 1960, a two-week All-States Wilderness Encampment at Todd Lake in the Deschutes National Forest hosted 107 Girl Scouts from throughout the United States. The girls took weeklong backpacking trips into the Three Sisters Wilderness Area, renamed the Three Sisters Wilderness after Congress passed the Wilderness Act of 1964. (US Forest Service, photograph by Leland Prater.)

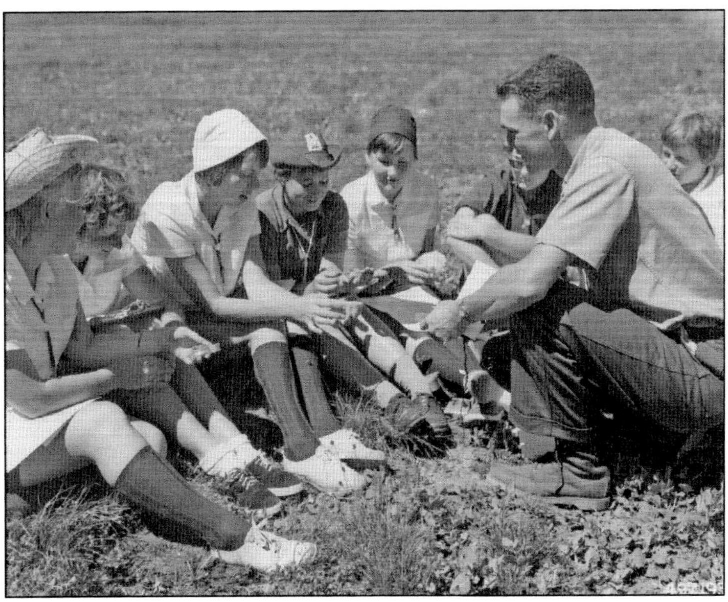

Before the Girl Scouts leave on their treks, a Metolius Ranger District forester named Wendall Jones shows them how to navigate the backcountry with a map and compass. Using those skills, they made their way through unfamiliar terrain to their wilderness destinations. (US Forest Service, photograph by Leland Prater.)

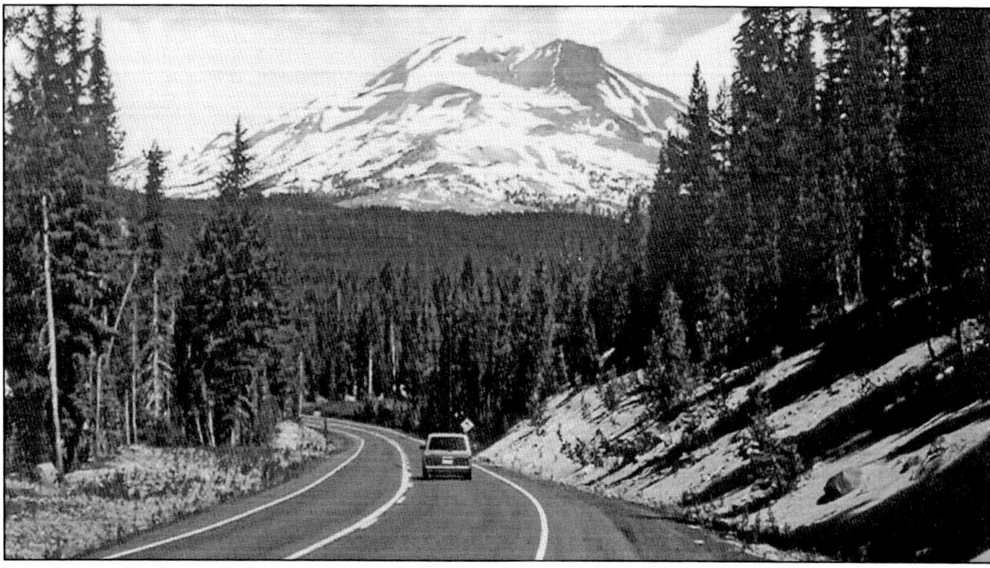

The beautiful Cascade Lakes National Scenic Byway leads into and through a forested volcanic landscape accentuated by alpine lakes—several surrounded by resorts, summer homes, and campgrounds—and to trailheads providing access to the magnificent Three Sisters Wilderness. South Sister looms on the skyline. (Photograph by the author.)

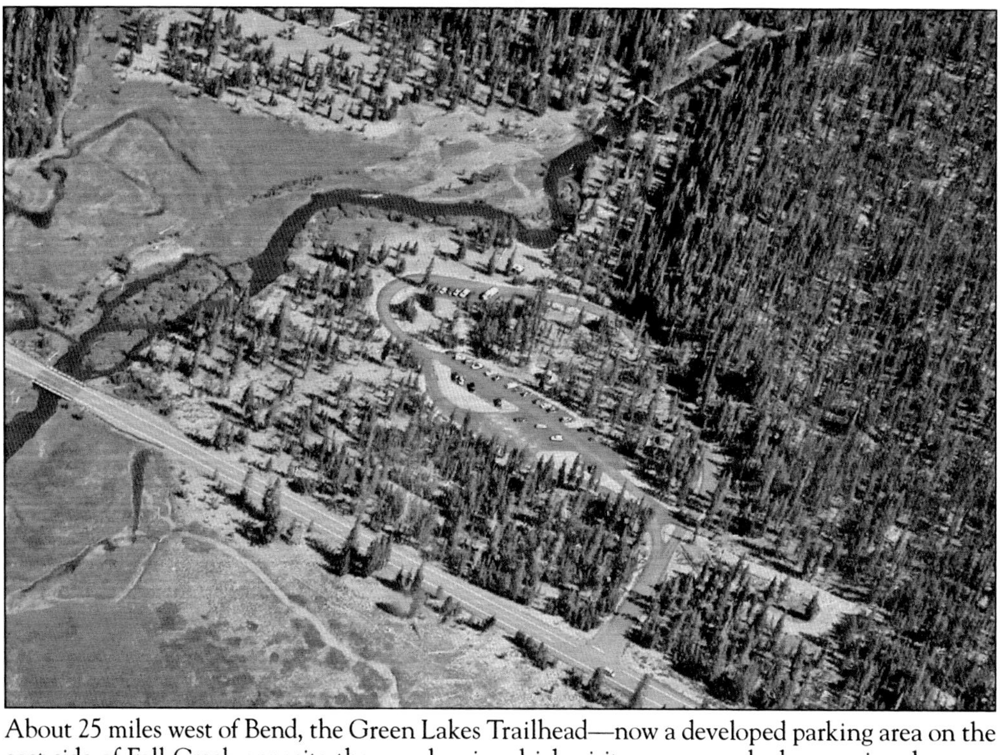

About 25 miles west of Bend, the Green Lakes Trailhead—now a developed parking area on the east side of Fall Creek opposite the meadow in which visitors once parked—remains the most popular entrance to the Three Sisters Wilderness. Most visitors follow the 4.5-mile trail up Fall Creek to the Green Lakes. Others walk about 3.7 miles to Moraine Lake. Still others enjoy the 12.5-mile Fall Creek–Soda Creek loop. (John Flood, MD.)

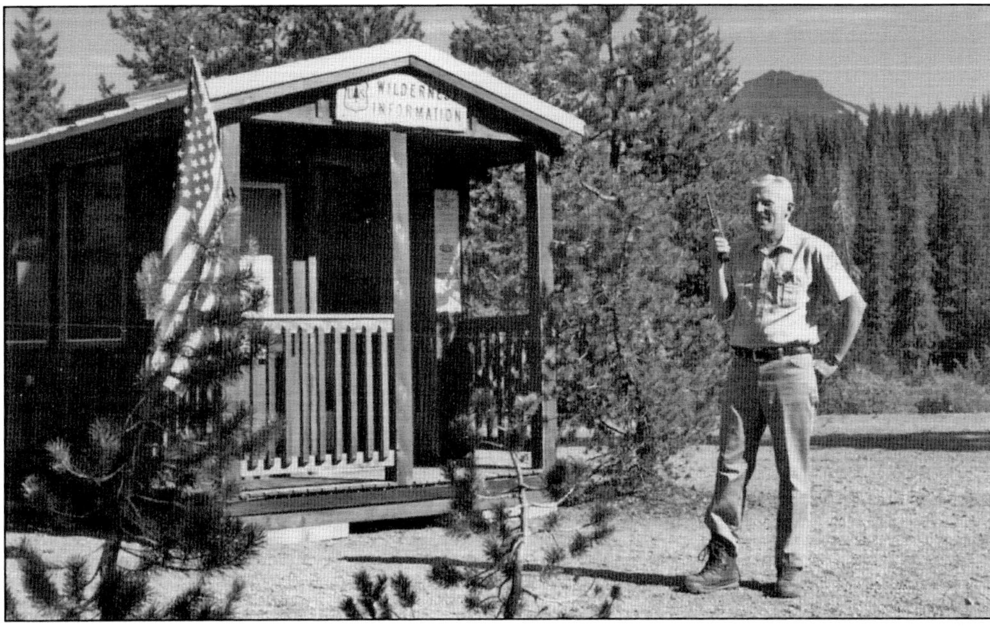

Three Sisters Wilderness visitors were welcomed by volunteer wilderness information specialists who staffed the Green Lakes Trailhead Information Station daily every summer from 1992 through 2005. Thousands of day-hikers and backpackers obtained useful information and maps at—and some got emergency assistance from—this most-used entrance to this most-visited in Oregon wilderness from volunteers such as John Flood, MD, a retired physician. (Photograph by the author.)

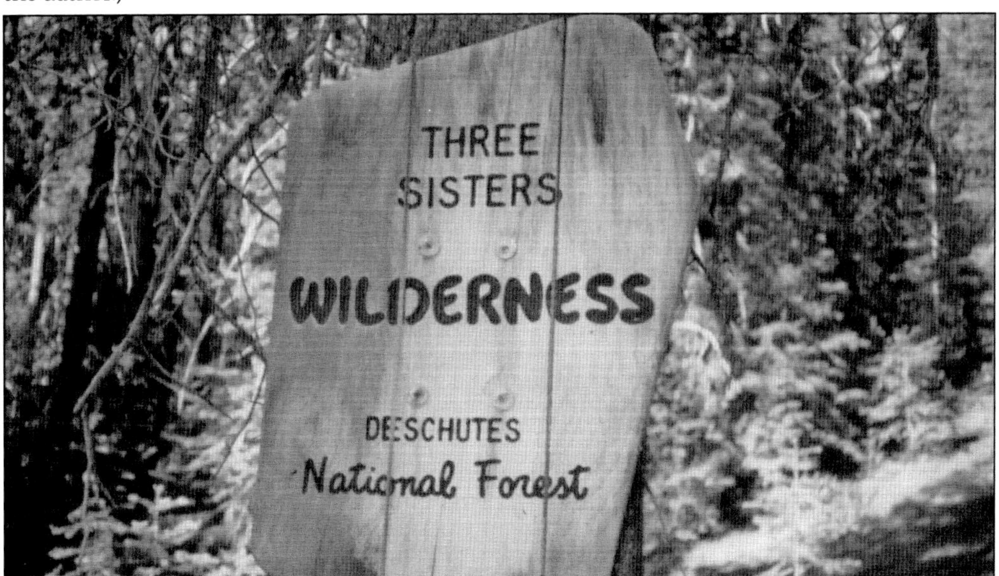

Three Sisters Wilderness boundaries, like all wilderness boundaries, are marked by distinctive signs that inform visitors they are entering a unit of the National Wilderness Preservation System, where things are different. Wilderness promises, in the words of the Wilderness Act of 1964, "solitude or a primitive and unconfined recreation experience," assured by observing a few simple practices and rules. (Photograph by the author.)

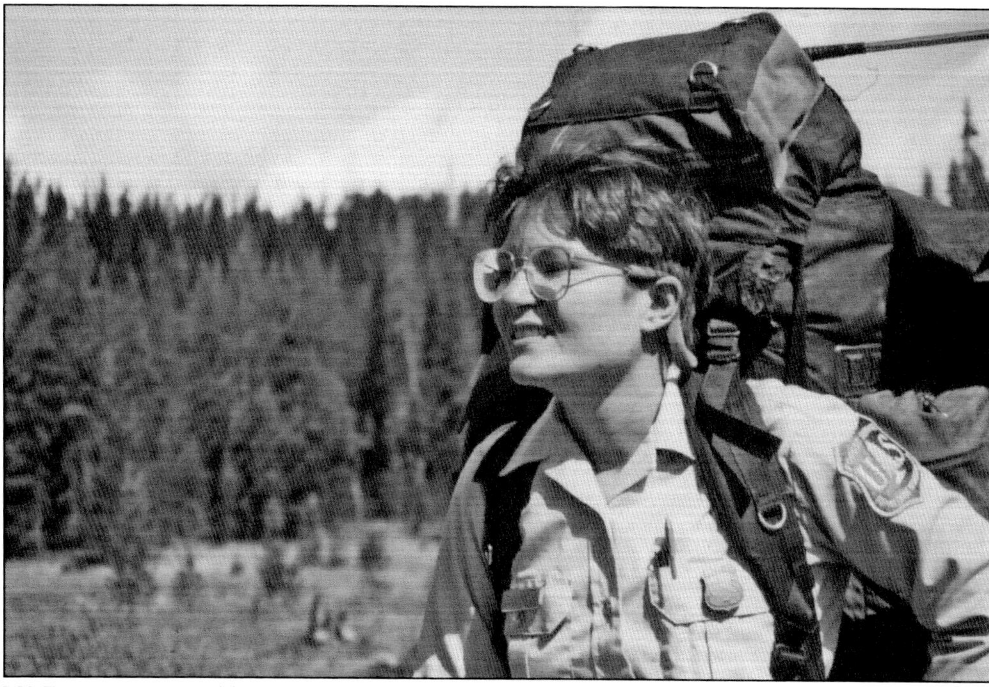

US Forest Service wilderness rangers—called "wilderness guards" early in the history of national forest wilderness management—patrol, protect the wilderness resource, and provide for visitor enjoyment and safety. Most serve during the summers. Wilderness ranger Melissa Merrifield served in the Three Sisters Wilderness during the early 1990s. (Photograph by the author.)

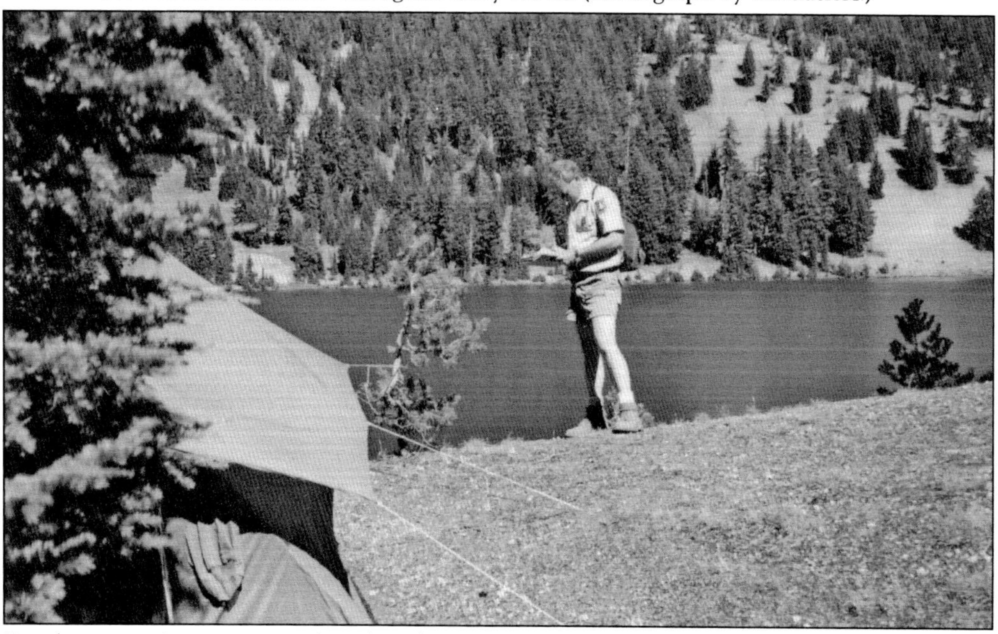

Popular visitor destinations within the Three Sisters Wilderness may suffer heavy visitor impacts. In 1990, this wilderness ranger collects camping impact data in the Green Lakes basin that was used to select designated campsites, use of which helped reduce camping impacts and retain wilderness values. (Photograph by Pat Joslin.)

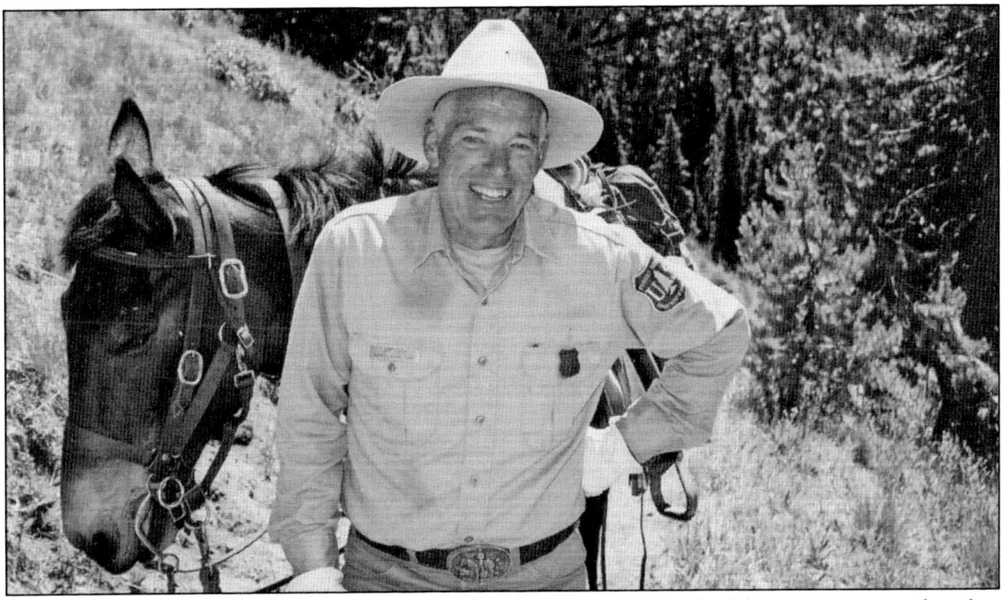

For a dozen summers during the late 1900s and early 2000s, mounted wilderness ranger and packer Jim Leep, a retired Portland, Oregon, police officer, served in the Three Sisters Wilderness. He welcomed and assisted thousands of visitors as he maintained trails and signs. Based on the edge of the wilderness, Leep was always on call for emergency fire operations support and search and rescue missions. (Photograph by the author.)

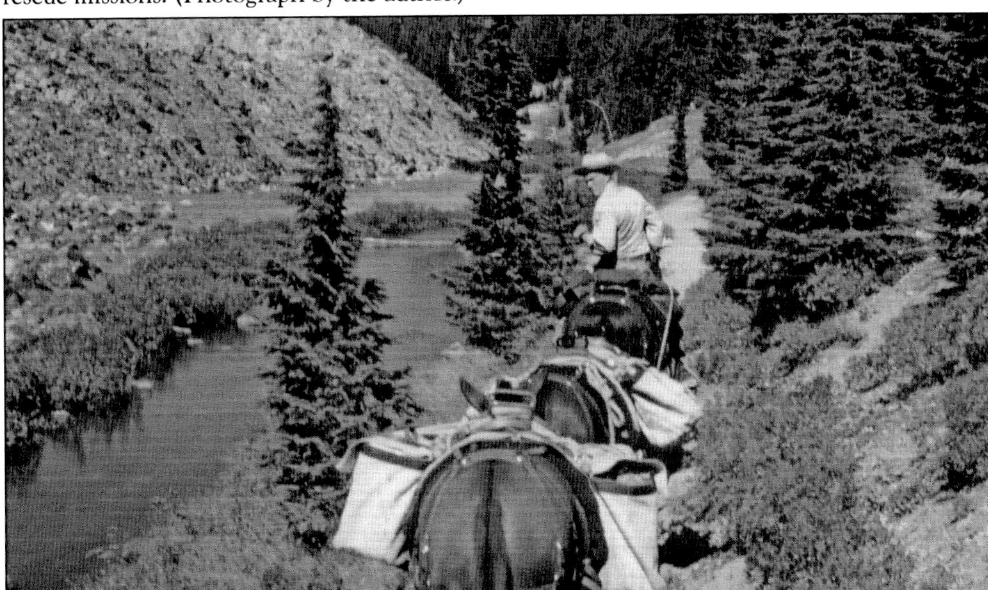

Mounted wilderness ranger and packer Jim Leep transported trail crew camps and supplies throughout the Three Sisters Wilderness—where travel and transport are by foot or saddle and pack stock only—with a pack string of up to five mules. He and his saddle and pack animals did the heavy lifting when it came to transporting bridge timbers, sign posts, and other heavy cargo. (Photograph by the author.)

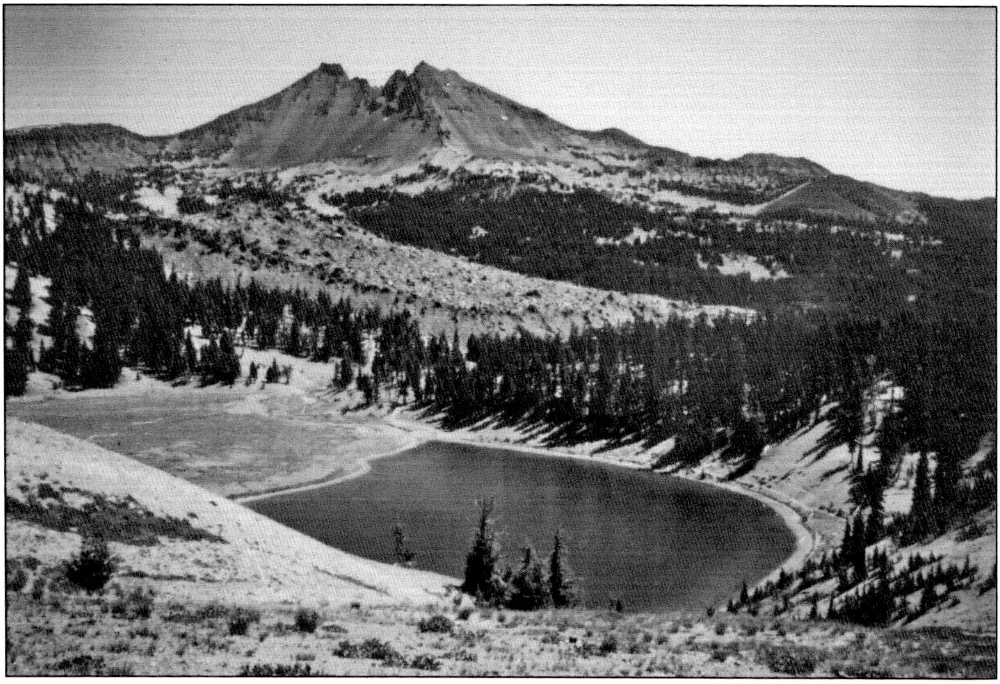

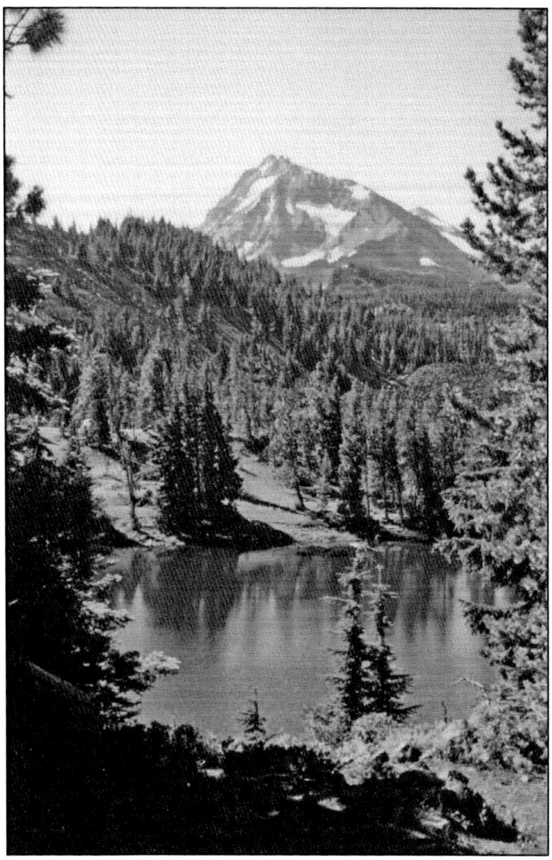

The Three Sisters Wilderness is truly a land of fire and ice. Broken Top, a heavily glaciated volcano; the Miller Lava Flow, on South Sister's southeastern slope; and Moraine Lake, impounded by a Lewis Glacier moraine at the southern base of South Sister, demonstrate that fact. Camping at this popular destination is at designated sites only. (Photograph by the author.)

At the northern end of the Three Sisters Wilderness, North Sister looms over South Matthieu Lake. Camping at this beautiful but delicate lake along the Pacific Crest National Scenic Trail, about 2.5 miles south of Oregon Highway 242 at McKenzie Pass, is at designated sites only. (Photograph by the author.)

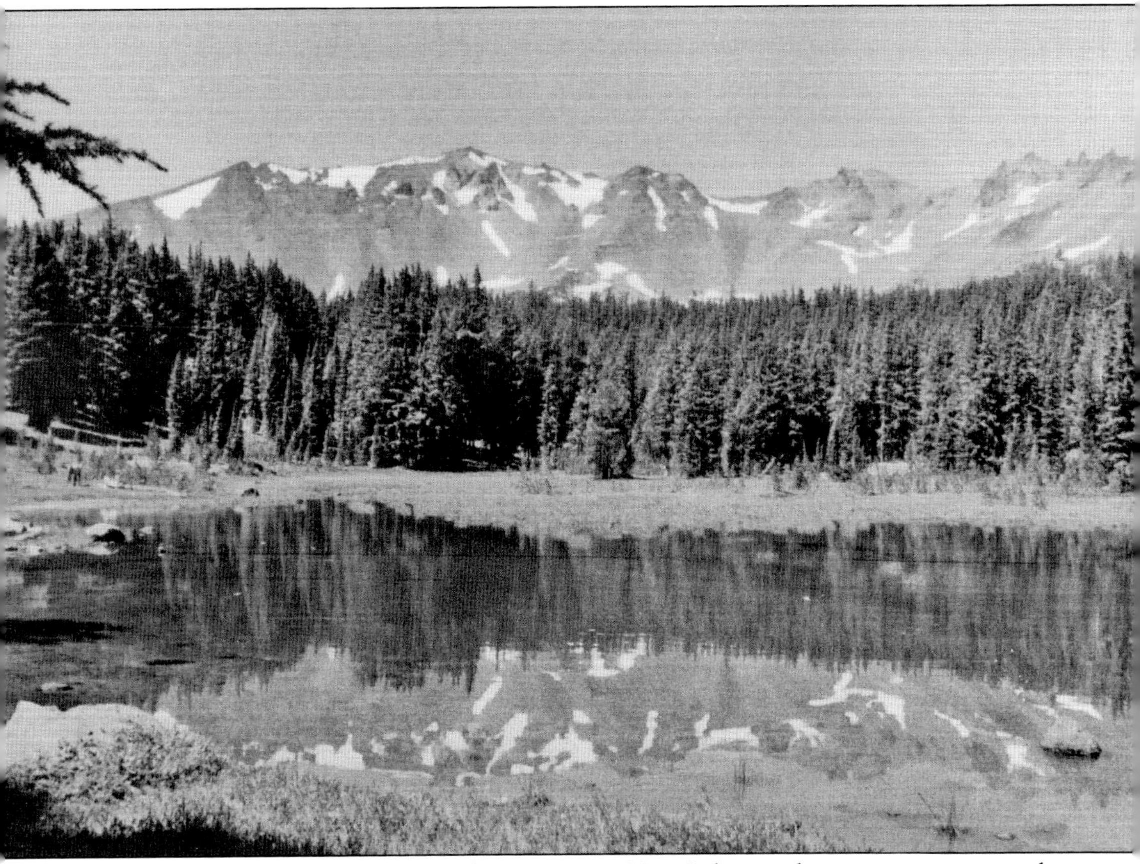

At 8,744 feet, Diamond Peak—reflected in Mountain View Lake—is the most prominent peak in the Diamond Peak Wilderness, which, like the peak itself, rests along the boundary between the Deschutes and Willamette National Forests. Administratively designated by the Richard E. McArdle, chief of the Forest Service, as the 36,637-acre Diamond Peak Wild Area in 1957, it became the Diamond Peak Wilderness when Congress passed of the Wilderness Act of 1964. Passage of the Oregon Wilderness Act of 1984 increased its size to 52,337 acres. The eastern 60 percent of this wilderness is within the Deschutes National Forest. (Deschutes National Forest, photograph by E.J. Parker.)

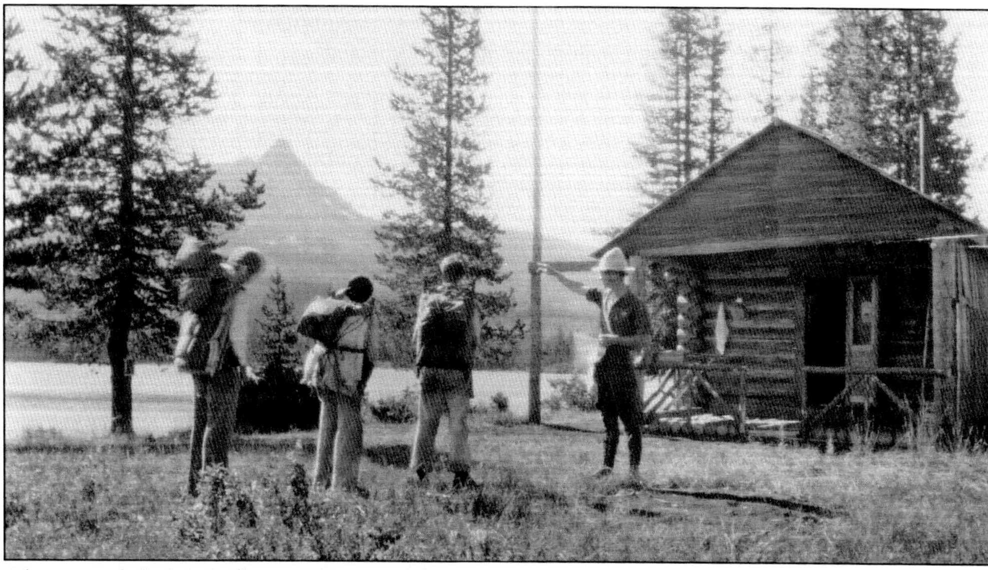

Also set aside by McArdle in 1957 as a wild area, the 46,635-acre Mount Washington Wilderness was established when Congress passed the Wilderness Act of 1964. Here, Boy Scouts who approached Mount Washington from the west in the 1920s are assisted by a forest guard from the Santiam National Forest (transferred to the Willamette National Forest in 1933) based at Big Lake Guard Station. (US Forest Service.)

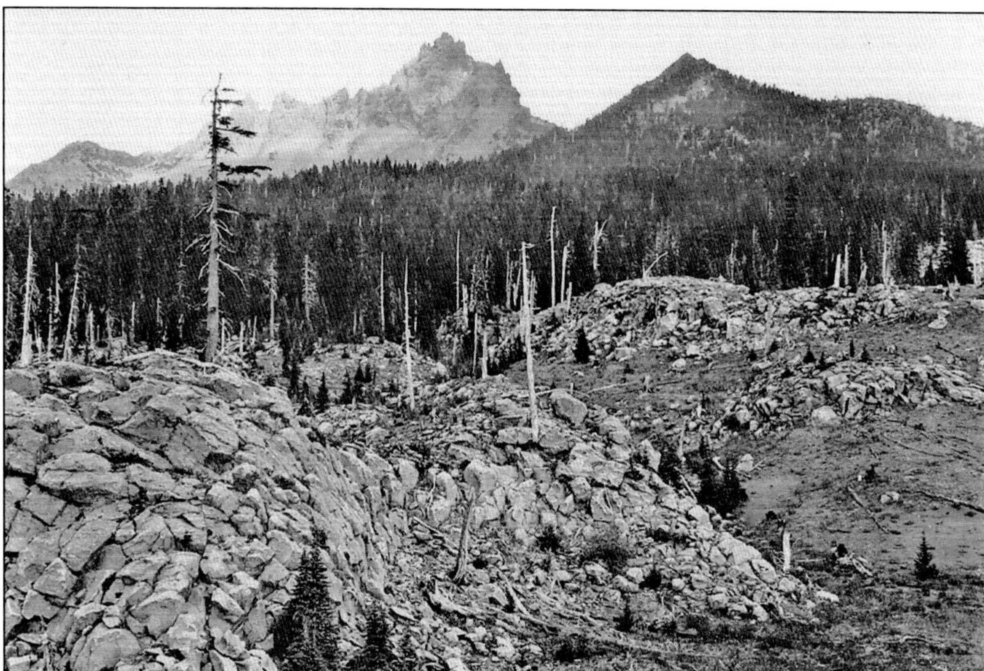

Three Fingered Jack, at 7,841 feet, is the most prominent peak within the 32,734 acres of the 107,008-acre Mount Jefferson Wilderness, administered by the Sisters Ranger District of the Deschutes National Forest. Named for Oregon's second-highest peak, which is shared by the Mount Hood National Forest and the Warm Springs Indian Reservation, the wilderness was designated by Congress in 1968 under the Wilderness Act of 1964. (Deschutes National Forest.)

Ten

Newberry National Volcanic Monument

The massive Newberry Volcano, one of the largest shield-shaped volcanoes in the Lower 48, dominates the southeastern third of the Deschutes National Forest. Not part of the Cascades Range, it erupted at the coalescence of three major faults and is one of the best places in the United States to observe and understand volcanism. The volcano's summit contains a 17-square-mile caldera, aptly characterized as "a stark, unforgiving volcanic bowl with a craggy rim [topped by Paulina Peak] overlooking two deep blue lakes, East and Paulina" in a September 19, 1989, editorial, "The Making of a Monument," in Bend's daily newspaper, the *Bulletin*.

The monument referred to in that editorial is Newberry National Volcanic Monument, established within the Deschutes National Forest in the autumn of 1990, when Congress passed and Pres. George H.W. Bush signed a locally inspired and crafted bill to create the monument. The result was the approximately 56,300-acre national monument that encompasses its namesake volcano and caldera and myriad other volcanic features as well as compatible outdoor recreation opportunities afforded by two resorts, several campgrounds, trails, and other facilities.

Among the volcanic features encompassed by the monument, which extends from the volcano and its caldera northwesterly along the northwest rift zone to the Deschutes River, are the Lava Cast Forest; Lava River Cave; Lava Butte, a cinder cone topped by a fire lookout and surrounded by its massive lava flow, at the base of which is the monument's Lava Lands Visitor Center just off US Highway 97; and Benham Falls, where the Deschutes River squeezes between Lava Butte's lava flow and older Benham Butte in a narrow blast of white water. All of this is within easy commuting distance of the city of Bend and surrounding recreation-oriented communities, including Sunriver.

Most of America's national monuments are administered by two Department of the Interior agencies, the National Park Service and the Bureau of Land Management. Newberry National Volcanic Monument is one of several national monuments administered by the Forest Service; an additional few are comanaged by the Forest Service and the Bureau of Land Management.

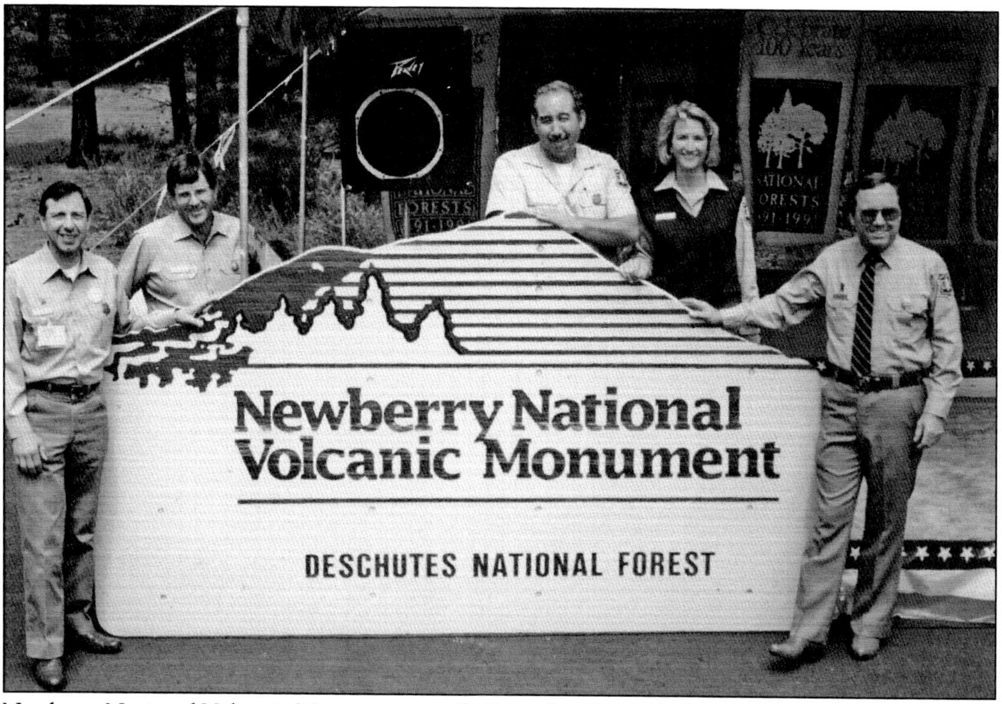

Newberry National Volcanic Monument was dedicated on June 30, 1991. Officiating were, from left to right, US Forest Service officials administration director Dick Ferraro and recreation director Lyle Laverty of the Pacific Northwest Region; Deschutes National Forest supervisor Joe Cruz and deputy forest supervisor Sally Collins; and deputy chief of the Forest Service for the National Forest System Jim Overbay. (Deschutes National Forest, photograph by Bob Jensen.)

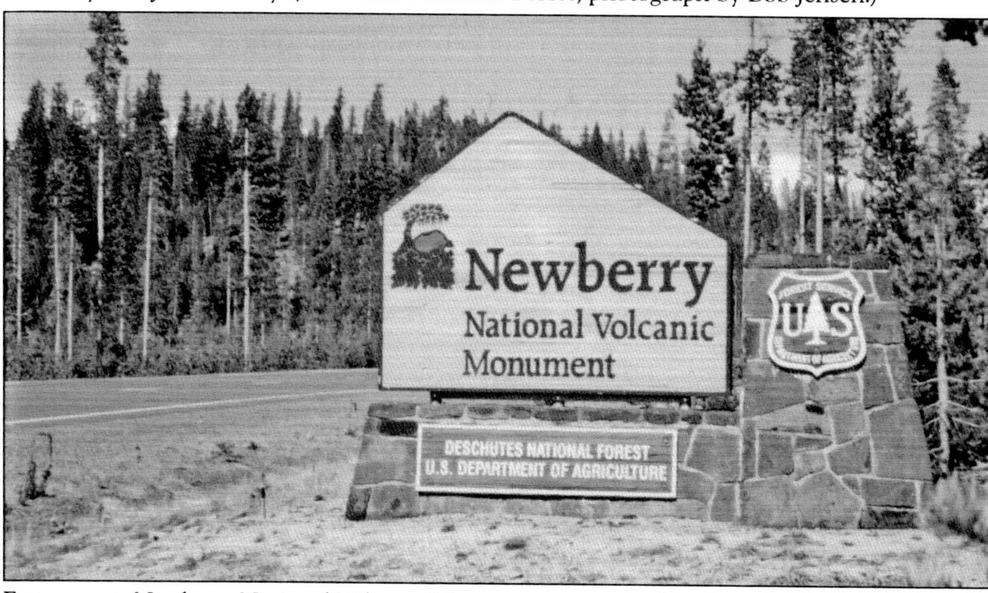

Entrances to Newberry National Volcanic Monument are marked by distinctive signs. These signs advise Deschutes National Forest visitors they are entering one of several national monuments within a national forest and administered by the US Forest Service rather than by the National Park Service, which administers most national monuments. (Photograph by the author.)

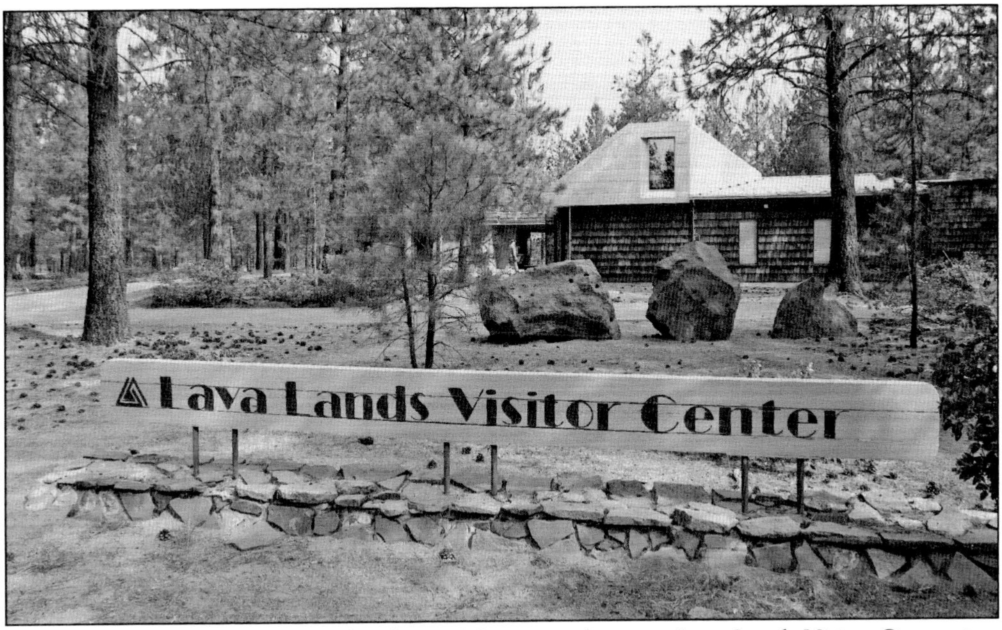

Most visits to Newberry National Volcanic Monument begin at Lava Lands Visitor Center, just off US Highway 97 about 10 miles south of Bend and one of the US Forest Service's earlier visitor centers. Here, visitors learn about the area's volcanic history and where to go to see various examples of volcanic activity. (Photograph by the author.)

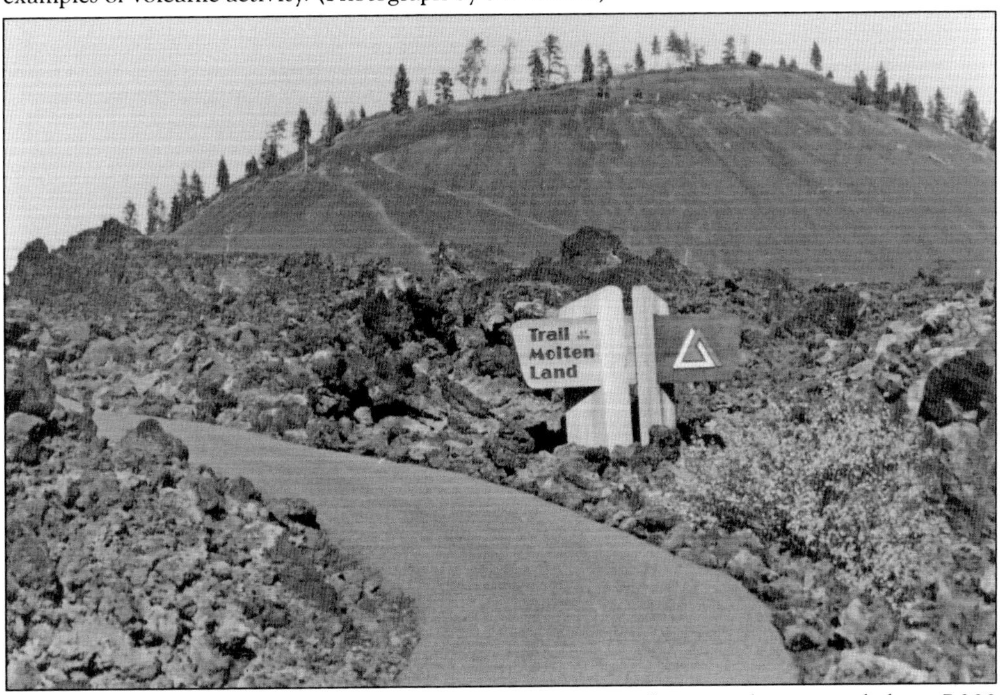

Lava Lands Visitor Center is at the base of Lava Butte, a cinder cone that erupted about 7,000 years ago. Beginning at the visitor center, the Trail of the Molten Land interprets the cinder cone, the over-nine-square-mile lava flow that resulted when molten lava breached its south side late in its eruption, and views of the Cascade Range to the west. (Deschutes National Forest.)

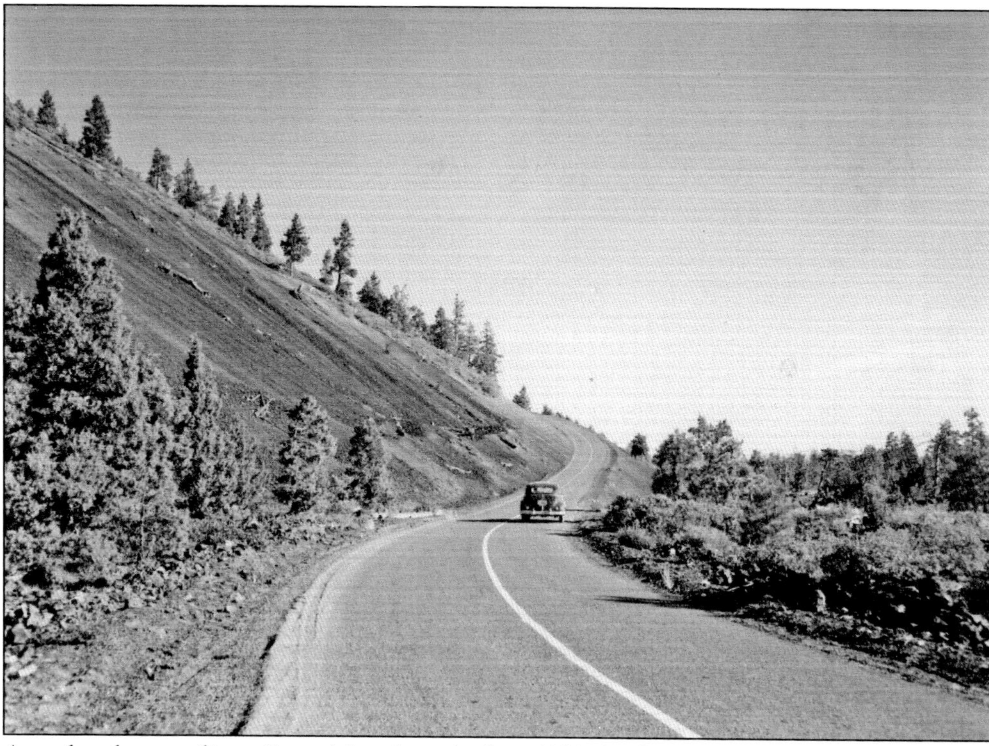

A road to the top of Lava Butte (above) was built in 1950. As this road winds up the butte, which towers 500 feet above the surrounding lava flows and ponderosa pine forests (below), it previews expansive views of the surrounding volcanic landscape seen from the top. (Both, Deschutes National Forest.)

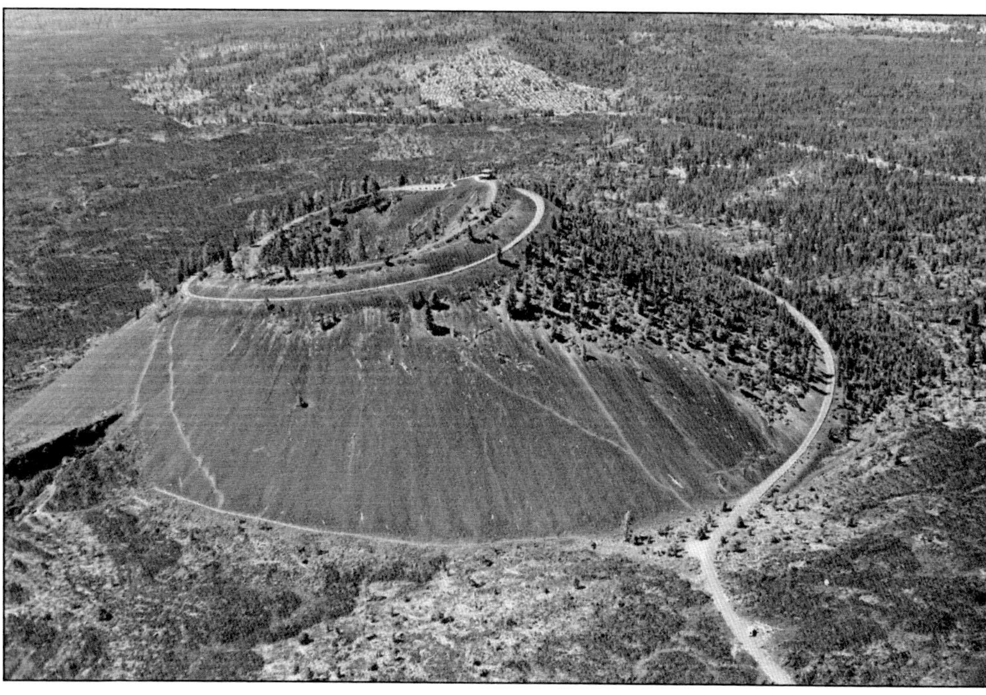

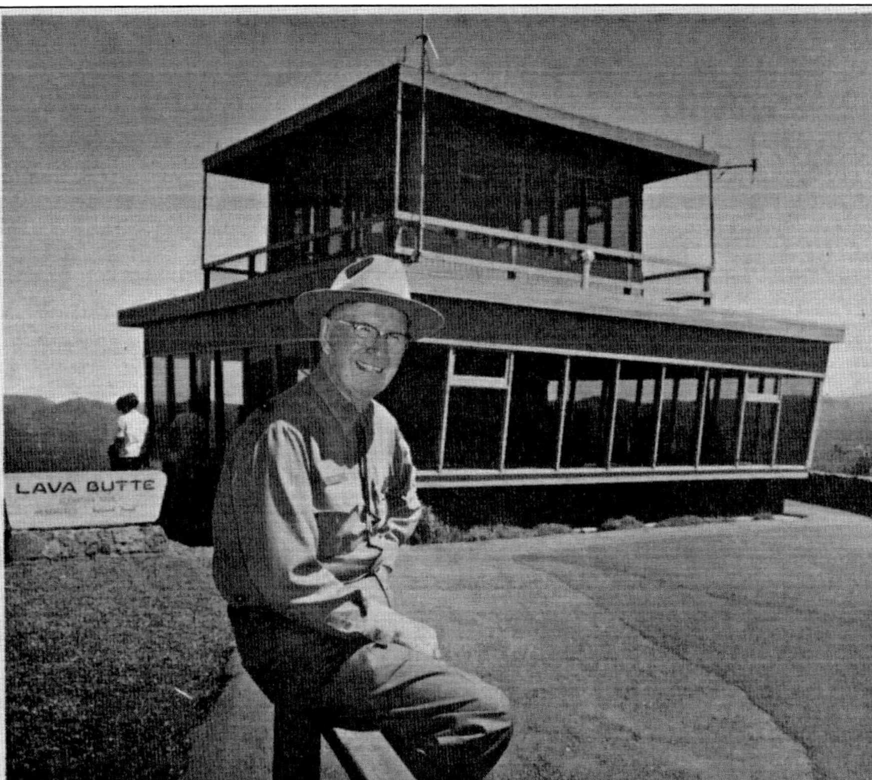

Phil F. Brogan, a Bend resident since finishing college in 1923, is a professional tourist host for the Deschutes National Forest this summer on Lava Butte. Viewpoint is one of the most popular tourist attractions in the area. (Bulletin Photo by Dave Swan)

Noted geologist plays tourist host

'Retired' newsman greets visitors at Lava Butte, tells volcanic story

By Ila Grant Hopper
Bulletin Staff Writer

Phil F. Brogan – author, historian, recognized authority on geology and related sciences – is running the show at the Lava Butte Visitor Information Center.

Atop the 500-foot red cinder cone, 10 miles south of Bend, Brogan tells visitors the Lava Butte story. The same facts are available in a brochure which Brogan wrote several years ago for the Forest Service. At the base of the 2,000-year-old volcanic hill, sight-seers can walk across the lava flow on a board-walk trail that was named for Brogan in 1965.

The seasonal stint as a professional tourist host is just one of Brogan's activities in his first summer of "retirement." Last September he ended his 44-

in the heavens. (Brogan is a director of the Pacific Northwest Meteor Society.) Some bring copies of his best-selling Central Oregon history, "East of the Cascades," for him to autograph. Some want to know where to look for thunder-eggs or lava bombs.

Brogan tells visitors how lava once boiled and bubbled in the 150-foot crater now filled with volcanic ash. How the liquid mass changed the ancient course of the Deschutes River, forming a big lake, islands and waterfalls. How tongues of fiery melted rock splashed into gutters and ridges, forming faults and pinnacles. How the surface crust was broken into slag and slabs by the energetic undertow.

Brogan points out spectacular features visible in the distance, using as a guide

The information center, established in 1962, is one of two in Oregon staffed by the Forest Service each summer. The other is at Cape Perpetua, on the coast.

Visitors from out-of-state, particularly those from distant points, are amazed by the spectacular panorama, Brogan says. Many express delight that they made the drive up the steep cone by chance, and say the stop should be a "must" for all tourists in the area.

The center is open daily from 8 a.m. to 8 p.m. The season this year started June 20 and will end September 15. On days when Brogan is not on duty, one of his assistants, Rose Putnam and Patricia Grimm, answer visitors' questions. The lookout tower above the center is out of bounds to the public. Mr. and Mrs. Larry

Before there was a Lava Lands Visitor Center, most visitors viewed and learned about the Deschutes National Forest's "Lava Lands" from the top of Lava Butte. There, a Lava Butte Visitor Information Center was established in 1962 on the lower level of the then-new Lava Butte fire lookout. The July 23, 1968, issue of the *Bulletin*, Bend's daily newspaper, reports that its retired famed writer Phil Brogan had pinned on a US Forest Service badge to interpret the volcanic landscape from that information center. (Deschutes County Historical Society.)

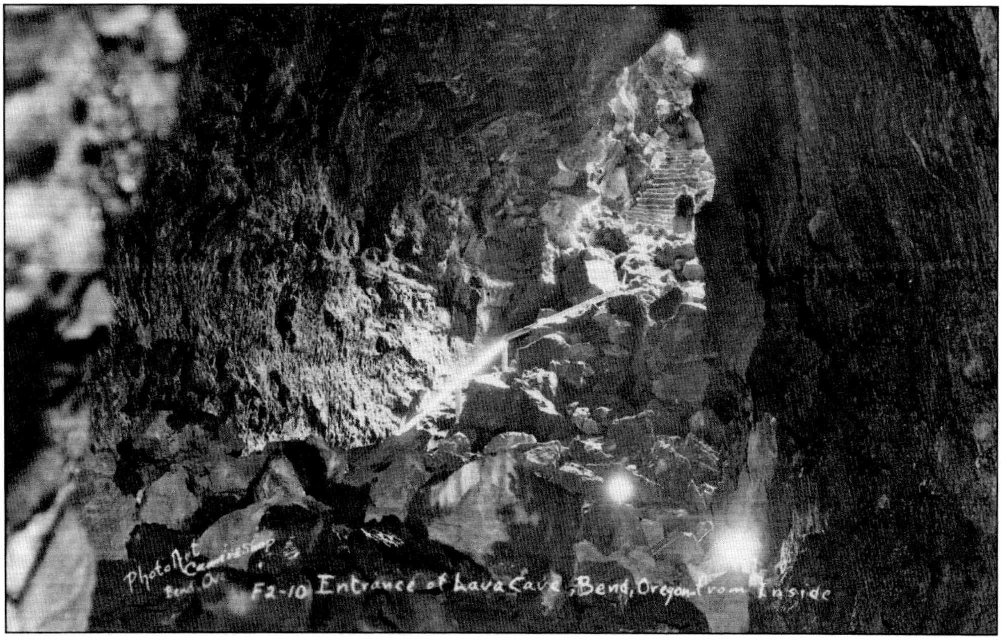

Just south of Lava Butte, Lava River Cave is a mile-long lava tube that follows the route of a fluid lava flow. Deeded to Oregon in 1926 for a state park, it became part of the Deschutes National Forest in a 1981 land exchange and is now explored by Newberry National Volcanic Monument visitors. (Deschutes National Forest.)

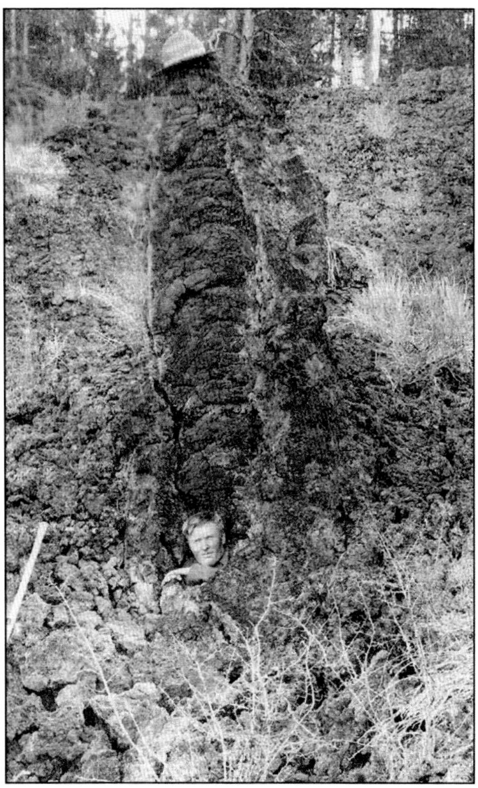

Twelve road miles south of Lava Lands Visitor Center, the Lava Cast Forest is an area within the Newberry Volcano's northwest rift zone through which molten lava flowed through a ponderosa pine forest some 7,000 years ago. This early-day forest ranger uses himself and his hat to show the depth and height of one of hundreds of tree molds or "casts" that resulted from that flow. (Walt Perry Group.)

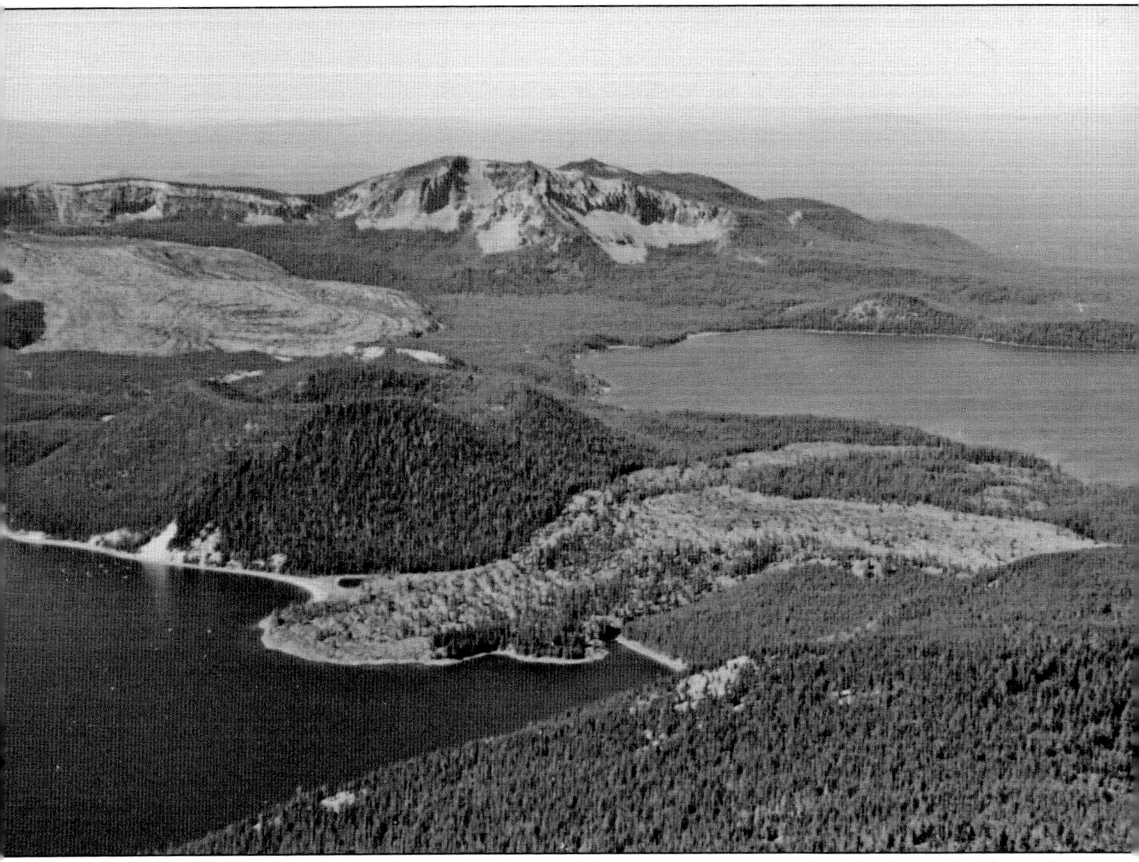

The southern half of Newberry National Volcanic Monument comprises the Newberry Caldera of the collapsed Newberry Volcano and its rim, surrounded by volcanic cinder cones of the Paulina Mountains. Paulina Peak (center), at 7,985 feet, is the highest point on that rim. Within the caldera are East Lake (left) and Paulina Lake (right), separated by Central Pumice Cone and interlake lava flows. Big Obsidian Flow (top left), about 1,300 years old, is Oregon's most recent major volcanic feature. The national monument and its caldera are named for Dr. John Strong Newberry, a prominent physician, geologist, and botanist who accompanied Lt. Henry Larcom Abbot's 1855 Pacific Railway Survey exploration of Central Oregon. (Deschutes National Forest.)

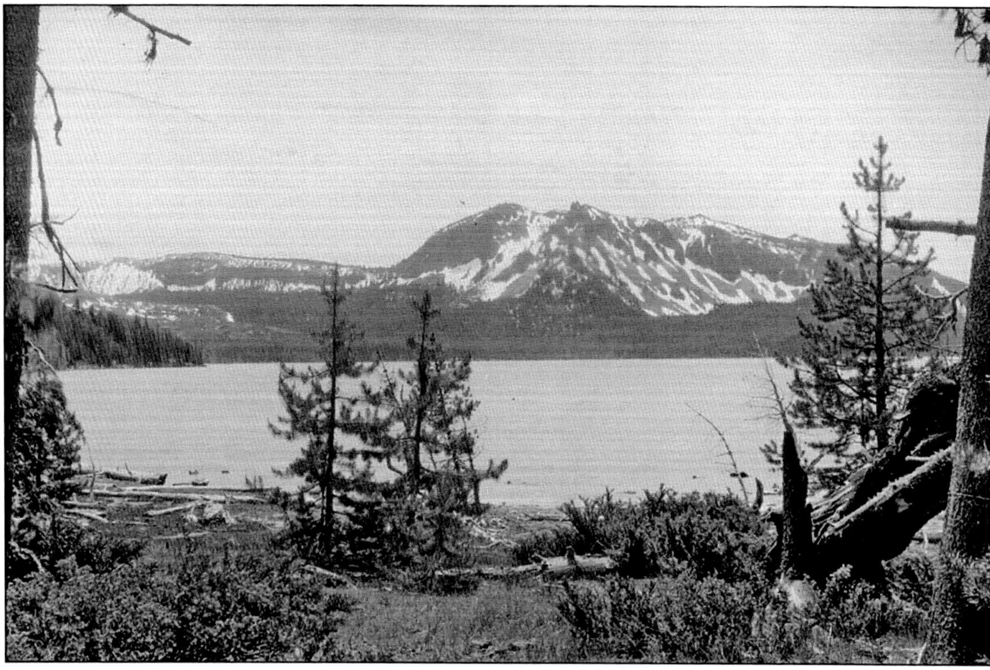

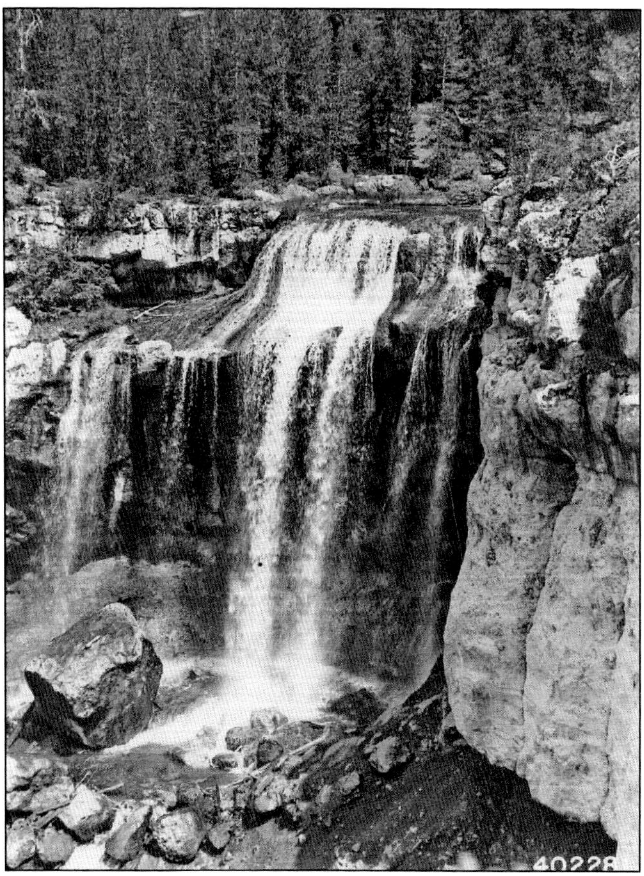

Paulina Peak rises above Paulina Lake (above), the larger of the two lakes within the caldera. Paulina Creek, the only stream within the Newberry Caldera–Paulina Mountains vicinity, drains Paulina Lake over Paulina Falls (left). This peak, lake, creek, and falls, along with other features and places in Oregon, are named for Paulina, of the Walpapi tribe of the Snake Indians, who led a band responsible for a series of raids against ranches in 1867. Pursued by ranchers led by Howard Maupin, Paulina was shot to death in the Trout Creek country. (Both, Deschutes National Forest.)

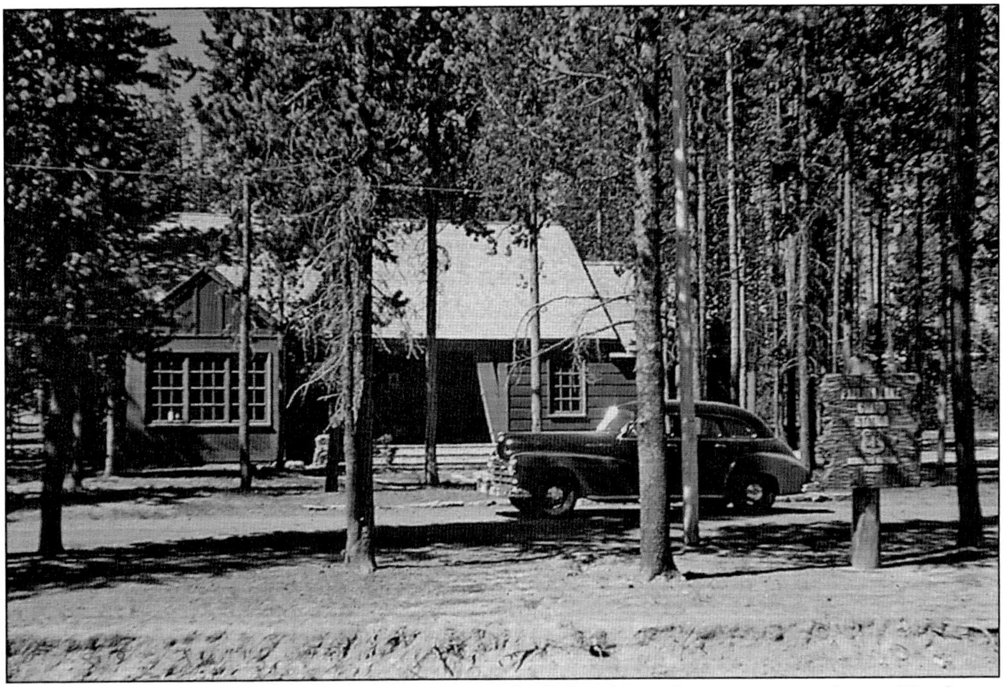

Paulina Lake Guard Station, close to its namesake lake along the western road into Newberry Caldera, was built by the CCC in 1941 and 1942. For its first 17 summers, it was staffed by forest guard John Robins, who lived there with his family as he carried out his many duties. Restored to its original appearance, it remains in service. (US Forest Service.)

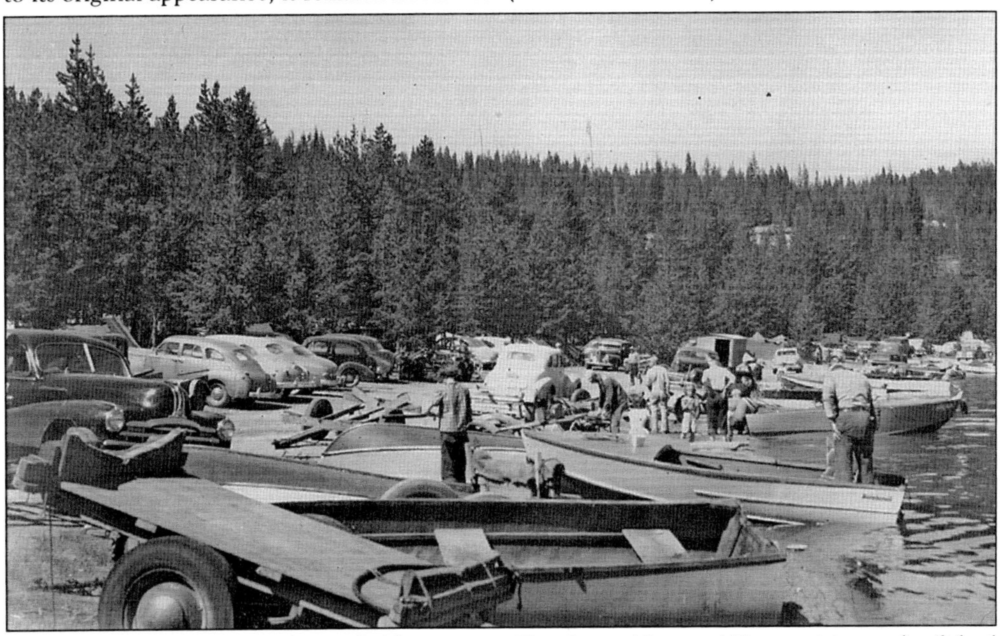

The popularity of the Newberry Caldera among Deschutes National Forest visitors who fished in Paulina Lake and East Lake, stayed at the resorts and campgrounds around both lakes, and enjoyed its many other recreation opportunities kept forest guard Robins busy. Here, fishermen launch their boats in East Lake on a late-1940s summer day. (Deschutes National Forest.)

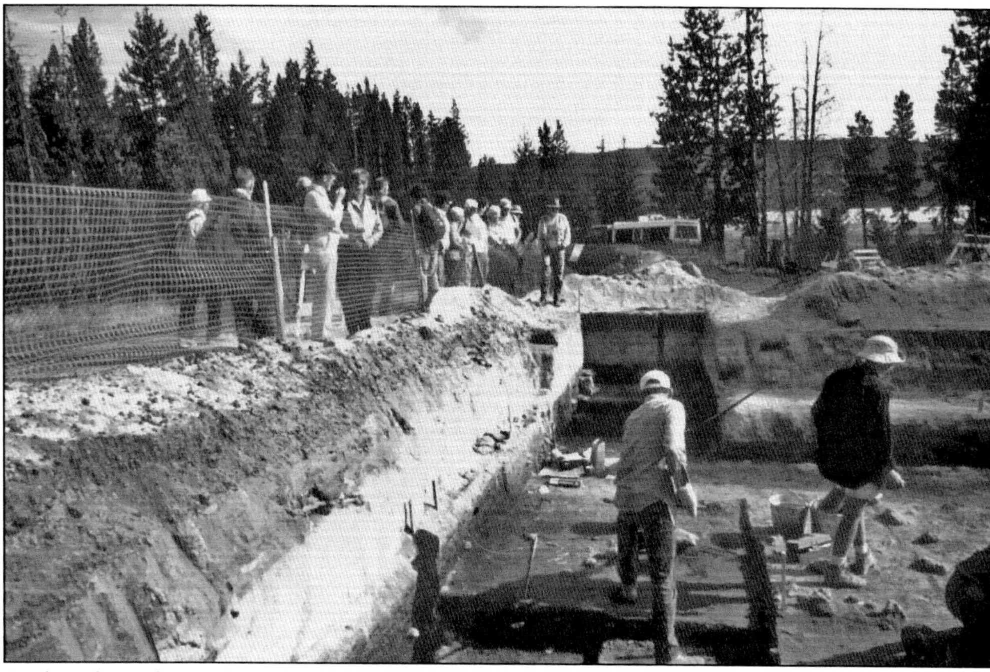

Archaeological excavations across the road from Paulina Lake Guard Station near Paulina Lake in 1992 (above) showed the Newberry Caldera has been a popular place for a long time. Visitors to Newberry National Volcanic Monument (below) read about the 10,000-year-old remains of a hearth that, along with projectile points and other stone tools of that time, evidences human occupation. The much later East Lake Obsidian Flow and Big Obsidian Flow eruptions drew Native Americans to the caldera in search of this valuable toolmaking volcanic glass. (Above, Deschutes National Forest; below, photograph by the author.)

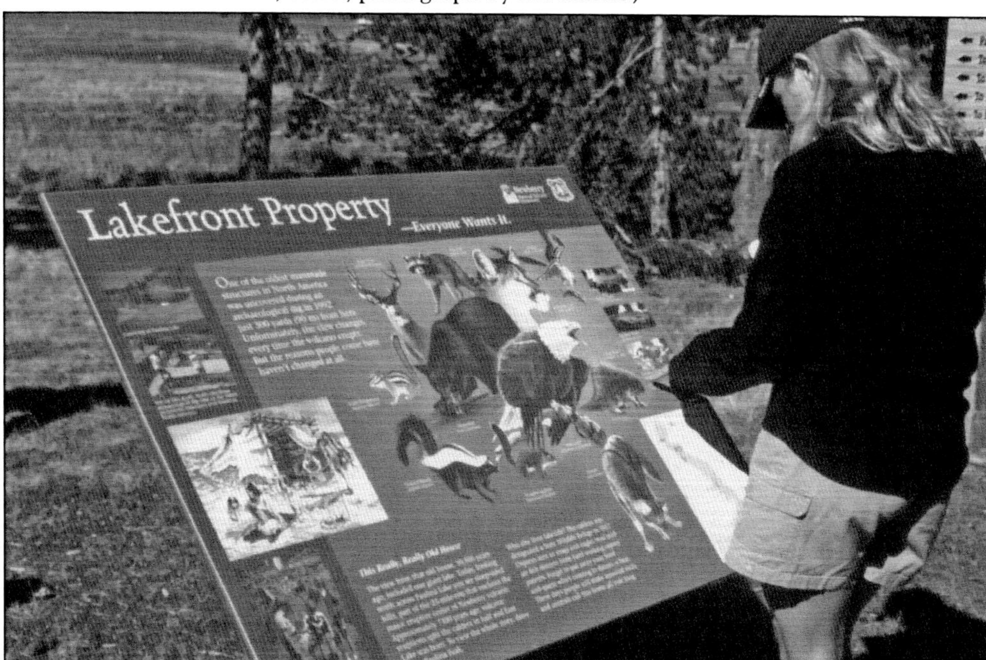

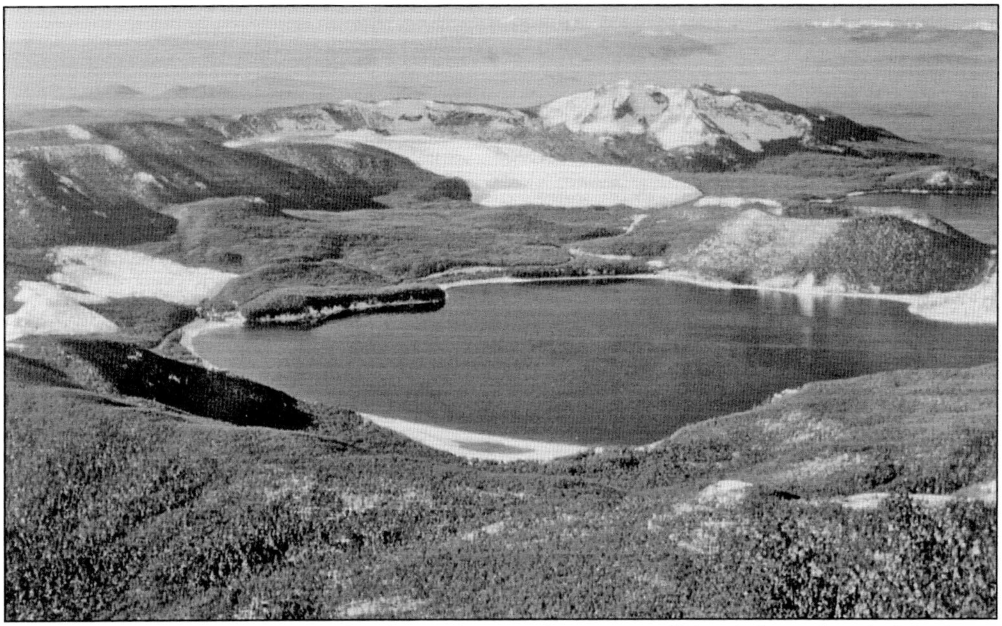

Winter snows define the volcanic landscape features that surround East Lake within the Newberry Caldera. Above the lake, the black volcanic glass of the Big Obsidian Flow shows starkly white, as does Paulina Peak. Central Pumice Cone, which erupted between and separated East Lake and Paulina Lake, is also evident. (Deschutes National Forest.)

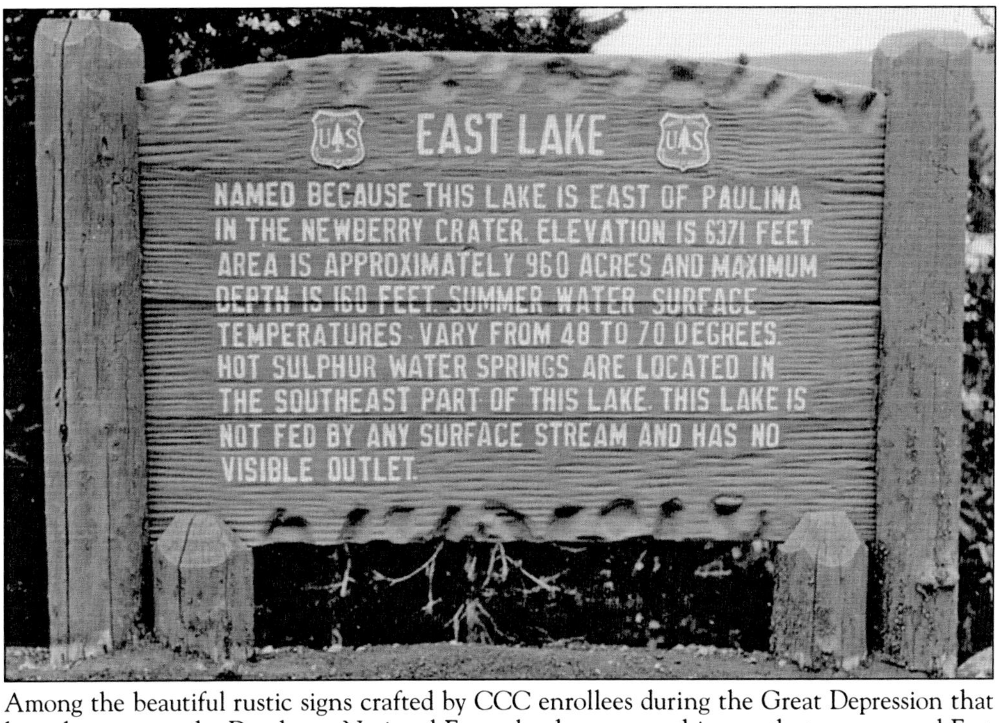

Among the beautiful rustic signs crafted by CCC enrollees during the Great Depression that lent character to the Deschutes National Forest landscape was this one that once graced East Lake's shore. This sign gave the facts and figures about the smaller of the two lakes that occupy the Newberry Caldera. (Deschutes National Forest.)

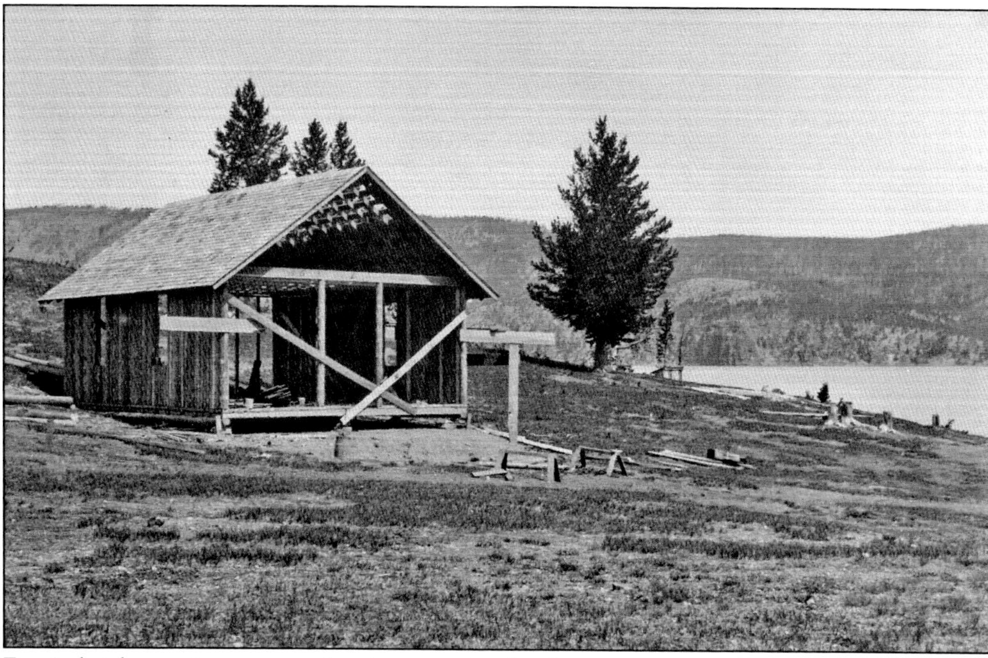

East Lake's hot springs attracted early recreation development interest. Construction of this East Lake Hot Springs resort cottage began under a US government lease dated February 28, 1899. Future recreation development included a larger hot springs resort, two fishing resorts, summer homes, and an Odd Fellows lodge and cabins built under US Forest Service permits. (Deschutes National Forest.)

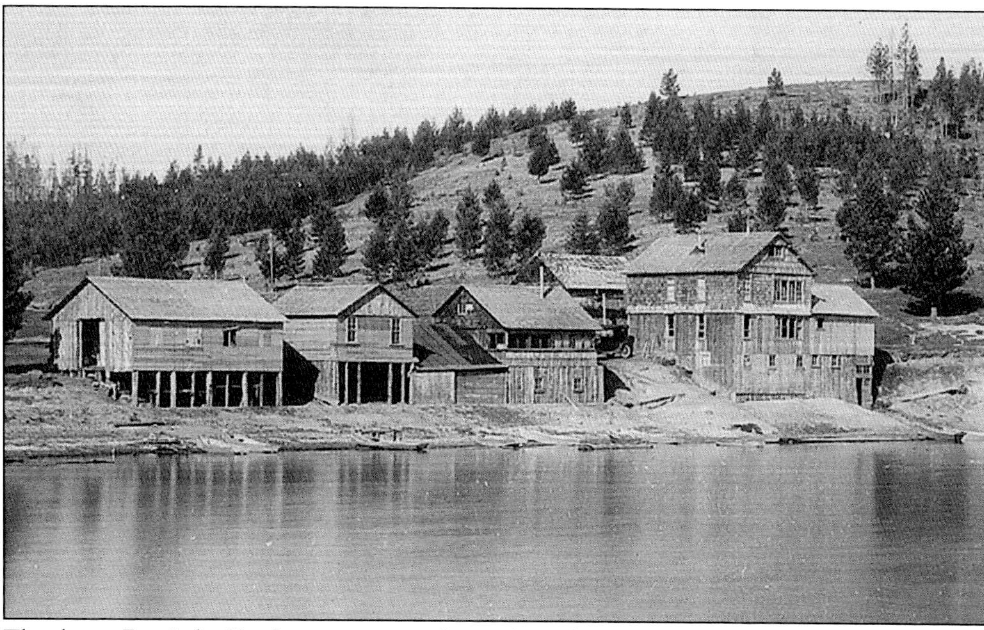

That larger East Lake Hot Springs resort welcomed Newberry Caldera visitors to the southeastern shore of East Lake from 1915 until it burned in 1922. Most of those visitors arrived via a road constructed by US Forest Service ranger John Curl and others in 1912 that entered the caldera from the west. (Deschutes National Forest.)

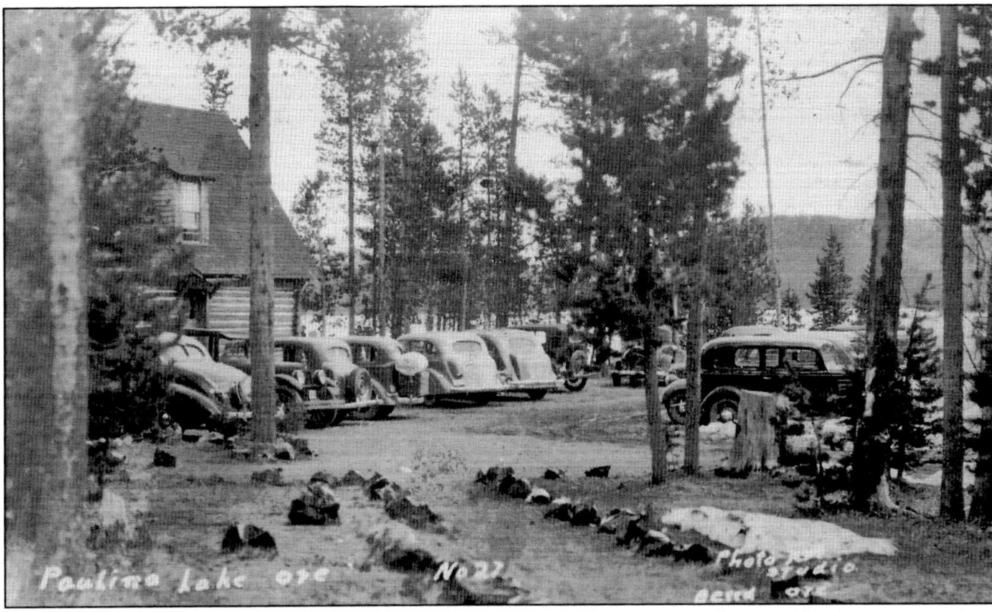

Paulina Lake Lodge, built in 1929, is a rustic resort on the western shore of Paulina Lake. Also long focused on summer fishing, it offers a range of summer and winter recreational opportunities. Just a snowcat shuttle from 10-Mile Snow Park, it hosts snowmobilers and cross-country skiers during the snowier months. Amenities include a restaurant and bar, a grocery store and tackle shop, and rustic log cabins. (Deschutes National Forest.)

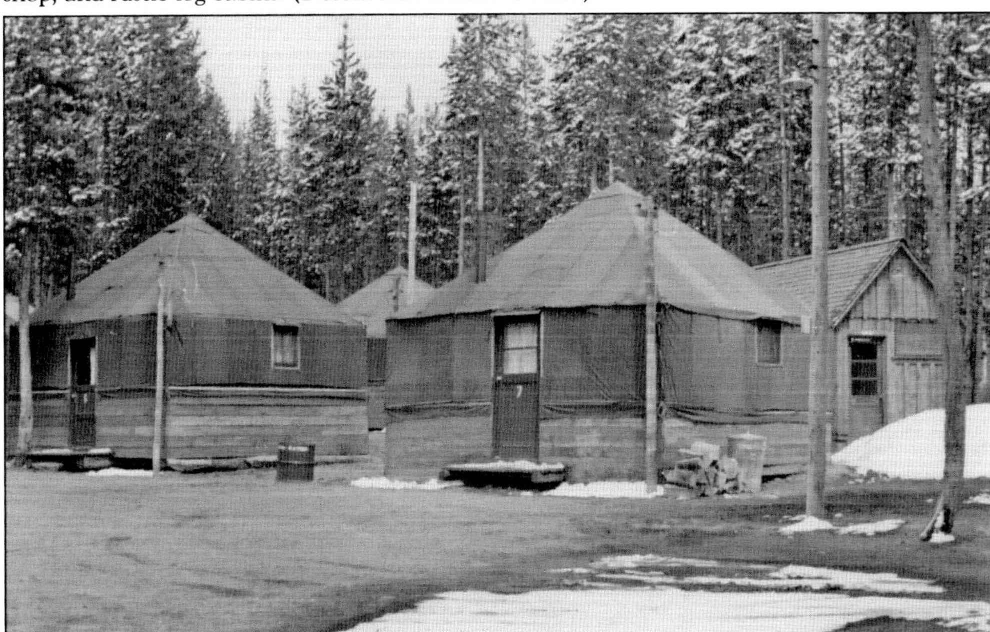

East Lake Resort, on the eastern shore of East Lake, caters to fishermen and other Newberry Caldera visitors who, in earlier times, enjoyed tent cabins such as these. Rebuilt in 1942 and well maintained since, it offers classic and newer lake view cabins, tent sites, recreational vehicle sites, and boats. A general store and tackle shop, a small restaurant, and a gift shop round out its amenities. (Deschutes National Forest.)

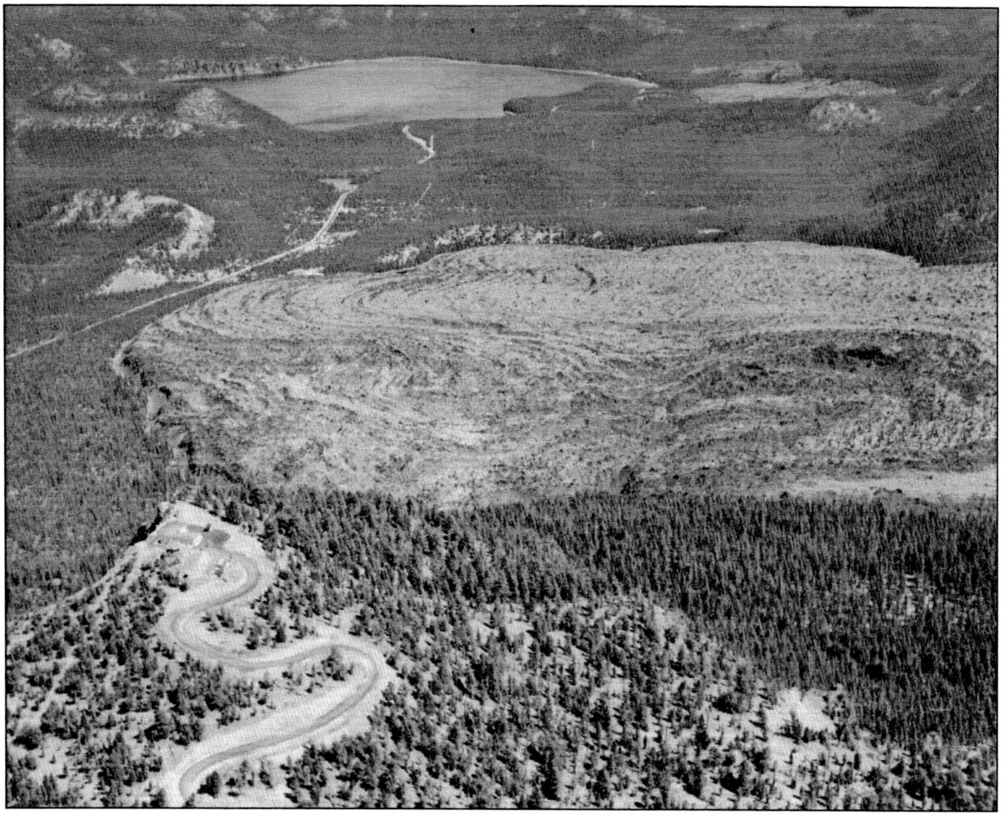

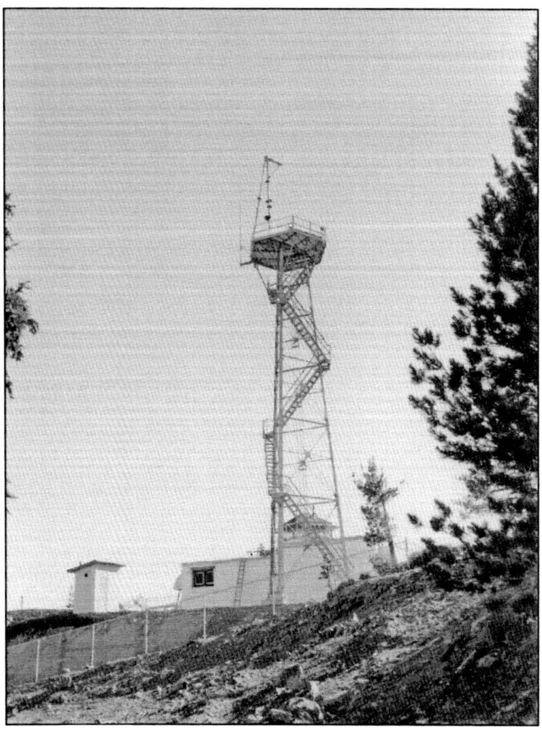

The road to the top of Paulina Peak (above) was built in 1959 during the Cold War for a US Air Force early warning system component called the La Pine Gap Filler Facility (left). A building that housed generators for a large radar antenna occupied the site along with the peak's last fire lookout. Harsh weather made system maintenance and repair extremely difficult even as advances in technology made the system obsolete. After only a year or two of operation, the system was dismantled. The road now provides access to spectacular views from Paulina Peak of the Newberry Caldera that include Paulina Lake, the Big Obsidian Flow (middle left), and East Lake (top left), as well as the Cascade Range to the west. (Both, Deschutes National Forest.)

The Deschutes National Forest entered the space age in August 1964 when astronaut Walter Cunningham and 15 NASA scientists conducted space suit mobility experiments on the Big Obsidian Flow in the Newberry Caldera as well as on the McKenzie Pass lava fields and the Crescent pumice flats. (Col. Walter Cunningham.)

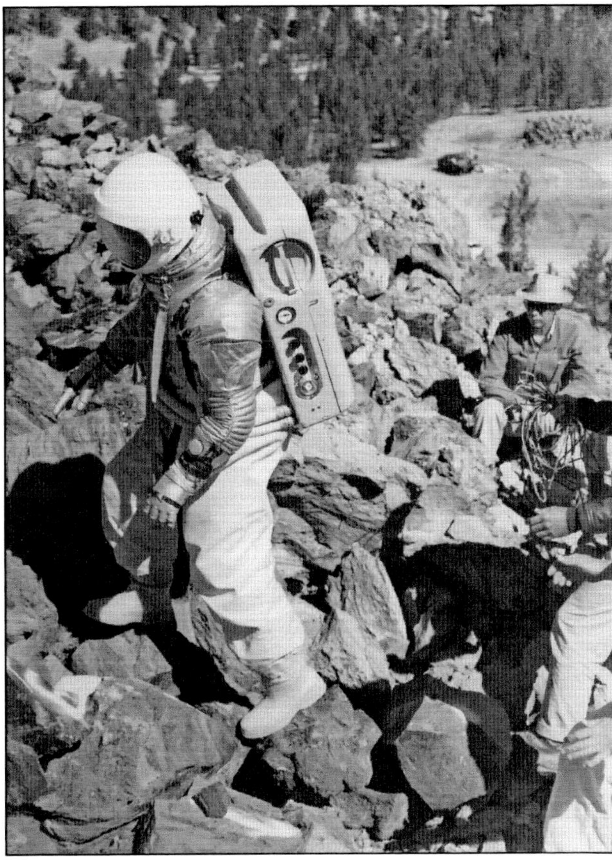

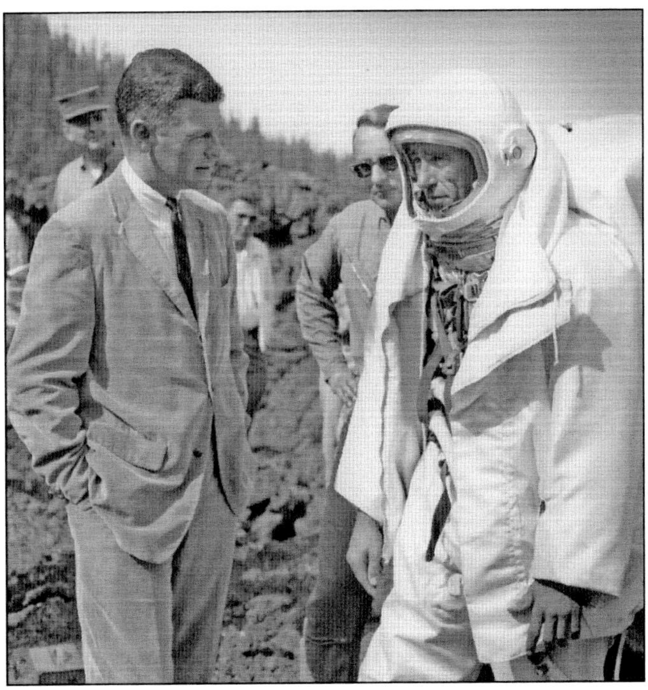

Gov. Mark O. Hatfield of Oregon visits with astronaut Walter Cunningham as he tests space suit travel on the Deschutes National Forest's moonlike terrain. These tests, along with the October 1968 Apollo 7 mission on which Cunningham was one of a crew of three orbiting the earth for 11 days, helped blaze the trail for Apollo 11 astronaut Neil Armstrong's "giant leap for mankind" onto the surface of the moon in July 1969. (Col. Walter Cunningham.)

Bibliography

Baker, Gail C. *Historical Writeup of the Deschutes National Forest*. Bend, OR: US Department of Agriculture, Forest Service, Deschutes National Forest, 1950.

Brogan, Phil F. *East of the Cascades*. Portland, OR: Binford and Mort Publishers, 1971.

———. *Visitor Information Service Book for the Deschutes National Forest*. Bend, OR: US Department of Agriculture, Forest Service, Deschutes National Forest, 1969.

Deschutes County Historical Society. *Bend*. Images of America. Charleston, SC: Arcadia Publishing, 2009.

Hatton, Raymond R. *High Country of Central Oregon*. Portland, OR: Binford and Mort Publishing, 1987.

———. *Oregon's Sisters Country: A Portrait of Its Lands, Waters and People*. Bend, OR: Geographical Books, 1996.

Jensen, Robert A. *Roadside Guide to the Geology of the Newberry Volcano*. 2nd ed. Bend, OR: CenOreGeoPub, 1995.

Joslin, Les. *Ponderosa Promise: A History of U.S. Forest Service Research in Central Oregon*. Portland, OR: US Department of Agriculture, Forest Service, Pacific Northwest Research Station, 2007.

———. *The Wilderness Concept and the Three Sisters Wilderness, Deschutes and Willamette National Forests, Oregon*. Bend, OR: Wilderness Associates, 2005.

Perry, Walter J. *Walt Perry: An Early-Day Forest Ranger in New Mexico and Oregon*. Les Joslin, ed. Bend, OR: Wilderness Associates, 1999.

Rakestraw, Lawrence, and Mary Rakestraw. *History of the Willamette National Forest*. Eugene, OR: US Department of Agriculture, Forest Service, Willamette National Forest, 1991.

Riis, John. *Ranger Trails*. Richmond: Dietz Press, 1937. Reprinted by Wilderness Associates, Bend, OR, 2008.

Robins, Dick, and Dave Robins with Les Joslin. *Seventeen Summers at Paulina Lake Guard Station, Deschutes National Forest, Oregon, 1942–1959*. Bend, OR: Wilderness Associates, 2006.

Steen, Harold K. *The U.S. Forest Service: A History*. Centennial ed. Seattle: University of Washington Press, 2004.

Vaughn, Thomas, ed. *High & Mighty: Select Sketches about the Deschutes Country*. Portland, OR: Oregon Historical Society, 1981.

Wilkinson, Charles F., and H. Michael Anderson. *Land and Resource Planning in the National Forests*. Washington, DC: Island Press, 1987.

Williams, Gerald W. *The U.S. Forest Service in the Pacific Northwest: A History*. Corvallis: Oregon State University Press, 2009.

Index

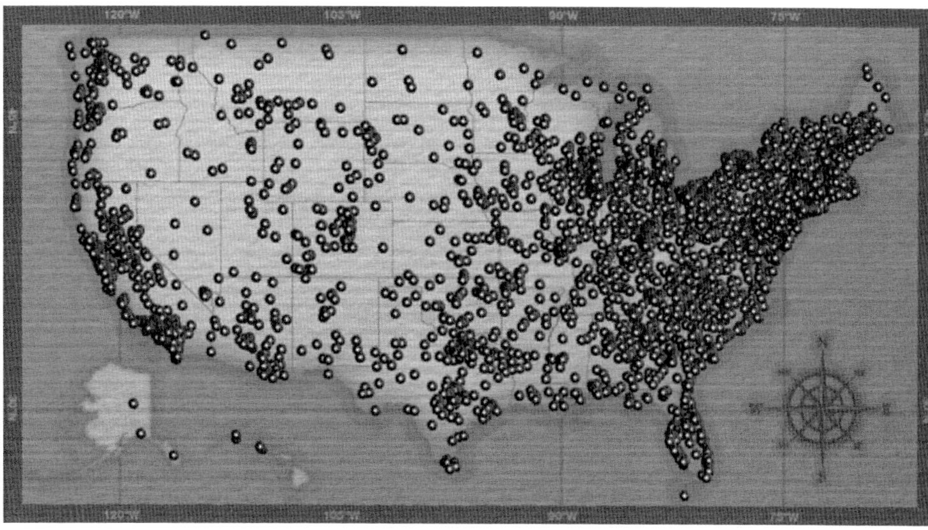